Praise for *Chine*

Chinese Laundries: Tickets to Survival on Gold Mountain is another important window into the history of the early Chinese immigrants to North America, one that transcends all regions. The tracing of the trail of Chinese migration into America's heartland and the Deep South as many entered the laundry business sheds light on their complex and difficult journey. The coverage of the virulent anti-Chinese sentiments in large cities as well as small hamlets exposes the hostility they had to overcome. The laundrymen faced struggles, challenges, and even disappointments; yet, the Chinese laundry became a valued and necessary enterprise in countless communities for several decades.

Sylvia Sun Minnick, Author,
SamFow: The San Joaquin Chinese Legacy and *Stockton's Chinese Community*

Professor Jung's book has made a significant contribution to the history of Chinese laundries in America. The story is best told by someone like Jung who experienced a 'laundry life,' and understands its psychological impact on the Chinese laundrymen and their families. It is hard to imagine the difficulties that the laundrymen encountered in making a living in a harsh and hostile environment. Bachelor laundrymen, like those with families back in China, suffered lonely lives. Those who had families with them worked hard to ensure that their children would have advantages that the laundrymen could never attain here.

Murray K. Lee, Curator of Chinese American History, San Diego Chinese
Historical Museum, and the son of a Chinese laundryman and restaurateur

A masterwork of definitive scholarship and heartfelt composition on this singularly important subject. Jung's own life in one such historic family business lends unique insight to a topic often cited but little explored until now. An academically solid effort that is much enhanced by several personal narratives from other "Children of the Laundries." This rewarding study of an era marked by invention born of dire necessity, an unforgiving host society that demanded Chinese laundrymen's services but then punished them for being too good at it, is a long overdue analysis of a familiar experience hidden in plain sight.

Mel Brown, Author,
Chinese Heart of Texas, The San Antonio Chinese Community, 1875-1975

CHINESE LAUNDRIES

Tickets to Survival On Gold Mountain

To Best wishes, John Jung

John Jung

 *Yin & Yang Press*

LCCN: 2006939696

Jung, John, 1937-

Chinese Laundries/Tickets to Survival on Gold Mountain

/ John Jung

p. cm.

Includes bibliographical references.

Front Cover Design by Lauren Doege

Back Cover Photograph:
Joe's Laundry in Atlanta for three generations,
And still in operation.

Online Orders: www.lulu.com/Chineselaundries

Let Us Now Praise Chinese Laundrymen

In search of Gold Mountain, you, your sons, and brothers came,

Some helped forge the rail that links the land from coast to coast,

Then, for problems not of your making, you were held to blame,

Racism denied you basic rights and liberties accorded to most,

You were taunted, assaulted, and then excluded from the land,

Undaunted, you persevered and worked long hours into the night,

Resourceful, you learned to survive by doing laundry by hand,

For many, apart years from wife and children was your plight,

You slaved, skimped, and saved to have money to send back,

Resilient, you endured hardships with a determined attitude,

Of courage, endurance, and determination, you did not lack,

For which your children, and theirs, owe you lasting gratitude.

Table of Contents

Foreword

Professor John Jung's present book, *Chinese Laundries: Tickets to Survival on Gold Mountain*, combined with his earlier memoir, *Southern Fried Rice: Life in a Chinese Laundry in the Deep South,* have expanded the frontier of overseas Chinese studies and made him an authority on Chinese laundries in America. Professor Jung goes beyond the laundryman's "sojourner and marginal mentality" aptly described in Dr. Paul Siu's ground breaking work, *The Chinese Laundryman: A Study of Social Isolation,* started in the 1940s but left unpublished until 1987. In contrast, *Chinese Laundries* provides a wider historical perspective, with painstakingly meticulous documentation of the immigration experiences of Chinese laundrymen. It achieves its goal through the inclusion of photographs, charts, cartoons, caricatures, posters, rhymes, popular media, stereotyped images, songs as well as oral narratives. These historical details include hitherto seldom-researched materials on the Chinese laundries in the Southwest, Midwest, Rocky Mountain regions and in the Deep South. What is remarkable is the combination of this historical perspective with Professor Jung's social psychological descriptions and analyses of laundrymen and their descendants. Their personal life stories, with inner thoughts, feelings, values, attitudes, work experiences and survival hardships are skillfully presented with penetrating insights and observations. This broad perspective presents an overall picture of the history and the life and labor of the Chinese laundrymen. ☐ From the late 19th century to the first half of the 20th century, Chinese laundries dotted the urban landscape of North America. Chinese laundrymen were so prevalent that it almost seemed as if they were genetically wired for this occupation. Even in asylums for the insane, Chinese inmates were asked to do laundry work. Laundry work was psychologically and physically demanding. One laundryman once told me that he washed his laundry with tears, and that if he had known that laundry work meant a lifetime of hardship and suffering, he would not have come to the Gold Mountain. However, despite all these difficulties of racial discrimination, hostility, violence and legal exclusion, they survived and prospered. Nowadays, many of their children are successful members of their communities who make valuable contributions to society. The laundrymen left a legacy of hard work, endurance, tolerance and an indomitable spirit to excel in life and work. This legacy is now benefiting all Chinese immigrants. Their descendants regard it as a significant part of their enduring heritage, one they can cherish and promote. As a Chinese saying goes, "To be able to taste the bitterest of the bitter, then you will be a step higher than the others." Professor Jung's seminal works have ably presented and preserved an important part of this heritage not only for those of Chinese ancestry but for all Americans.

Ban Seng Hoe, Ph.D.
Vanderbilt University
Curator of Asian Studies, Canadian Museum of Civilization
Visiting Professor of Ethnology and Chinese Studies, Peking University

Preface

A confluence of adverse circumstances in the impoverished villages of Guangdong province in southeastern China led thousands of young men to leave and seek their fortune abroad in the mid to late 19th century. California, or "Gold Mountain," as it was called after gold was discovered there in 1848, was an attractive destination, and soon gold finds in Canada, Alaska, and Australia lured others. But Chinese were not allowed to work the best mining sites anywhere and then they were similarly driven out of other work in fishing, farming, and manufacturing.

Many Chinese had to spend their Gold Mountain days washing and ironing laundry for a living under conditions of cultural isolation and racial oppression. For over a century, the hand laundry was the stereotypical occupation for the Chinese. The laundry was made obsolete by social and technological changes by the last part of the 20th century.

The laundry *ticket* became an emblem of the Chinese hand laundry. Although a laundry ticket is nothing more than a small piece of paper that serves as a claim check linking each customer with his laundry items, it came to be used to ridicule Chinese as in the well-known mocking expression, "no tickee, no washee." Chinese laundrymen, if they ever used the actual phrase or its variants, "no tickee, no laundee" or "no tickee, no shirtee," were justified in their demand. Requiring a customer to present a ticket to claim their laundry is not unreasonable because without it, locating the customer's clothing is made difficult. Furthermore, someone might claim clothing that was not his own.

Whites looked down at Chinese, their attire, their food, and their language. They derogated the Chinese characters the laundryman scribbled on the ticket to inventory the customer's laundry, as 'chicken feet scratches.' This response reflected as well as reinforced white views that the Chinese had alien and inscrutable Oriental ways. Whites enjoyed poking fun at the difficulty Chinese had in pronouncing English, and "no tickee, no washee" was a popular phrase for ridiculing the laundryman.

No one is sure how the expression arose but it may have started with a story from 1903 by a humorist, Calvin Stewart, in which Uncle Josh takes his clothes to a Chinese laundry.[1] The narrator of the tale relates that:

> " ... he giv me a little yaller ticket that he painted with a brush what he had, and I'll jist bet a yoke of steers agin the holler in a log, that no livin' mortal man could read that ticket; it looked like a fly had fell into the ink bottle and then crawled over the paper."
> Confused, he asked a man what the ticket was and he was conned, "Wall sir that's a sort of a lotery ticket; every time you leave your clothes thar to have them washed you git one of them tickets, and then you have a chance to draw a prize of some kind." Not wanting to enter the lottery, Josh sold the "lottery ticket" to the stranger for 10 cents. "... and in a couple of days I went round to git my washin', and that pig tailed heathen he wouldn't let me hev em, coz I'd lost that lotery ticket. So I sed -- now look here Mr. Hop Soon, if you don't hop round and git me my collars and ciffs and other clothes what I left here, I'll be durned if I don't flop you in about a minnit, I will by chowder."

This type of confrontation between customers and laundrymen over attempts to claim laundry without presenting a ticket was not

---

[1] Cal Stewart, *Uncle Josh's Punkin Centre Stories.* Chicago: Thompson and Thomas, 1905.

uncommon. In the story, it was Uncle Josh, and not the laundryman, who was in the wrong. But the story nevertheless vilifies the unfortunate laundryman who receives the unwarranted pummeling from Josh.

"No tickee, no washee" has since come to be used as a catch-phrase for an impasse in conflicted transactions quite unrelated to laundries, or even ones involving Chinese. Still, the term casts a derogatory tone toward Chinese and it is unfortunate that it remains in use long after Chinese laundries have almost completely disappeared from modern life.

Although less well known, there is an old parlor trick called the "Chinese laundry ticket." The performer take a slip of paper covered with ersatz Chinese characters and tears it into several pieces, while bantering that even without this laundry ticket, a laundryman can find the laundry. Then the performer 'magically' reproduces the ticket in one piece. The name of this stunt conveys the view that Chinese laundrymen are mysteriously odd or different.

A completely different meaning of ticket, a means of gaining admission beyond a barrier, is the sense that is intended by its inclusion in the title of this book. The laundry was the best, and at one time, the only, 'ticket' available to Chinese immigrants to rise from their low position in society. They came here in the middle of the 19th century to seek fortune on "Gold Mountain," but were denied opportunities by discriminatory barriers. The laundry became their economic lifeline, the meal ticket for the Chinese and their descendants that enabled them to overcome the obstacles confronting them and achieve success on Gold Mountain.

The inspiration for writing *Chinese Laundry Tickets* was my recently acquired awareness and understanding of the vital role of the hand laundry in the survival of Chinese immigrants from the late 19th century until the end of World War II. I knew first-hand how difficult it was to earn a living running a laundry from growing up in the only Chinese family in Macon, Georgia, where my parents operated a laundry. But, I did not realize that thousands of earlier Chinese laundrymen had endured equally, or greater, hardships than my family experienced until I did research for writing a memoir about our experiences.[2] In fact, I did not even know that for almost 50 years prior to my father coming to Macon in 1928, other Chinese had operated the very laundry he acquired.

I am a psychologist by training, and have a love for history, so my approach in this book blends the two disciplines. In the early chapters, I focus on historical documents and resources to explain why and how hand laundries assumed increasing importance for Chinese during the years of their exclusion, 1882-1943. Laundrymen, classified as laborers, not only were excluded during these 61 years, but those already here were not allowed to bring their families here. Yet, laundrymen, as well as other Chinese, found ways to circumvent these unfair laws to gain entry. Although tactics such as the "paper son" method do not directly pertain to laundries, I discuss it at length because without it, the thousands of Chinese laundries here could never have existed.

The laundry, in view of the exclusion of Chinese from many other occupations, had an essential role in the development of the economic, social, and psychological status of the early Chinese immigrants and their

---

[2] John Jung, *Southern Fried Rice: Life in A Chinese Laundry in the Deep South (Cypress, Ca.: Ying & Yang Press, 2005).*

families, both here and in China. Their success was not an easily gained victory as laundry work soon also became contested by discriminatory laws and taxes in the context of persistent hostile media images of Chinese laundrymen as well as the demeaning, belittling, and sometimes physically abusive treatment they suffered from the prevailing racist attitudes of white society.

My psychology background surfaces in later chapters. I examined first- and second-hand accounts of the work activities and daily experiences of laundrymen and, in some instances, their families. This evidence shows how much laundrymen achieved through their labor and resolve despite years of racial prejudice, discriminatory laws, and cultural isolation.

The social networking among laundrymen is the focus of one chapter. This analysis, based on 19 male relatives of my great, great-grandfather that ran laundries in the American South spanning over 100 years, focuses on a neglected but vital aspect of immigration. How did familial networks develop to create migration chains of men who came over earlier helping later arriving relatives in gaining entry into the country and in surviving with financial, informational, and emotional support.

Another chapter presents recollections about daily life in laundries from a small sample of individuals from varied regions of the U. S. and Canada that literally grew up above or behind their family stores. These inside perspectives provide invaluable insight on how laundry families functioned from day to day. I am grateful to these 'children, and two grandchildren, of the laundry' for their trust and willingness to make public their laundry experiences. The reflections of Eliz Chan, Laura

Chin, Bill Eng, Ken Lee, Lucy Wong Leonard, Harvey Low, Jeff Low, Donna Wong, and Elwin Xie testify to the resourcefulness and strength of their laundry parents in surviving and raising their children successfully. Their observations about their adult lives illustrate the powerful impact that their laundry experiences had on their personal development.

A final chapter examines the significant economic influence of the laundry for Chinese immigrants, and their families, throughout North America well into the past century. It concludes with a discussion of factors leading to the inevitable obsolescence of the hand laundry and the emergence of the restaurant after the end of World War II as the primary family-run business for Chinese immigrants.

The insightful suggestions and guidance from Sylvia Sun Minnick and Judy Yung improved the manuscript considerably, and I am grateful to them for their warm friendship and generous support. I appreciate the collegiality of Ban Seng Hoe, an authority on Chinese laundries himself and author of *Enduring Hardship: The Chinese Laundry in Canada,* in preparing the generous commentary in the Foreword. Many thanks go to Margo Kasdan and Mel Brown for expert editorial guidance and encouragement. Finally, I owe thanks to my wife, Phyllis, for invaluable editorial assistance, discussion of many issues, and for putting up with the hours I spent absorbed in the project while deferring household chores.

John Jung

April, 2007
Cypress, Ca.

CHINESE LAUNDRIES

Tickets To Survival On Gold Mountain

1. Did The Chinese Come To Do Laundry?

"Laundry is a problem that will not go away." [3]

With the discovery of gold at Sutter's mill in the Sierra foothills of northern California in 1848, Chinese men came from the impoverished regions of Guangdong province by the thousands to seek their fortune on "Gold Mountain," as the United States was called in China. Thousands of other Chinese came later in the 1860s under contract to help build the transcontinental railroad. Why, then, did laundry work instead become for many years the primary occupation of Chinese immigrants to the U. S. as well as to Canada well into the twentieth century? What social conditions led them into washing and ironing America's dirty clothes as a livelihood to such an extent that the laundry became the occupational stereotype for the Chinese?

NO LAUNDRIES IN CHINA.

"It's the funniest thing to me," said an old sea captain who for many years was in the China trade, as he settled himself comfortably in his chair and blew a few rings of smoke into the air, "that nine out of every ten Chinamen who come to this country open laundries and engage in a business which does not exist in their native land.

As everyone knows, the Chinese at home wear soft cotton and woolen garments, according to the season, and there is not a pound of starch in all China. Stiffly starched clothes are unknown, and the Chinese men do not do the washing, as they do in this country. Neither is there any regular laundry in the Flowery Kingdom. Therefore it is more than passing strange that Chinamen should all come to America to engage in a trade so foreign to their home industries."

Figure 1 A trade comment on Chinese laundries. *National Laundry Journal*, 1905, 41.

---

[3] Arwen P. Mohun, *Steam Laundries: Gender, Technology, And Work In The United States And Great Britain* (Baltimore, MD.: Johns Hopkins University Press, 1999).

As an American laundry trade publication noted in 1905 (See Figure 1), the Chinese men who came to the United States during the mid-19th century were not laundrymen in their homeland. In China, as throughout most of the world, women did the laundry.

The first Chinese laundry in America is said to have opened over 150 years ago, when Wah Lee hung a sign in front of his shop in the Chinese quarter of San Francisco in 1851 that simply read "Wash'ng and Iron'g."[4] However, it was not until the 1870s that Chinese laundries really began to proliferate. In San Francisco 1333 Chinese were listed in the 1870 U. S. manuscript census as working in laundries, rising to 2148 by 1880, but declining slightly to 1924 by 1900.[5] These numbers represented from about 50 to 60 percent of California's Chinese working in laundries during that period.[6] Countless Chinese immigrants earned their living from hand laundries over the next 100 years. Chinese laundries opened in small and large cities and towns all across the country.[7] The majority of these men from China worked in or owned Chinese laundries, and for a few years in the late 19th century they dominated the trade throughout the U.S and Canada.

---

[4] Some evidence suggests that a Chinese laundry existed as early as 1845 in Philadelphia. David Te-Chao Chen, "Acculturation of the Chinese in the United States: A Philadelphia Story" (Ph.D. diss., University of Pennsylvania, 1948), 66-67. Quoted by Joan Wang, "'No Tickee, No Shirtee:' Chinese Laundries in the Social Context of the Eastern United States: 1882-1943." (PhD diss., Carnegie Mellon University, 1996), 20.

[5] Census counts usually are aggregated data, but do not identify individuals. In contrast, the "manuscript census" identifies each person's name, address, sex, age, birthplace, occupation plus a few items that differ across decades, but to protect confidentiality they are not public for 72 years.

[6] Sucheng Chan, *This Bittersweet Soil: The Chinese in California Agriculture, 1860-1910.* (Berkeley: University of California Press, 1987): 62-63, 68-69, 74-75.

[7] Sucheng Chan, *Asian Americans: An Interpretive History* (Boston: Twyane Publishing, 1991), 33.

The story of Chinese laundries cannot be fully understood without considering the historical and cultural context in which they originated. We first need to see what led to the Chinese diaspora from Guangdong province in southeast China starting in the middle 19th century. Thousands of Chinese men left their villages during these years to work in distant regions of North America such as California, the Pacific Northwest, and western Canada. Why did so many of them spend most of their lives abroad washing and ironing laundry for a living, one of their primary occupations in most of these regions for many years.[8]

Why Chinese Left Guangdong In The Mid-1800s

The province of Guangdong in the southeastern part of China, not far from Hong Kong, was beset by many problems during the early 1800s that made it extremely difficult to earn a decent living. The peasant villagers of the region, a fertile agricultural area for centuries, were primarily farmers. Figure 2 summarizes the major factors behind the exodus. Alternating floods and droughts during those years destroyed their crops. China was a weak nation, forced to make humiliating concessions to open the country to commerce with foreign powers following the disastrous Opium wars with England (1839-1842) and with England and France (1856-1860) as they were powerless to stop England from selling opium to China. From 1850 to 1864, there was also civil

---

[8] Chinese laundries were not limited to North America, but also became a primary livelihood during the late 1800s in New Zealand, James Ng, "A laundry background." http://www.stevenyoung.co.nz/chinesevoice/history/lanundrymay03.htm, (accessed June 1, 2006) Australia, "Tracking the dragon –A guide for finding and assessing Chinese-Australian heritage places." http://www.ahc.gov.au/publications/chineseheritage/trackingthedragon/background.html#e (accessed Dec. 17, 2006) and England. "How the Chinese came to Wales," www.bbc.co.uk/.webloc . www.sacu.org/britishchin#14A8A7, (accessed Dec. 17, 2006).

unrest leading to millions of deaths in the bloody Tai-ping rebellion against the ruling Qing or Manchu dynasty. Warlords fought for control of local regions while bandits attacked and robbed food from villagers.

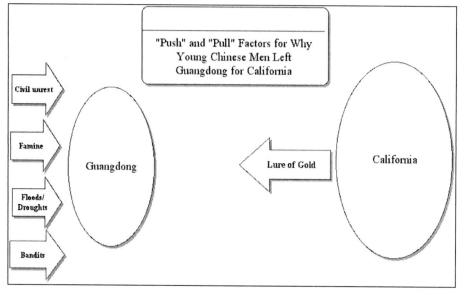

Figure 2 Push and pull factors for large-scale Chinese immigration to the U.S.

Desperation, born from these dire circumstances, "pushed" many of the sons, starting with the oldest, of families in these rural villages to leave home in search of work. California held an especially strong "pull" with the 1849 discovery of gold there. The cost of passage by ship from China to California was about $50, a large sum in those days, and equivalent to over $500 today, but relatives pooled their money to help purchase steerage passage for sons to cross the Pacific on arduous voyages that took about a month. The hope was that they would find work and send money home to assist their impoverished kin and then return to China.

Swallows and magpies, flying in glee:
Greetings for New Year.
Daddy has gone to Gold Mountain
To earn money.
He will earn gold and silver,
 Ten thousand taels.
When he returns, we will build a house and buy farmland.[9]

YOKOHAMA AND HONGKONG,

Connecting at Yokohama with Steamers of the Mitsu Bishi Company for Hiogo, Nagasaki, Shanghae, and other Japanese and Chinese Ports, and at Hongkong with Steamers for East Indian, Australasian and European Ports.

SAILING SCHEDULE, 1883.

FROM SAN FRANCISCO FOR *HONGKONG.*	STEAMER.	FROM YOKOHAMA FOR SAN FRANCISCO
Thursday, January 18th	ARABIC	Saturday, March 10th.
Tuesday, January 30th	OCEANIC	Friday, March 23d.
Saturday, February 10th	COPTIC	Tuesday, April 3d.
Tuesday, March 6th	GAELIC	Friday, April 27th.
Saturday, March 17th	BELGIC	Tuesday, May 8th.

PASSAGE RATES AS FOLLOWS, SUBJECT TO CHANGE:

PAYABLE IN U. S. GOLD COIN.	First Class or Cabin.	European Steerage.	Chinese Steerage.	Distance from San Francisco.
San Francisco to **Yokohama, Japan**	$250 00	$ 85 00	$51 00	4,800 miles.
" **Hiogo,** "	268 00	98 00	58 00	5,100 "
" **Nagasaki,** "	285 00	111 00	63 50	5,550 "
" **Shanghae, China**	305 00	125 00	71 00	6,000 "
" **Hongkong,** "	300 00	100 00	51 00	6,400 "
" **Singapore, India**	380 00	.....	.....	7,850 "
" **Penang,** "	400 00	.....	.....	8,250 "
" **Calcutta,** "	450 00	.....	.....	9,900 "

Figure 3 Steerage class passage rates from San Francisco to China in 1883.

Their departure also meant one less mouth to feed at home. The married men left wives and children behind, because it would be difficult enough to survive in a foreign country without having the added costs for passage, travel problems involved with bringing families across the Pacific, and the burden of providing for them in a new land. Besides, the original intention of the early waves of immigrants was to stay abroad temporarily, long enough to hopefully strike it rich on "Gold Mountain"

---

[9] Marlon Kau Hom, *Songs of Gold Mountain: Cantonese Rhymes From San Francisco Chinatown* (Berkeley and Los Angeles: University of California Press, 1987), 41.

and then return to China. Little could they foresee that most of them would never return, or only for short visits, to their villages. Instead they would live the rest of their lives in a foreign, and often, hostile land.

In the years immediately after the discovery of gold in California in 1848, over two-thirds of Chinese immigrants on the continent worked in mining or as unskilled laborers. Despite facing discriminatory laws and taxes as well as physical violence during the 1850s aimed at preventing their work in mines, half of the Chinese in California were still involved with mining in 1861, but only around 25 percent were by 1870.

The passage of the Burlingame Treaty in 1868 expanded commerce and trade with China. It established cordial immigration policies between the United States and China, a nation that historically had not approved of its citizens leaving the country. This treaty broke through this barrier and opened opportunities for large-scale immigration to the U. S. where great supplies of cheap labor were needed to help build the rapidly expanding western regions. Under the Burlingame Treaty, the United States promised protection and fair treatment of Chinese immigrants.[10] Chinese came from Guangdong by the thousands starting around the middle of the 19th century to seek work, which was not available in their rural villages. However, the treaty still denied them, unlike European immigrants, the possibility of becoming naturalized citizens.

Unfortunately, the protection and fair treatment promises were not upheld as racial discrimination led to unfair treatment of Chinese immigrants. Not allowed to engage in mining to the same extent as

---

[10] McClain, *In Search of Equality*, 30-31.

whites, they turned to other work that they were knowledgeable about such as fishing and farming. They acquired skills in logging, manufacturing shoes, cigars, and woolen goods.[11] But eventually racially based discrimination excluded them from work in these areas as well.[12]

A similar plight confronted the thousands of laborers recruited as contract workers for construction of the western section of the transcontinental railroad by the Central Pacific Railroad. They filled a need for plentiful and inexpensive labor. Similarly, a decade later, thousands of Chinese came to fill the need for railroad construction in western Canada. But once the transcontinental railroad was completed at Promontory Point, Utah, with the linking of the Union Pacific and the Central Pacific in 1869, more than 10,000 Chinese who had worked on its construction for over four years became unemployed overnight.[13] The same problem occurred in 1885 for thousands of Chinese laborers left without work by the completion of the Canadian Pacific Railroad.

Actually these men were in demand and many continued with construction work on smaller railroads located all over the country such as the Southern Pacific line between San Francisco and Los Angeles and the line between Los Angeles to Yuma, Tucson, and El Paso.[14] Other Chinese went to work on construction projects like the extensive set of levees in the Sacramento-San Joaquin River Delta in California that transformed

---

[11] Stanford M. Lyman, *Chinese Americans* (New York: Random House, 1974), 70-80.

[12] Wang, "No Tickee, No Shirtee," 22-23.

[13] Chan,. "*Asian Americans: An Interpretive History*" 32.

[14] Loren Chan,. "The Chinese in Nevada: An Historical Survey, 1856-1970." In *Chinese on the American Frontier* Edited by Arik Dirlik with the assistance of Malcolm Yeung (Lanham: Rowman & Littlefield, 2001: 92.

swampland into highly productive farmlands and on the building of the canal in Augusta, Georgia, that provided electricity to power textile mills to manufacture cotton goods. These activities introduced the Chinese to other regions than the west, and some remained after these construction projects were finished and found other means of earning a livelihood. Still others struggled as migrant farm workers, fruit pickers, and vegetable peddlers. Others became domestic servants, performing duties that included washing, ironing, and cooking while others did the same tasks by starting laundries and restaurants.

Chinese were not always unwelcome in America, as they would become by the 1870s. Before their large-scale arrival here in the mid 1800s, Chinese visitors had been welcome when they came to the United States, viewed with a mixture of interest and curiosity.[15] Chinese civilization and its achievements were highly respected from as far back as the time of Marco Polo when Chinese goods such as silk and tea were prized. China's culture, technology, and arts were envied and admired by American gentry.

In addition, the exotic appeal of the different language, attire, and customs attracted attention to visitors from the "Celestial Empire" during the early part of the 19th century. Opportunistic promoters like the showman of the century, P. T. Barnum, shamelessly involved exploitation of exotic aspects of the Chinese, appealing to the need for Americans to gawk at the strange ways of the 'Orientals.'

However, Chinese were never fully accepted in North America. They were denied important rights, even though they paid taxes to work

---

[15] John Kuo Wei Tchen, *New York before Chinatown. Orientalism and the Shaping of American Culture, 1776-1882* (Baltimore, Md.: Johns Hopkins University Press, 1999).

in their major occupations such as mining and laundries. They were not allowed to become naturalized citizens; hence, they could not vote and were unable to exert any political influence.[16] The list was long; they could not testify in court against whites,[17] marry whites,[18] and their children could not attend white schools.[19]

The anti-Chinese sentiment may have started well before Chinese came in any numbers to these shores. Many Western traders, diplomats, and missionaries dealt with China as early as the 16th century and they gave unflattering accounts of Chinese customs, values, and people.[20] By the time Chinese arrived in the mid 19th century, these writings had instilled strong negative stereotypes of them. The Chinese rulers were described as despotic, Cantonese merchants were depicted as shrewd and cunning, and Chinese people were portrayed as immoral, godless pagans of inferior racial stock bearing exotic and loathsome diseases.[21]

Faced with the lack of work opportunities, laundry work happened to be one of the few avenues open to Chinese in the latter half of the 19th century. Several factors created an unprecedented and unfilled need for laundry service during the mid 1800s. In the frontier west, few

---

[16] Chan, *Asian Americans: An Interpretive History*, 70-72.

[17] Charles J. McClain, In Search of Equality: The Chinese Struggle Against Discrimination in Nineteenth-Century America (Berkeley: University of California Press, 1994), 20-22.

[18] Chan, *Asian Americans: An Interpretive History*, 59-60.

[19] McClain, *In Search of Equality*, 133-139.

[20] Stuart Creighton Miller. *The Unwelcome Immigrant: The American Image of the Chinese, 1785-1882* (Berkeley: University of California Press, 1969), 30-31.

[21] Lyman, 58.

women were available to do laundry. Ships transported laundry to Hawaii for washing, an expensive and slow solution requiring several weeks.[22]

Many factors served to create an increasing need for laundry services in the industrial east, making it possible for the first time in history for laundry to be a business opportunity. In the large cities, crowded housing conditions did not allow laundry to be done easily in city residences, flats, and apartments. At the same time, increased knowledge, awareness, and concern over the 19th century about the diseases caused by germs enhanced the desire for clean clothes as well as bathing as a form of personal hygiene. In addition, being able to afford clean clothes became a marker of higher social standing. Finally, from a moral view, cleanliness became a virtue "next to Godliness."[23]

Not surprisingly, laundry work, which involved physically demanding and time consuming labor, was not a highly contested occupation. Washing and ironing laundry for many hours each day and night, week after week, and year after year was by no easy way to earn a living. It was unattractive to most whites, allowing Chinese almost exclusive control of this occupation around the 1870s.

What Laundry Work Involved

> *Chink, chink, Chinaman,*
> *Wash my pants;*
> *Put them into the boiler,*
> *And make them dance.*[24]

---

[22] Betty Lee Sung, *The Story of Chinese in America. Their Struggle for Survival, Acceptance, and Full Participation in American Life.* (New York: Collier Books, 1967), 190.

[23] Wang, "No Tickee, No Shirtee," 132-135.

[24] Ban Seng Hoe, *Structural Changes of Two Chinese Communities in Alberta, Canada.* Ottawa: National Museum of Canada, 1976: 349.

The procedures involved in doing laundry are not mysterious or complex. It is simple but tedious, tiring, and repetitive. Clothing becomes soiled from wear, and the unacceptable appearance and odors of garments require washing to remove the dirt, stains, and bodily secretions from them. Once cleaned, clothes are worn and get dirty again, and the cycle is repeated.

Figure 4 Black washerwomen doing laundry, Dahlonega, Ga. c. 1900. Georgia Archives, Vanishing Georgia Collection, LUM 092.

Until relatively recent times, laundering was done entirely by hand. For most of history, there was no plumbing for running water or electricity for powering washing and drying machines. A washerwoman had to go to a source of water such as a stream or river or had to bring water, pail by pail to the house. She would soak clothes to loosen dirt and stains, use a paddle to pound the clothes lying on a solid surface to remove dirt, wring out excess water by hand, and then hang clothes on a line to dry in the sun and wind before finally ironing them.

Laundry work was universally considered a domestic chore, and traditionally relegated to women. Those with financial means assigned this drudgery to servants. In some regions, black washerwomen (See Figure 4) did laundry for white families and businesses when few commercial laundries existed. It was their major source of income, but the work was hard and the wages low.

When Chinese started laundries during the 1880s in the South, black laundresses challenged this threat to their livelihood.[25] The conflict was fairly mild as Chinese laundries focused on items from businessmen such as collars and white shirts and blue-collar work clothes rather than on domestic items such as bedding, linens, or women's clothing. The laundry 'business,' involving a needed service rather than a product, was an occupation well suited to their circumstances, requiring long and hard labor but no costly facilities or equipment.

Chinese were not the first to open commercial laundries; white-owned laundries existed since the early 1800s in England, and soon after in the U. S., using mechanized or steam driven laundry equipment.[26] These large power laundries competed with washerwomen, domestic servants, and Chinese hand laundries, with the advantage of being able to do larger amounts of laundry in less time. Still, for many years, the Chinese competed successfully against larger white-owned laundries.

---

[25] Black laundresses held a successful strike for higher wages from their white clientele in Atlanta in 1881. Tera W. Hunter, *To 'Joy My Freedom: Southern Black Women's Lives and Labors after the Civil War* (Cambridge: Harvard University Press, 1997).

[26] Mohun, *Steam Laundries.* **50-60.**

Chapter 1 examines factors that led Chinese immigrants to enter the laundry business from the mid 19th to the mid 20th century. Chapter 2 focuses on the social and economic conditions leading to the Chinese Exclusion Act, in effect from 1882-1943, and related discriminatory laws that adversely affected Chinese, leaving hand laundries as one of the few occupations available to them. Chapter 3 looks at how Chinese learned to be laundrymen, financial aspects of buying and running laundries, and how Chinese laundries survived initially against larger white-owned steam laundries. Chapter 4 discusses challenges to Chinese laundries from unjust laws and racist actions ranging from vandalism, assault, and robbery to even homicide. It describes how laundrymen lived, depending on region of the country and on the number of Chinese in their communities.

How kinship ties forged chains of migration for Chinese laundrymen is the focus of Chapter 5, using 19 laundrymen in the South descended from my great, great, great grandfather as a case study. Chapter 6 describes the hardship of laundry work and the austere living conditions of laundrymen and their families. We 'hear the voices' of children who grew up in their laundries describe their lives and laundry experiences in Chapter 7. Their vivid accounts give a first-hand glimpse into an important understudied topic. Finally, Chapter 8 examines the historical place of the Chinese laundry, serving as the primary economic launching pad for almost a century that enabled Guangdong immigrants to gain admission to Gold Mountain. Its declining role over the past century is contrasted with the rise of the Chinese restaurant as its replacement over the first half of the 20th century.

2. The Chinese Must Go

"We make no pretense that the exclusion of Chinese can be defended upon a high ideal, ethical ground... Surely, America's workmen have enough to contend with, have sufficient obstacles confronting them in their struggle ...without being required to meet the enervating, killing, underselling, and under-living competition of that nerveless, wantless people, the Chinese... it is our essential duty to maintain and preserve our physical condition and standard of life and civilization, and thus to assure us the opportunity for the development of our intellectual and moral character." [27]

An understanding of why Chinese here, and in Canada, had such limited work opportunities by the 1870s requires a closer examination of the extremely virulent and blatant racism directed toward them during that period by whites. Some of this hostile climate stemmed from the competition between whites and Chinese against a background of economic depression. The animosity was so intense that some journalists branded the Chinese as the 'yellow peril,' but this may have only been an excuse to justify movements to stop further Chinese immigration and to mistreat those already here.

In the mid 1800s, many members of these "inferior" races were allowed into the country primarily to meet the need for substantial supplies of cheap labor on many construction projects and to replace the freed slaves in the South. In many respects, American attitudes involved the 'negroization' of Chinese immigrants, treating their labor as similar to that of blacks, unfree and inferior, in contrast to that of whites. [28]

---

[27] American Federation of Labor. *"Report of Proceedings of the Twenty-Fifth Annual Convention,"* 1905.

[28] Najia Aarim-Heriot. *Chinese Immigrants, African Americans, and Racial Anxiety in the United States, 1848-82* (Urbana: University Of Illinois Press, 2006).

Thus, the U. S. and Canada both benefited by exploiting the abundant cheap labor of Chinese railroad workers. However, they became expendable, and undesirable, once the major rail construction was completed in 1869 in the United States and a decade later in Canada. The overnight supply of thousands of unemployed Chinese railroad construction workers posed a major threat to whites for jobs.

Whether the Chinese were 'willing' to work for less or whether racial prejudice led to them being offered lower wages can be debated. In any case, Chinese *did* work for lower wages than whites, giving them a competitive advantage at first. Willing to work hard and perform undesirable, and often dangerous, work for low wages, Chinese were more likely to be hired than whites, arousing white hostility.

The problem was compounded by the panic of 1873 stemming from bank failures that led to the economic depression that persisted until the late 1890s. The Chinese were blamed for these conditions. A bitter irony was that the transcontinental railroad, which the Chinese had been so instrumental in completing in 1869, failed to have the expected boost to the economy in the West and actually had the opposite effect by bringing cheaper goods as well as new supplies of white laborers from the east. Chinese were easy targets to scapegoat because their physical appearance, dress, language, and customs clearly distinguished them from whites. Moreover, they lacked political power to fight back.

Additionally, the fact that they sent money back to their families in China rather than spending it here fueled more resentment. But still the Chinese continued to come from the rural villages of Guangdong, not only to California, but also to the Pacific Northwest, and to western Canada as well, regions that had major gold strikes during approximately the same period.

Chinese proved to be capable, industrious, and reliable workers who generally were good members of their communities. The fact that they worked for low wages may have provoked resentment among the working class, but the capitalists who benefited from their cheaper labor did not want them excluded. Thus, after the Civil War, plantations in the South needed cheap labor to replace slave labor and a proposal to bring Chinese as contract workers to the region was made at a Memphis convention in 1869.[29]

Similarly, in the northeast, capitalists sought the cheap labor of the Chinese to help break strikes of white workers. In 1870, 75 Chinese were brought in from California to replace white strikers in a shoe factory in North Adams, Massachusetts.[30] In the same manner, 68 Chinese laborers were contracted in 1870 as replacement workers for striking Irish women in white-owned steam laundries in Belleville, New Jersey. One journalist denigrated the Chinese as "a plodding, viewless animal community who seem hardly cognizant of being in a place called Belleville, and utterly indifferent to all things beyond laundry and rice and tea. Their movements are slow and furtive, but they work with extreme regularity." [31] Ironically,

---

[29] Andrew Gyory. *Closing The Gate: Race, Politics, and the Chinese Exclusion Act.* (Chapel Hill, N.C.: University of North Carolina Press, 1998): 30-35.

[30] Ibid., 39-41.

[31] "The Chinese Washermen. A Visit to the Laundry at Belleville, New Jersey," *New York Times,* Dec. 26, 1872.

some of these Chinese replacements probably later became laundrymen in that part of the country using skills acquired in the white-owned laundries.

Other industrialists also turned to recruiting Chinese workers for lower wages. In 1872, a cutlery factory in Beaver Falls, Pennsylvania, recruited about 200 Chinese contract workers from California to replace white striking workers.[32] The use of Chinese to replace striking white workers added to the resentment among white labor.

Political pressures eventually led to a series of laws over the next decade in the U. S., and in Canada, that excluded Chinese laborers from mining, logging, fishing, farming and other occupations that they sought after railroad construction work was completed everywhere. They had little recourse but to compete for work by accepting lower wages. Many discovered there was less competition with whites for laundry work. This factor, rather than any special skills or experience in washing and ironing clothes, contributed to the sudden involvement of Chinese in this occupation with which they had no previous experience. Hundreds of small Chinese hand laundries appeared from one coast to the other over the last quarter of the 19th century.

Shaping Anti-Chinese Attitudes

Exclusionary laws denying entry to Chinese were not passed overnight. The groundwork for widespread support for outright exclusion first required a period of demonizing the Chinese as not everyone felt the Chinese should be excluded. Moreover, such treatment was unfair, if not illegal, under the 14th Amendment to the Constitution. Still, numerous

---

[32] Edward J. M. Rhoads, "Asian Pioneers in the Eastern United States: Chinese Cutlery Workers in Beaver Falls, Pennsylvania, in the 1870s" *Journal of Asian American Studies*, no.2 (1999): 119-155.

vociferous objections, especially among labor unions, were raised against the continued presence of Chinese in America.

Figure 5 Cover of music based on Bret Harte's 1870 poem, "The Heathen Chinee."

The attitude of white racial superiority rejected the Chinese. Disparaged as the 'heathen Chinee,' a term popularized by Bret Harte in 1870,[33] they were roundly condemned on moral grounds because of their propensity for engaging in gambling, prostitution, and opium smoking. Relegated to crowded living quarters, often in undesirable and segregated

---

[33] Harte's song about Ah Sin, a Chinese who feigned not knowing how to play cards but won by outrageous cheating. The last verse captures the negative view of Chinese that it fostered.

Which is why I remark,
And my language is plain,
That for ways that are dark,
And for tricks that are vain,
The heathen Chinee is peculiar-
Which the same I am free to maintain.

parts of town, they lived in unsanitary and offensive smelling hovels. The prejudicial treatment of Chinese helped make the biases become self-fulfilling.

Popular depictions of the Chinese focused on their 'Orientalism,'[34] emphasizing their irreconcilable differences with Occidental or western cultural customs. Christian missionaries who had gone to China in the 1700s to gain converts wrote home about the unusual food preferences, the queues or pigtails worn by the men, arranged marriages, concubines, foot binding of women, ancestor worship, and other exotic Chinese cultural traditions that clashed with American ways.

A popular argument against the Chinese was that they were sojourners who did not assimilate to American society. Yet, others have maintained that many Chinese did intend to resettle in America.[35] Of course, it is difficult to determine how much control the Chinese had over their fate. Did some Chinese want to return to China because of the hostile reception here or was their unwelcome presence in part a result of their intentions to be here only temporarily?

Still another view is that many Chinese had two identities, as they were 'Chinese' while in America but 'American' when they were in China. They had been Chinese when they first came, but over time they became

---

[34] Robert G. Lee, *Orientals: Asian Americans in Popular Culture* (Philadelphia: Temple University Press, 1999).

[35] In favor of the "sojourner hypothesis," 48 percent of Chinese, coming between 1848 and 1882 did return to China. This rate may be an underestimate, as others may have wanted to return but could not pay passage, or felt they would lose face for not being successful here. Still, it was a much higher rate than for European immigrants. It is likely that later immigrants were less likely to have been sojourners because conditions for them in the U. S. improved over the 20th century while it worsened in China. See Philip Q. Yang, "Sojourners or Settlers: Post-1965 Chinese Immigrants," *Journal of Asian American Studies*, 2 no. 1 (1999): 61-91.

somewhat Americanized and were no longer regarded as Chinese during their visits to China. And, in the United States, they were not totally regarded by Americans to be American. Instead of being either Chinese or American, they had a transpacific[36] identity reflected in their movements back and forth between both countries.

Whether Chinese were unable or simply unwilling to assimilate, advocates of exclusion felt Chinese would not establish roots here but eventually return to China. Eastern European immigrants assimilated into the American mainstream, but the Chinese stayed in their own enclaves, did not learn English, and gave allegiance to their families in China to whom they sent some of their earnings rather than spending it here.[37]

Increased Violence Against The Chinese

In the 1870s, the national economic downturn increased hostility among working class whites toward Chinese laborers. Labor unions were militantly opposed to the increased number of Chinese laundries. The Workingmen's Party led by its vociferous spokesman, Denis Kearney waged vicious campaigns in California against capitalists and the Chinese alike, both viewed by him as enemies of the working man.[38] Rallying around his battle cry, 'The Chinese must go,' open hostility soon erupted

---

[36] Yong Chen, *San Francisco Chinese: 1850-1943: A Trans-Pacific Community* (Stanford: Stanford University Press, 2000).

[37] Indeed a Supreme Court Justice wrote an opinion in the later case of Wong Kim Ark in 1898, "Large numbers of Chinese laborers of a distinct race and religion, remaining strangers in the land, residing apart by themselves... and apparently incapable of assimilating with our people, might endanger good order and be injurious to the public interests."

[38] Elmer Clarence Sandmeyer, *The Anti-Chinese Movement in California* (Urbana: University of Illinois Press, 1939), 66-67.

into violence against Chinese who were assaulted and, in some instances, killed throughout the west.

In the 1870s, sporadic and small incidents of white violence against Chinese workers occurred in some western communities. Eventually several riots occurred in western towns, with many Chinese assaulted and some even killed. Angry white rioters destroyed Chinese stores and homes.

In Los Angeles in 1871, a dispute between some rival Chinese factions attracted a crowd. Gunfire erupted among members of these tongs, support groups originally formed for protection that later engaged in illegal activities. One white bystander was accidentally shot and killed, prompting the crowd to riot against the Chinese. They looted homes and businesses of the Chinese, and killed at least 19 Chinese.[39]

In 1880, an argument between white railroad workers and Chinese in a Denver, Colorado bar led to violent attacks (See Figure 6). Over 2,000 rioters became involved in the destruction of Chinese laundries, and even the lynching of one Chinese.[40]

In Chicago, the Trades and Labor Assembly made a resolution in 1882 supporting strikers in a labor dispute. It also used the opportunity to rail specifically against Chinese laundries and their patrons. Their platform included a Chinese Plank stating: "That 'Scabs' shall be treated as traitors and enemies to those who raise and maintain the standard of life so as to afford the greatest good to the greatest number; those that

---

[39]http://www.cr.nps.gov/history/online_books/5views/5views3h54.htm (accessed Dec. 1, 2006).

[40] Sharon M. Lee, "Asian Immigration And American Race Relations From Exclusion To Acceptance," *Ethnic and Racial Studies* 12, no. 3 (1989): 369-390.

exercise in their capacity as 'Scabs' and aliens must not settle among people which tend to an industrial self-government. We detest all men who patronize Chinese laundries, and hope the Chinese nuisance will soon be abated."[41]

Figure 6 Anti- Chinese riot, Denver, Oct 30, 1880. Library of Congress LC-USZC2-760.

Another atrocious episode of violence, the Rock Springs Massacre, described in Figure 7, occurred at a work site in Wyoming in 1885.[42] Angered by the replacement of whites by about 500 Chinese brought to work in the coalmines, a mob decided to drive them out of town. With no weapons or barriers to hold off the surprise attacks, 28

---

[41] "Chicago Workingmen Resolve," *Los Angeles Times*, March 20, 1882, 1.

[42] Craig Storti. *Incident at Bitter Creek: The Story of the Rock Springs Chinese Massacre* (Ames, Iowa: Iowa State University Press, 1991).

defenseless Chinese workers were killed and 15 others injured. Most of their homes were destroyed. The survivors fled to other towns where they were also threatened with bodily harm. The U. S. Army had to send 300 soldiers to enable them to return to bury their dead and retrieve what was left of their possessions. No one was ever convicted and all suspects were released a month after the incident.

THE MASSACRE OF THE CHINESE.

SIXTEEN KNOWN TO HAVE BEEN KILLED AND MANY WOUNDED.

ROCK SPRINGS, Wyoming, Sept. 4.—A glance over the battle ground of Wednesday reveals the fact that many of the bullets fired at the fleeing Chinamen found their mark. Lying in the smoldering embers where Chinatown stood were found 10 charred and shapeless trunks, sending up a noisome stench, while another, which had evidently been dragged from the ashes by boys, was found in the sage brush near by. A search resulted in the finding of the bodies of five more Chinamen, killed by rifle shots while fleeing from their pursuers. All were placed in pine coffins and buried yesterday afternoon. Some six or eight others were found seriously wounded, and were cared for by the railroad officers. The Coroner's jury has rendered a verdict to the effect that the men came to their death at the hands of parties unknown. Reports from along the line of the railroad are to the effect that Chinamen have been arriving at small stations east and west of here, and they say that a large number of the fugitives were wounded by Wednesday's attack, and that many have perished in the hills. It is feared that it will be found that no less than 50 lost their lives when all the returns are in. This trouble has been brewing for months. The contractors who run the mines have been importing Chinamen in large numbers and discharging white men, until over 600 Celestials were in their employ. It is said that mine bosses have favored the Chinamen to the detriment of white miners, and it needed only a spark to kindle the flames. This was furnished by a quarrel between a party of Celestials and whites in mine No. 6 over their right to work in a certain chamber. A fight ensued and the Chinamen were

Figure 7 The Rock Springs, Wyoming Massacre. *New York Times*, Sept. 5, 1885, 5.

When nothing was done to punish the perpetrators of the Rock Springs massacre, violence against Chinese quickly spread across the Pacific Northwest. Shortly later in the same year, strong anti-Chinese sentiment in Seattle led to a manifesto that all Chinese must leave the Washington Territory. They were rounded up and ordered to leave on a steamer. Anti-Chinese sentiment led to similar expulsions of Chinese from Tacoma, Washington (See Figure 8), Eureka, California, and other western cities.[43]

Figure 8 Anti-Chinese rally poster. Courtesy, Washington State Historical Society, Tacoma.

A popular stereotypical image used to represent Chinese was a caricature of a laundryman. The imagery in Figure 9 vividly urged the expulsion of Chinese laundrymen, but the larger message was that all Chinese must go, and by force, if necessary. The enforcer was not depicted as a mob of workers but in the form of Uncle Sam himself.

---

[43] Jean Pfaezler, *Driven Out: The Forgotten Was Against Chinese Americans* (New York: Random House, 2007).

Figure 9 An 1886 soap ad endorsed Chinese exclusion. The caption: "We have no use for them since we got this WONDERFUL WASHER: What a blessing to tired mothers: It costs so little and don't injure the clothes." Library of Congress LC-USZC4-2045.

Anti-Chinese Legislation

Discriminatory laws in California in the mid 1800s denying Chinese access to many forms of work and restricting their civil rights were intended to discourage new Chinese immigrants from coming and motivate those already here to leave.[44] That these efforts failed to stop immigration was in large measure due to successful appeals of the Chinese for protection from the courts. Nor did the rising tide of violence stem the flow of Chinese immigration. Pressure mounted for national legislation to make it more difficult for Chinese come to, or stay, here.

Page Act

The Page Act, aimed at preventing the kidnapping or importation of 'Mongolian, Chinese, or Japanese' females for immoral purposes, was

---

[44] McClain, *In Search of Equality*, 278-282.

passed in 1875. Thousands of Asian women, sometimes involuntarily, were being brought to the United States for prostitution. The wording of the law, however, also had a chilling effect on Chinese women who had legitimate reasons for immigration because the statute required all women to present evidence that they were persons who were coming voluntarily and "of correct habits and good character." In short, Chinese women immigrants were generally presumed to be prostitutes unless they could prove otherwise.

This legal barrier further reduced the already small number of Chinese women coming to the U. S. so there were few families in Chinese communities. Anti-miscegenation laws opposed white women marrying men of other races. Chinese taboos against out-marriages also worked for many years to relegate most Chinese men to bachelorhood unless they could return to marry in China. Despite these barriers, a few men did enter interracial marriages with whites as well as blacks. Others resorted to patronizing brothels. The absence of wives and children prevented most Chinese from having a normal family life and undoubtedly contributed toward increasing the number of men gambling or smoking opium.

Based on census data, the ratio of Chinese men to women in the U. S. was already high at 21:1 in 1880,[45] It rose to a peak of 27:1 by 1890 after exclusion and did not approach parity unless after 1970. This imbalance was partly because most immigrants were young men, about half of whom were unmarried. Few unmarried women came since few jobs existed for women. In 1900, ratios of men to women in California

---

[45] Judy Yung, *Unbound Feet: A Social History of Chinese Women in San Francisco* (Berkeley: University of California Press, 1995), 293.

were 12:1 and in San Francisco at 5:1 and even higher in the east at 45:1 in New York State and 47:1 in New York City.[46] As many of these few women were prostitutes, marriage prospects for laundrymen were low.[47]

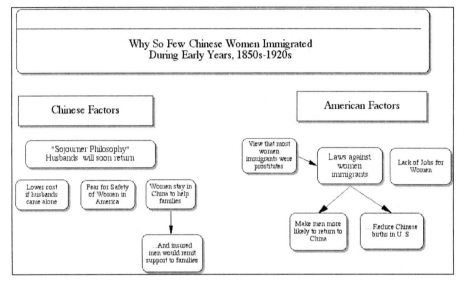

Figure 10 Overview of early factors affecting Chinese women coming to America.

Married men generally left their wives behind in Guangdong for several reasons.[48] First, some barely had enough money to pay their own passage and they would not have been able to afford the costs of bringing a wife, or children. The uncertainty and dangers of life in a new country also discouraged them from bringing their wives until they could first establish themselves in the new land. Some wives who came over

---

[46] Xiaolan Bao, *Holding Up More Than Half The Sky: Chinese Women Garment Workers in New York City, 1948-92.* (Urbana: University of Illinois Press, 2001).: 44-45; Wang, "No Tickee, No Shirtee," 47-48.

[47] Chan, "Against All Odds," 56. A surprisingly high, over 62, percent of Chinese women in the 1900 San Francisco census were single when they entered. A conjecture is that many were brought in to be prostitutes, and in many cases, under coercion.

[48] Huping Ling, *Surviving Gold Mountain: A History of Chinese American Women and Their Lives* (Albany, N.Y.: State University of New York Press, 1998).

eventually decided to return to China because in many respects they were actually were better off there, provided their husbands sent money back. Living in a land where they did not know the language and customs and also where they faced strong racial prejudices made their lives very difficult. In addition, there were cultural reasons for remaining in or returning to China because wives were expected to fulfill obligations to assist their in-laws.

In the view of one American woman observer in 1892, the Chinese do not want their women to come to America because:

> Very few have brought their wives and families, largely because they are unwilling to expose their families to the persecutions which they themselves suffered. The women are not anxious to come. Respectable women in China live in strict seclusion, and they dread the long journey from home, and life among the "foreign devils." ...The parents of the men also object to letting the wives and children go, lest their sons should never return, and there should be no one to worship their memories.[49]

Whites opposed to Chinese felt that by preventing them from legally bringing wives and families to the U. S,[50] immigration would be reduced. The logic was that without Chinese women, fewer men would come and some of those already here would leave sooner.[51] An additional benefit was that fewer Chinese would be born here.

---

[49] Mary Chapman, "Notes on the Chinese in Boston" *The Journal of American Folklore*, 19, no. 5 (1892): 321-324.

[50] A social reformer argued that many problems of the Chinese would be lessened if they were allowed to bring their wives to America. See Jacob A. Riis, *How The Other Half Lives: A Study among the New York Tenements* (New York: Charles Scribner's, 1890).

[51] George A. Peffer, *If They Don't Bring Their Women Here: Chinese Female Immigration Before Exclusion* (Urbana: University of Illinois Press, 1999).

Chinese Exclusion Act (1882)

Anti-Chinese sentiment and violence against them continued to mount over the 1870s.[52] In 1882, despite the major contributions Chinese made to the economic growth and development of the nation in building the railroads, constructing irrigation systems, and farming the land, the Chinese Exclusion Act was passed to bar further entry of Chinese laborers.[53] It is the only law in American history ever aimed at excluding a specific ethnic group.[54]

Opposition to the exclusion law also existed, coming mainly from capitalists and politicians who felt that lucrative trade with China would be jeopardized by such policies.[55] Their stance, however, was motivated by self-interests rather than moral or legal concerns. Objections were also voiced from religious groups that saw exclusion as indefensible on moral grounds but they had little power to stem the tide. The gross unfairness of the law and the screening process led the Chinese to devise illegal methods of entry. Many laborers used false documents they purchased

---

[52] In this negatively charged atmosphere, many terms of the 1868 Burlingame Treaty beneficial to Chinese immigrants were nullified when it was revised in 1880 in response to political pressure. These initial changes put limits on entry of laborers but stopped short of outright exclusion. The terms still allowed entry of teachers, students, merchants, or those coming from curiosity, together with their body and household servants as well as reentry of Chinese laborers who were in China for visits but had previously lived in the United States.

[53] In 1893, the McCreary Amendment essentially expanded the definition of 'laborer' by narrowing the definition of merchant to "a person engaged in buying and selling merchandise at a fixed place of business, which business is conducted in his name, and who during the time he claims to be engaged as a merchant does not engage in the performance of any manual labor, except such as is necessary in the conduct of his business as such merchant."

[54] In 1885 Canada first imposed a Head Tax of $50, which was unsuccessful even though it was raised to $500 by the Canadian Immigration Act of 1903, equivalent to two years' wages for a laborer in 1903. Over 80,000 Chinese came despite the tax so it was abandoned in 1923 in favor of an outright ban of laborers until the law was repealed in1947.

[55] Lucy E. Salyer, *Laws Harsh as Tigers: Chinese Immigrants and the Shaping of Modern Immigration Law* (Chapel Hill: University of North Carolina Press, 1995), 16.

while others acquired merchant status by paying to become "paper partners" in existing Chinese businesses. Many laundrymen, restaurant workers, miners and other laborers had gained entry posing as bankers, merchants, or students. Chinese felt these methods were morally defensible in view of the injustices they suffered.

Consequently, inspectors developed intensive interrogations to detect fraud involving a barrage of questions about minute details of the immigrant's background, number and characteristics of relatives, living conditions in their homes, and physical details of their houses and villages. Inconsistencies in testimony among witnesses or within the applicant's own answers could be used to deny entry. These methods were sometimes successful in identifying imposters, but they also excluded some applicants entitled to enter.   The net effect was to intimidate all immigrants, but thousands of applicants still applied. The success of Chinese in answering the questions lay partly in the fact that the same basic types of questions were always asked, allowing the earlier arriving Chinese to insure that later arrivals knew what questions to expect.[56]

Exclusion was not based entirely on race, but also involved social class. Thus, where it was advantageous to the United States interests in trade with China, as in the admission of merchants, the law allowed exemptions.   Merchants were admitted because, unlike laborers, they could contribute to the economy of the country especially those involved with trade between the U. S. and China.   They were also acceptable

---

[56] Prior to arrival, immigrants memorized answers to stock questions that they would be likely asked. Immigration officials, on the other hand, viewed the success of many immigrants in passing the hurdles as proof that they were cunning, devious, and untrustworthy aliens. Adam McKeown, "Ritualization of Regulation: The Enforcement of Chinese Exclusion 1898-1924," *American Historical Review*, 108, (2003): 377- 403.

because they were more educated than laborers. This externally imposed class differentiation divided and adversely affected the Chinese American community for many decades.[57]

This law was intended to last only 10 years but political pressure of white labor activists kept it alive. In a 1902 address to Congress, Samuel Gompers, the first President of the powerful AFL/CIO labor union, argued that the Chinese were taking away work from whites.[58] This helped renew the exclusion law, and its indefinite extension in 1904.

> Beginning with the most menial avocations they gradually invaded our industry they gradually invaded one industry after another until they not merely took the places of our girls as domestics and cooks, the laundry of our poorer white women, but the places of the men and boys, as boot and shoemakers, cigarmakers, bagmakers, miners, farm laborers, brickmakers, tailors, slippermakers, etc.

How The Chinese Fought Exclusion

The Chinese combined their resources to seek legal redress and to contest the many legal obstacles imposed on them. Chinese

---

[57] Other laws against the Chinese soon followed. In 1888, the Scott Act severely restricted Chinese laborers who were already residing here from returning to China for visits. They could not reenter unless they owned property or held a business investment of $1,000 or more. More than 20,000 laborers who had gone to China for visits before the Act passed were denied reentry even though they held valid return certificates obtained prior to leaving the U. S.

The Geary Act of 1892 required Chinese to carry a Certificate of Residence at all times. During periodic unannounced sweeps of areas with large Chinese populations, failure to have it with them when a U. S. Marshal or deputy asked to inspect it could result in deportation.

The National Origins Act of 1924, which changed to a quota system for immigration prevented Chinese Americans here from bringing their wives from China. American-born Chinese women lost their citizenship if they married someone who did not qualify for citizenship. The criteria for merchant status were tightened, requiring international trade, adversely affecting entry of wives and families of laborers as it was harder to acquire merchant status by purchasing partnerships in existing businesses.

[58] American Federation of Labor, *Some Reasons for Chinese Exclusion. Meat Vs. Rice. American Manhood Against Asiatic Coolieism .Which Shall Survive?* Senate Doc. No. 137, 57th Congress, 1st Session (Washington D. C.: Government Printing Office, 1902).

had already formed *gongsi,* organizations for mutual aid for men from the same districts in Guangdong, and *huiguans* or family or clan associations. Such organizations provided new arrivals to America a place where they could stay for a few days, get assistance in locating relatives, and help in finding work.[59] As the anti-Chinese sentiment grew in the late 19th century, Chinese unified these smaller organizations into a single organization, the Chinese Consolidated Benevolent Association (CCBA), to better defend their rights and provide members with legal assistance.[60]

"Paper Son" Method of Entry

Despite imposing barriers to entry, Chinese still found ways (See Figure 11). A laundryman, or any other laborer, wanting to bring family members over had to first locate someone trusted that was exempt from exclusion such as a merchant, someone born in the U. S. and thus holding U. S. citizenship (or claiming their U. S. birth records had been destroyed in the 1906 San Francisco fire).

Many men in these exempt groups had, on previous return visits to China, 'created' entry slots for fictitious or 'paper sons' by falsely declaring the birth of a child, usually a son which could be used in future years for the son to immigrate.[61] Immigration officials could not readily

---

[59] Renqui Yu, *The Chinese Hand Laundry Alliance of New York.* (Philadelphia: Temple University Press, 1992), 12-19.

[60] Also known as the Chinese Six Companies, this merchant-led organization promoted economic interests and handled disputes among Chinese. Competing factions sometimes led to violent tong wars among rivals for control.

[61] Erika Lee, *At America's Gates: Chinese Immigration during the Exclusion Era, 1882-1943.* (Chapel Hill: University of North Carolina Press, 2003), 194-195, 201-207.

refute these claims, as China did not have registries of births and marriages.

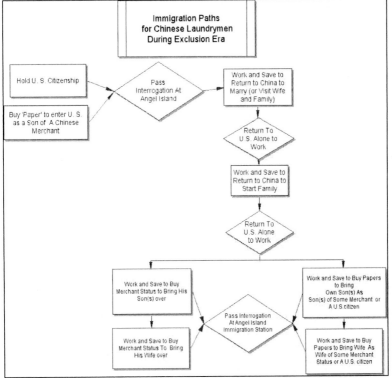

Figure 11 Different methods for Chinese immigrants to gain entry to the U. S.

Upon arrival in San Francisco, 'paper sons,' as they came to be known, still had to pass a difficult interrogation at Angel Island by immigration officers who vigorously sought to detect imposters to deny their entry. Paper sons memorized extensive family histories of people they typically had never met and geographical facts about their village where they had usually never been. Their answers had to be consistent with testimony of prior relatives, which were available to immigration officers from files that extended back for many years in some cases.[62]

Unused slots not needed to bring their family members were sold to relatives of a laborer whose family was ineligible to enter the U. S. These 'paper' relatives would apply for entry to the U. S. claiming to be the son, wife, or other relative of a member of the exempted categories already cited, merchant, U. S. citizen, or student. [63]

Habeas Corpus Challenges to Denial of Entry

When Chinese immigrants were detained or denied entry, the CCBA hired American lawyers to aid Chinese plaintiffs in gaining entry by filing writs of *habeas corpus*.[64] This legal action challenged the immigration

---

[62] Use of false papers, *gai chee*, was not an ethical issue among Chinese, as they felt unfairly excluded in the first place. Their concern was to memorize the information about their paper identity and family history that was needed to pass the immigration interrogation.

[63] For a better understanding of the convoluted gauntlet Chinese immigrants faced, it is instructive to see the actual documents they had to file and the transcripts of their interrogations. Excellent websites created by descendants of immigrants provide this valuable information.

Yee Jock Leong opened a laundry in 1920 in Dayton, Ohio, which he ran until he died in 1936. A great grandson created a website, http://fuzzo.com/genealogy/YeeJo#E34FA (accessed June 15, 2006), that provides a chronology of his life. Copies of his immigration file documents are included. Yee's address books, also posted, show that even though he was isolated in the Midwest, he had addresses of over 100 Chinese immigrants all over the U. S., although how often he corresponded with them is unknown.

Gong Bow Gwun, came in 1912 and had a laundry in Merced, California during the 1920s A year later he was finally able to bring his wife, Lock Shee using the identity of the wife of his brother. In 1925 they moved to Woodland, California where they operated another laundry until 1947. An excellent family website, http://www.tonaidin.net/Bios/Gong-Din_history/history.htm (accessed Aug 15, 2006) covers the Gong/Din family immigration history detailing intricate immigration procedures and includes copies of documents and transcripts of the interrogations.

[64] From 1891 to 1905 over half of 2,228 appeals won. See Robert Barde, "An Alleged Wife. One Immigrant in the Chinese Exclusion Era. Part 2." (Prologue: Quarterly of the National Archives and Records Administration, 36 no. 1, 2004): 24-35. Another analysis found that between 1910 and 1924, over 93 percent of appeals were successful. See Erika Lee, "Defying Exclusion: Chinese Immigrants and their Strategies during the Exclusion Era," In *Chinese American Transnationalism: The Flow of People, Resources, and Ideas between China and America during the Exclusion Era.* Edited by Sucheng Chan (Philadelphia: Temple University Press, 2006), 1-21.

authorities to provide evidence that individuals should be denied entry or to release them (See Figure 12). Judges, committed to adherence to legal principles and procedures, often found insufficient grounds for exclusion in specific cases, and discharged the deportation.[65] [66]

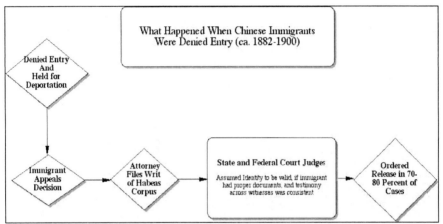

What Happened When Chinese Immigrants Were Denied Entry (ca. 1882-1900)

Denied Entry And Held for Deportation

Immigrant Appeals Decision

Attorney Files Writ of Habeas Corpus

State and Federal Court Judges

Assumed Identity to be valid, if immigrant had proper documents, and testimony across witnesses was consistent

Ordered Release in 70-80 Percent of Cases

Figure 12 Inspectors denied entry of many Chinese but a majority won their appeals.

Advantages of Merchant Classification

The importance of holding a merchant rather than laborer status cannot be overstated. It is dramatically illustrated by specific cases of two laundrymen that Chinese Inspectors suspected were not merchants, as they had claimed to be.

Lee Wong Hing, age 45, of Holyoke, Massachusetts had lived for 27 years in the U. S. when he made a visit to China. Upon his attempt to reenter the U. S. in January 1904 at Port Townsend, Washington, he was

---

[65] Salyer, *Laws Harsh as Tigers*, 18-19.

[66] This right to have a "day in court" to contest decisions denying entry lasted only about 20 years. In the Ju Toy case in 1905, an initially favorable ruling of a U. S. District Court was reversed by the U. S. Circuit Court (San Francisco) and then upheld by the U. S. Supreme Court. After this historic case, courts no longer could overrule immigration decisions. "Due process" for immigrants now was limited to appeals within the executive branch, except for claims of unlawful or arbitrary actions. See *U. S. v. Ju Toy 198 US 253* (1905). China boycotted American goods in protest.

detained while an Inspector in Boston went to Hing's store in Massachusetts to inspect his place of business. He was denied reentry based on the Boston Chinese Inspector's report on Feb. 11, 1904 that concluded his store included a laundry and a grocery.

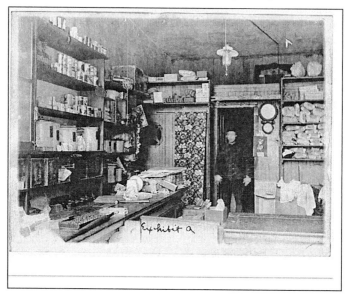

Figure 13 Interior of Lee Wong Hing's store in Holyoke, Ma. ca.1904. File Unit from Record Group 85: Records of the Immigration and Naturalization Service, 1787 – 1998. NARA's Pacific Alaska Region (Seattle), Seattle, WA. ARC Identifier: 298983 Accessed 7/20/2006.

As Figure 13 shows, the interior of the store had shelves of canned foods on the left side and wrapped packages of laundry on shelves on the right side. A doorway in the middle led into the back of the store where there were spaces for several people to sleep so that it appeared the building also served as a rooming house. Another photograph (See Figure 14) of the front window of Hing's store clearly indicates it was a laundry. In contrast, the only external indication that it was a grocery store appears only in a small inconspicuous sign reading, "Quong Hing Wah & Co.," posted on the telephone pole outside the store at the curb. This discrepancy led the immigration officer to conclude that Hing was not a merchant but in fact only a laundryman, a laborer who was not exempt from exclusion.

Figure 14 Exterior of Lee Wong Hing's store at 141 High St., Holyoke, Ma. File Unit from Record Group 85: Records of the Immigration and Naturalization Service, 1787 – 1998. NARA's Pacific Alaska Region (Seattle), Seattle, WA. ARC Identifier: 298983 Accessed 7/20/2006.

Two white lawyers testified on his behalf that they had never seen him engaged in any laundry labor during their visits to the store. This type of evidence was essential whenever an immigrant claimed exemption from exclusion as a merchant. Witnesses not only had to be white, but they had to declare in their affidavit that they were non-Chinese. Despite their supportive testimony, the Inspector ruled that Hing was a laundryman, not a merchant. Hing was given two days in which to appeal, but his attempt failed. The extent to which the authorities investigated cases with such zeal is not known, but this case was not an isolated incident.

Another case involved Lock Doon who attempted to reenter the U. S. in 1903 after a visit to China. The Chinese Inspector at Port Townsend, Washington was not convinced that he was a merchant in

Olympia, Washington. This case was similar to the Lee Wong Hing case as the inspector had photographic evidence that made him conclude that Lock was actually a laundryman rather than a merchant. His ruling was based on photographs of Doon's store, which showed there was an inside passageway connecting his store with a laundry.

Figure 15 Lock Doon's Hong Yek Merchantile Store (middle building) had an inner door connecting to the Kwong Hong Yick (building on the corner). File Unit from Record Group 85: Records of the Immigration and Naturalization Service, 1787 – 1998. NARA's Pacific Alaska Region (Seattle), Seattle, WA. ARC Identifier: 298993. Accessed 7/20/2006.

From the street (See Figure 15), it appears that the laundry on the corner is a different store from the one on its left. But inside the building (See Figure 16), clearly there is an open doorway that connects Doon's Hong Yek merchandise store with the laundry. Lock Doon enlisted four white citizens, one an attorney, to testify that he was a merchant and they had never seen him engaged in any labor or laundry work. One witness claimed that the connecting door between the two stores had been closed since the photograph had been taken. Unlike the unfortunate Lee Wong Hing, eventually Lock Doon won his appeal and was readmitted.

Figure 16 Interior of Hong Yek Store leads across doorway into Kwong Hong Yick Laundry. File Unit from Record Group 85: Records of the Immigration and Naturalization Service, 1787 – 1998 NARA's Pacific Alaska Region (Seattle), Seattle, WA. ARC Identifier: 298993 Accessed 7/20/2006.

These two cases, with opposite outcomes, clearly show how advantageous it was to be classified as a merchant rather than a laborer. However, the evidence is unclear as to why one man won his appeal and the other one did not. Perhaps minor factors often affected the decisions of Chinese inspectors, rulings that had the power to determine the future lives of Chinese laundrymen.

3. Chinese Enter The Laundry Business

Laundry work is a thankless lot.
You work day and night; you work round the clock.
Ironing, washing, it's full of anxiety and all fatigue.
You miss your meals; you don't have enough sleep.
Everyday, every year, that's the way it is indeed.
You work yourself to poor health;
You hurt yourself at work.
Alas, it's a hell of a way to work for a lousy living![67]

By the 1880s, the hand laundry emerged as a major occupation of Chinese immigrants.[68] Growing numbers of Chinese entered the laundry business in the U. S. and Canada during these years and into the first quarter of the 20th century. Chinese preferred entrepreneurial and business opportunities, which allowed them more independence than work as laborers for white employers.

The Chinese immigrants of the late 19th century arrived on the West Coast at a time when domestic servants, almost all women, had the task of doing laundry. However, the ratio of men to women in the West during the mid 1800s was so high there was a severe shortage of providers of this service. Since washing and ironing was regarded as women's work, the Chinese were able to engage in that occupation for a while without serious objection from whites. Chinese accepted this niche near the bottom of the social ladder. As noted earlier, denied access to many other forms of work, many Chinese had little choice but to become domestic

---

[67] Xu Yan *China Daily News*. Dec. 14, 1946.

[68] Joan Shiow-Huey Wang, *"'No Tickee, No Shirtee:' Chinese Laundries in the Social Context of the Eastern United States: 1882-1943."* (PhD diss., Carnegie Mellon University, 1996): 21-32.

servants or houseboys. Working as servants they acquired experience in doing laundry and cooking meals, skills that they later used in laundry and restaurant businesses that served the predominantly male populations of the early west. They realized doing the 'dirty work' of cleaning laundry for other people was a relatively uncontested opportunity for work.

After Chinese immigrants expanded their presence in the laundry business during the last part of the 19th century, a decade or so later they began to enter the restaurant business. They became involved with these occupations more from chance and the necessity for survival than from the application of any skills they had brought with them from China. The hand laundry served as their first long-term avenue to economic survival, providing the Chinese immigrants and their descendants the foothold they needed to grab a step onto the bottom rung of the ladder that they might climb to greater economic success in America.[69] Operating their own business was not easy, but they were no longer dependent on the decisions of employers, many who were prejudiced against Chinese.

Chinese faced little or no initial opposition to their operation of hand laundries. Even where they faced anti-Chinese sentiment and had to compete with non-Chinese laundries and washerwomen as in Virginia City, Nevada, they managed to survive because the need for laundry service exceeded the supply.[70] By 1870 there were about 2,600 Chinese

---

[69] Paul M. Ong, "An Ethnic Trade: The Chinese Laundries in Early California" *Journal of Ethnic Studies*, 8, no. 4 (1981): 95–113.

[70] Virginia City, Nevada thrived from the Comstock silver mines during the 1860s to the 1880s. Diverse ethnic groups, ages, and genders co-existed in competing for laundry work. Although 29 percent of the Chinese there ran a high percentage of the 40 Virginia City laundries in 1880, there were also Native American and Irish washer women, German male-owned small laundries, and large Euro-American-owned laundries that carved out their own segments of the large market for laundry service during the Comstock lode years. Although Chinese faced racism they survived

laundrymen in California, about half located in San Francisco and they constituted roughly 12 percent of the Chinese there. By 1880 Chinese operated over three-fourths of all laundries in California, according to census records.[71]

Impact of Exclusion Law on Chinese Laundries

However, life became much more difficult for laundrymen after the Chinese Exclusion law passed in 1882. Classified as laborers, Chinese laundrymen were no longer permitted to bring family members into the country.

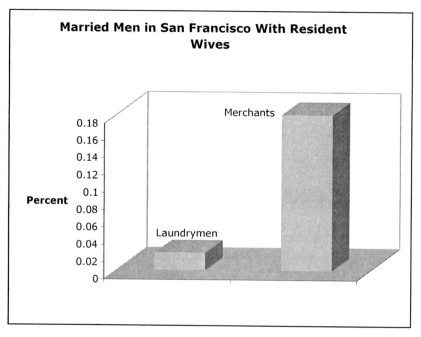

Figure 17 Married laundrymen vs. merchants in San Francisco whose wives lived with them. Based on 1900 U. S. Census data compiled by Sucheng Chan, 2006., Table 3.3A

---

with low prices for efficient work. Their eventual closings were due to the end of the mining boom rather than to the competition from other groups or from anti-Chinese sentiment. Ronald M. James, Richard D. Adkins, and Rachel J. Hartigan, "Competition and Coexistence in the Laundry: A View of the Comstock," *The Western Historical Quarterly*, 25, no. 2 (1994): 164-184.

[71] Wang, "No Tickee, No Shirtee," 26.

Based on U. S. Census data for 1900 (See Figure 17), less than 2 percent of the married laundrymen in San Francisco had their wives with them, irrespective of whether they were born in the U. S. or China whereas 18 percent of the married merchants had resident wives.[72]

Overall, although 62 percent of the China-born men in San Francisco were married, only 13 percent had wives here in the U. S. with them. Among Chinese born in San Francisco, only 17 percent were married. Only 21.5 percent of the U. S. born married men had their wives living with them reflecting the possibility that many who went to China to marry, as was common then, left wives there when they returned here.

Some laundrymen arranged fake merchant status by purchasing partnership shares in a store. Other laundrymen paid a merchant to bring relatives over using identities of the merchant's kin. Not surprisingly, in some laundries one might find a father, his brothers, and sons working together but not all of them bearing the same surname as the father.

In some cases, a laundryman unable to gain merchant status was able to find a merchant willing to claim the laundryman's wife as his own by selling a false identity for her. For example, if a merchant's wife in China died, and it was not disclosed to immigration authorities, a laundryman's wife could attempt to enter using the deceased woman's papers. Of course, she would have to memorize extensive information about the family history, names and ages of all relatives, the village, the home, and other matters to answer the detailed questions she would

---

[72]Analysis of U. S. Census 1900 data in Table 3.3A from Sucheng Chan, "Against All Odds: Chinese Female Migration and Family Formation on American Soil During the Early Twentieth Century," In *Chinese American Transnationalism: The Flow of People, Resources, and Ideas between China and America during the Exclusion Era,* edited by Sucheng Chan (Philadelphia: Temple University Press, 2006), 84-85.

receive when she tried to enter the U. S. The task was especially difficult because often she had never met the relatives or been in their village. She also had to avoid confusing facts about her real and fictive families.

The harsh reality was that even a laundryman who had enough money to buy papers still had to locate brokers who could obtain and sell him papers for each relative. If they succeeded on those tasks, there was still considerable risk that they might be detected as an imposter upon interrogation at San Francisco or other ports of entry. Given the distance separating the laundryman and his relatives in China, and the slow and expensive means of communicating with them, the logistics of arranging and planning entry into the U. S. required an extensive network of assistance to succeed in such a difficult undertaking.[73]

Laundry Work Becomes A Primary Chinese Occupation

About 20 percent of all Chinese men in San Francisco in 1900 were laundry workers (See Figure 18). The rates varied only slightly by marital status and whether they were born in the U. S. versus China.[74] In southern California, about 25 percent of the 102 Chinese in San Bernardino in 1880 were laundrymen while another 25 percent were cooks and domestic servants. Another 38 percent were laborers, including

---

[73] Paul C. P. Siu, *The Chinese Laundryman: A Study in Isolation* (New York: New York University Press, 1987), 84-85. If unable to bring relatives over, they typically chose those who worked for the lowest pay, usually black women. Before the 1930s, black women, many who had migrated to northern cities from the South, were employed in many Chinese laundries in Chicago as hand ironers.

[74] Analysis of U. S. Census 1900 data in Table 3.1A from Sucheng Chan, "Against All Odds: Chinese Female Migration and Family Formation," 72-73.

farm, railroad, and miscellaneous jobs. Less than 2 percent were merchants.[75]

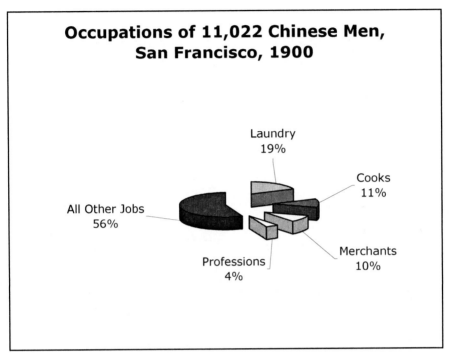

Occupations of 11,022 Chinese Men, San Francisco, 1900

Laundry 19%

Cooks 11%

All Other Jobs 56%

Merchants 10%

Professions 4%

Figure 18 Leading occupations for Chinese men in San Francisco, 1900. Based on U. S. Census data tabulations by Sucheng Chan, 2006.

In cities where many Chinese immigrants lived, work opportunities other than laundries existed. Many worked for or owned businesses that provided services to other Chinese such as grocery stores, restaurants, and Chinese merchandise stores. In El Paso, Texas, where it was relatively easy for Chinese immigrants to cross the Mexican border undetected, a growing Chinese population of about 300 existed in 1910. The U. S. Census manuscripts (See excerpts in Figure 19) showed that many Chinese there operated laundries, but even more worked as cooks,

---

[75] "Asians in the Inland Empire," http://kstephens.topcities.com/soc590/census1880.htm (accessed Aug. 11, 2006).

dishwashers, and waiters. In addition, there were merchants as well as druggists and three physicians. In the much larger Chinese community of Philadelphia, laundrymen were numerous in 1910 but surpassed in numbers by merchants and restaurant workers.

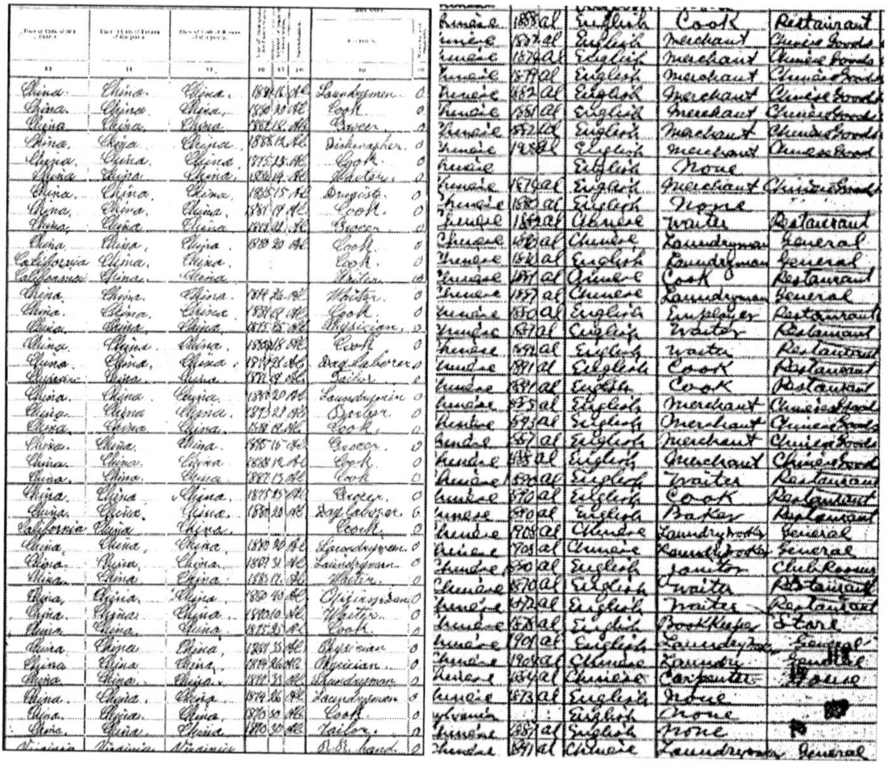

Figure 19 Comparison of sample of jobs, El Paso, Tx. (left) and Philadelphia, 1910 (right).

However, laundry work was virtually the exclusive occupation in the countless communities where very few Chinese lived. A representative sampling of communities across the U. S. showed that in the 1900 U. S. Census almost all of the 41 Chinese in Atlanta, Georgia, and all 32 Chinese in Tampa, Florida, were listed as Heads of, or as workers in laundries. In Milwaukee, Wisconsin, 20 of 21 Chinese were laundrymen and 11 of 13 Chinese in Boulder, Colorado, in 1900, worked in laundries. In Iowa, all 75 China-born Chinese listed in the 1900 census were laundrymen. In 1910, 11 of 12 Chinese living in Litchfield County, Connecticut, were laundrymen as were all 10 Chinese in Richmond, Virginia.

Inspection of 1910 U. S. Census manuscript records for an arbitrary sample of 100 towns located across the country that each had only one Chinese resident, revealed that over 95 percent of these men ran laundries. The few who did not run laundries around the start of the 20th century were most likely to be cooks, waiters, and servants.

Popular alternatives to laundry work varied across regions. Many Chinese were found in cannery work in Washington state, vegetable farming in rural California, and placer mining in the mountain regions of many western states.

Becoming A Laundryman

A common scenario for how Chinese men began their laundry lives on Gold Mountain was for them to apprentice in the laundry of a relative for several months or longer. Most laundrymen who worked alone probably welcomed apprentices because operating a laundry by oneself was a daunting task. Washing, ironing, and in some cases, pickup and delivery, required two or more men. Having several partners or workers in the store offered protection against assault or robbery. It also proved invaluable whenever a laundryman was incapacitated by illness.

Newcomers would have difficulty surviving without apprenticing or partnering with a seasoned laundryman. An apprenticeship taught them the procedures and techniques of laundering and ironing clothes. The guidance of an experienced laundryman taught them about important aspects of business operation including laws, business regulations, and licensing requirements.   They learned that the Chinese newspaper contained ads for sources of laundry supplies and equipment.[76]

And, importantly, working as an apprentice, their living expenses were lower so they were able in a few years to save enough money, in many cases, to purchase their own laundry. Many then returned to China to find a wife, typically through a matchmaker. In other cases, men had married first in China, and even had children, before they came to the United States to work in laundries. Some laundrymen were able to take extended trips back to China periodically to visit family because they had partners, often relatives, who could maintain the operation of the laundry during the often, lengthy absences. Some fathered children during these visits, but they had to leave them in China when they returned to the U. S. until they had the money and legal documents to bring them over, often after many years, if ever.[77]

Examples of Entry Into Laundry Work

Chinese first had to gain entry to a hostile land in the face of exclusion, adjust to new customs and language, earn a living, and try to support a wife, and sometimes children, left behind until they could bring them over. Although the details vary, the experiences of thousands of Chinese immigrants who came here and earned living in laundries and similar work, shared many common features. Several examples of men who came and managed to survive running laundries will be provided here which can vividly portray the difficult lives they had.

---

[76] Siu, 98-102.

[77] This 'script' outlines life experiences that many Chinese laundrymen had in coming to North America as described in many published narratives and interviews of laundrymen. It also matches my impressions formed as a child from hearing conversations among a small sample of laundrymen in the South during the 1940s.

Yee Jock Leong came to the U. S. in 1903 when he was 19. He actually was born in San Francisco in 1884 but his parents had taken him to Guangdong when he was 2. His mother raised him there while his father, Yee Kim Wo, returned alone to the U. S. to work as a partner of a merchant, returning on two other occasions for brief visits to his family in China and having 2 more children. [78]

Yee Jock Leong returned to China in 1905 to marry Dong Shee, probably in an arranged match. They had a son but three years later he returned alone to the U. S. to operate a laundry in Irwin, Pennsylvania, sending remittances to support his family. In 1914, Yee Jock Leong returned to China with the intention of bringing his son to the United States, but for unknown reasons came back alone in 1915. Yee Jock Leong relocated to Dayton, Ohio, marrying a woman of Chinese and Mexican descent in 1915 and began a new family. He operated a laundry there for about 20 years.

During the Depression, laundries, like many businesses faced very hard times and many went out of business. An illustration of the difficult struggle for survival faced by many laundrymen during these years is seen in a letter (Figure 20) sent by Yee Jock Leong from Chicago to his wife in Dayton, Ohio. Apparently he had gone to Chicago in search of work, leaving his wife or a partner to continue running the Dayton laundry. In any event, it appears clear from his poignant letter dated in 1936 that he had gone to Chicago to find a source of additional income to supplement the income from the Dayton laundry. Leong's letter reveals his tenuous

---

[78] "The Life of Yee Jock Leong." http://fuzzo.com/genealogy/YeeJo#E34FA (accessed June 15, 2006).

financial and work situation, as he worked at any jobs he could find in restaurants and laundries in Chicago, but eked out an uncertain income.

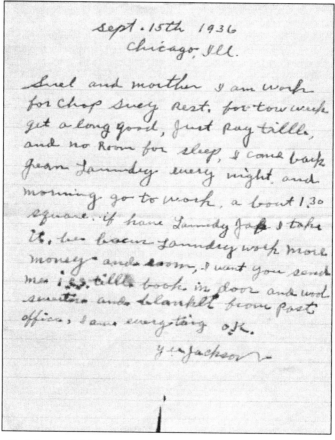

Figure 20 Yee Jock Leung 1936 letter to his wife in Ohio. Courtesy, David M. Lawrence & Kathleen Y. Lawrence.

Li Hong came to Canada shortly before 1920 to work in his uncle's laundry in Montreal. In 1921 he went back to China to an arranged marriage to Jiu Thue Loon. He returned alone to Canada to resume work in the laundry where eighteen-hour days were the norm. Due to Chinese exclusion, he was unable to bring his wife over so for more than 30 years he made 4 visits back, fathering two daughters and a son. He continued with the laundry until 1952 when he joined a group to buy a restaurant.

Working conditions in the restaurants proved difficult as well, involving 12-hour workdays for 6 and one half days a week, with an annual 2 weeks vacation. When the Communist assumed control of China in 1948, Li Hong's plan to retire in China died. He realized the need to become a Canadian citizen, which enabled his family to join him in Canada finally in 1957.[79]

Gong Yuen Tim came in 1920 from Huaxian, Guangdong, as a paper son under the sponsorship of his older brother who had come a few years earlier with the aid of his uncle. Yuen Tim was only 15, and left his new 14-year old bride, Low Hop Yee, behind when he came to the U. S. He worked first as an apprentice at Hop Lee laundry in San Francisco, a large laundry that had 10 partners. For the first 20 weeks he learned how to iron shirts and sometimes delivered laundry. During this training, he received only room and board but no money. He then earned about $10 a week and eventually his salary increased to as high as $20 to $30 during the best weeks. During other weeks, however, he earned much less so that his total income was less than $500 a year.

By age 23, he had managed to save $450, which enabled him to visit home in 1928. Returning to Gold Mountain in 1930, he resumed working in the laundry trying to save enough to bring his wife over. After working in laundries for 11 years, in 1931 with the aid of a loan from his uncle, he was able to return to China to bring his wife to the U. S. Although she carefully memorized her coaching papers, she failed the immigration interrogation and was detained at Angel Island. Fortunately she was 6 months pregnant, so deportation was delayed which gave Gong

---

[79] "Li Hong, (1899-1962)." http://www.legacy1.net/d_hong.html (accessed Jan. 12, 2006).

Yuen Tim enough time to get a lawyer and borrow $300 from his uncle for bribes that got her admitted. Eventually he ended his laundry work to enter the produce business and was successful operating a supermarket in California's Central valley.[80]

Kwock Jung Huey came to work in his father's San Francisco laundry in 1931. Four years later he returned to Toishan to an arranged marriage. He soon returned to work in the U. S., making a few visits back during the next 17 years, fathering one son. His wife, Git Ling Huey, was unable to immigrate until 1952. She immediately went to work in their large laundry, preparing daily meals for over 40 workers, while raising five children.[81]

Financial Aspects of Hand Laundries

The low cost of starting and operating a hand laundry was a major reason why so many Chinese immigrants from the late 1800s up to about 1950 entered this type of work. Around 1900, it cost about $500 to buy a laundry, a considerable sum at that time especially since white-run banks would not make loans to Chinese. Whereas opening a business requiring a large inventory of goods such as an import business or restaurant, starting a laundry required much less capital. Still, according to one estimate,[82] the costs were still considerable and beyond the means of new immigrants. It would take many years for an individual to save enough from his meager wages to buy his own laundry.

---

[80] Gong Yuen Tim, "A Gold Mountain Man's Memoirs," Translator: Marlon K. Hom, *Chinese America: History and Perspectives* (1992): 211-237.

[81] Patricia Yollin, "Git Jing Huey -- matriarch who loved food, family," *San Francisco Chronicle*, August 7, 2005, A-21.

[82] Anthony Chan, *Gold Mountain: The Chinese in the New World* (Vancouver, Canada: NewStar, 1983).

Pooling and rotation of credit were common practices for starting small business enterprises by Chinese and other Asian immigrant groups as a strategy for quickly raising larger sums of capital for an individual with insufficient funds.[83] The *woi* or *hui* [84] was a mechanism that provided a pooled source of funds from, say, about 20 to 30 other Chinese who each contributed the same amount. Everyone wanting to obtain the pooled amount made a secret bid as to how much interest they would be willing to pay to receive the total amount, and the highest bidder wins. The other participants had the right to bid again in future months. This process is repeated each month until every member gets a chance to receive the large amount.

Owning a laundry involved a high risk of failure, as there was often fierce competition from other laundries, Chinese or non-Chinese. If an American steam laundry opened nearby, it could destroy a laundryman's business and cost his life savings. Thus, from 1874-1880, about half of the laundries in Chicago failed each year.[85] In 1900, Philadelphia had 525 Chinese laundries. By 1910, there were 364 Chinese laundries left in Philadelphia, and two years later only 224 had survived.

In 1902-3 the average pay of a Chinese laundry worker in Philadelphia was around $30 a month, with a range from $16 to $50, according to return certificates that Chinese had to file with immigration

---

[83] Ivan Light, *Ethnic Enterprise in America: Business and Welfare among Chinese, Japanese, and Blacks* (Berkeley: University of California Press, 1972).

[84] Siu, 92-96.

[85] Siu, 25-26.

when they made visits to China.[86] Although the typical proprietor averaged $138 monthly, after expenses for supplies, rent, and business licenses, he only netted about $50. If he understated revenues, his business license fees would be lower, as would be his federal income tax.

Accurate comprehensive records of how much laundrymen earned are not available. Some anecdotal information[87] showed that a newcomer in the 1890s earned about $8 to $15 per week, not counting lodging and board. In 1922, a novice in Pittsburgh started at $5 a week and made about $15 a week soon afterwards. In 1926, 42 percent of Chinese laundrymen in Chicago earned a weekly income of between $20 and $29, and 28 percent earned between $30 and $40 weekly, which was moderate in comparison with the income of other ethnic groups. At these levels, it would require years to buy one's own laundry and cover operating expenses without the rotating credit system described earlier.

Even if he managed to buy his own laundry, given the low income generated by even a successful laundry, it would have probably been necessary for most laundry owners to have partners and/or have unpaid labor from family members to turn a profit. Another benefits of not having paid employees was that the owner did not have to contribute to their retirement accounts when the program federal social security was instituted in 1935.[88]

---

[86] Dongzheng Jin, *"The Sojourner's Story: Philadelphia's Chinese Immigrants, 1900-1925"* (PhD diss. Temple University, 1997).

[87] Wang, "No Tickee, No Shirtee," 68-69.

[88] Ibid.,293.

How Did Chinese Laundries Get Their Names?

Although some Chinese laundries were named with their owners' names, many laundry names reflected strong hopes for financial success.[89] Thus, Sing Lee Laundry and Sam Lee Laundry, probably the two most commonly occurring Chinese laundry names, use words that refer to large, glorious, or eternal prosperity.[90] The character for the common Chinese surname, Lee, sounds like the character for 'profit.' Thus, a Sing Lee Laundry is not, as customers might assume, named after its owner. "Sing" refers to victory, and combined with "Lee," means "victorious profit." "Sam" is the Chinese pronunciation for the number three, and when combined with "Lee" also refers to making profits so that a Sam Lee Laundry is not usually owned by someone named "Sam Lee."

Unfortunately many laundries did not live up to their promising names. Perhaps, owners anticipated the difficulty of success, and engaged in a form of magical thinking to improve profits in selecting names for their laundries.

---

[89] I thank Daniel Bronstein for confirming this view by translating names of all laundries in San Francisco and New York listed in a 1946 business directory.

[90] Sing Lee and Sam Lee were two of the most common Chinese male names in the U. S. from 1900 to 1920. For example, the 1910 Census lists 280 Chinese men named Sing Lee (also 182 with the reverse name, Lee Sing) and 234 named Sam Lee. Some Sing Lees were probably listed as Lee Sings, and vice versa, because census takers, confused by Chinese surnames preceding given names, were known to have reversed some names. Most Sing Lees and Sam Lees ran laundries. In a sample of 50 Chinese named Sing Lee and 50, Sam Lee, from the 1910 census, 73 percent were listed as laundry heads. It is not known how often the laundry and owner names matched. Many Chinese did not speak English well so census takers may have often assumed it was the same as the laundry name, inflating the number of laundrymen recorded as Sing Lee and Sam Lee. Customers in my father's laundry, made precisely this assumption, thinking his name was Sam Lee.

The Chinese term for "laundry," *yi guan or yishangguan*, translates as "clothes store," hardly an image that depicted washing and ironing dirty clothes. Why did laundrymen use this misleading term rather than one that more accurately described their actual work of washing and ironing the soiled clothes of other people? One explanation is that family members in poverty-stricken villages in China were convinced that the laundrymen were prosperous merchants in America because of their regular remittances and the presents they brought with them on their visits.[91] Most of them were probably unaware that the laundrymen labored long hours washing and ironing dirty clothes for a small income and lived in the backs of their shops. When laundrymen returned to visit relatives in China they enjoyed the admiration they received. It was a welcome respite from their wretched laundry existence living in the back of small and dilapidated stores and working in a land where racial discrimination and hostility confronted them daily. They would have lost face by telling their families what their actual work involved.[92]

Regional Shifts in Chinese Laundry Locations

Figure 21 provides an overview of key events surrounding the Chinese in the Pacific coast and Rocky mountain region as they expanded their participation in the laundry business from around the 1870s. Laws restricting their civil rights as well as assaults, killings, and property damage against Chinese during the last quarter of the 19th century occurred in many

[91] Yu, 28-30.

[92] An example of their 'illogical' beliefs during WW II was to stop putting paper bands around folded shirts that held them together because the usual light blue paper was in short supply and replaced by dark blue, a color that symbolized death. Paul Louis Fletcher, SR. "The Chinese wholesale shirt laundries of New York." *Management Research News*, 25, no. 2 (2002): 36.

communities. Some towns tried to forcibly drive all Chinese out of their communities.

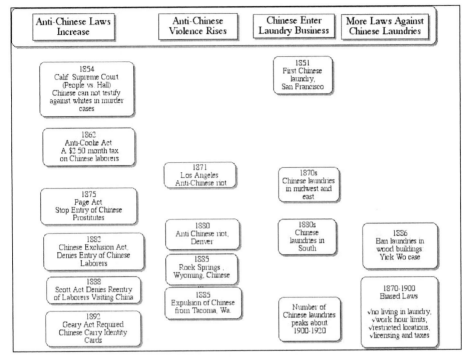

Figure 21 Social and historical context surrounding the entry of Chinese into the laundry business in the last quarter of the 19th Century.

Combined with numerous discriminatory local ordinances and taxes imposed on the operation of their laundries, discussed in detail in the next chapter, these adverse conditions prompted some to return to China and many others to flee to other parts of the country, especially to the northeastern states. They hoped they would be better treated in regions where Chinese were less numerous and less of a threat to white workers

Figure 22 shows that during the exclusionary years the Chinese population dropped the most in the west, from 75,000 in 1880 to 45,000 by 1900 whereas some regions such as the northeast had large gains.

These patterns generally held through the 1930 census. Then the number of Chinese increased in most regions over the remaining exclusion years, as reflected by the 1950 census, the first one after the 1943 repeal of exclusion. The largest number was always in the west coast states.[93]

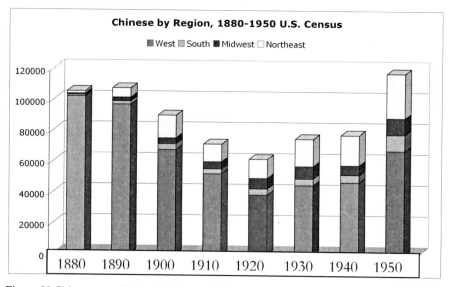

Figure 22 Chinese population in different U. S. regions from 1890 to 1950.[94]

Chinese Laundries in the Mountain States

Small Chinese communities developed throughout the Rocky Mountain region as well as in the southwestern states in the 1870s. When the Central Pacific Railroad was completed in 1869 at Promontory Point,

---

[93] Overall, however, there was a net loss of about 15,000 Chinese in the U. S. between the 1880 and 1900 census, reflecting the possibility that many of them returned to China, moved to other countries, or died. The U. S. Chinese population recovered slowly but it was not until 1950 that it managed to surpass the pre-exclusion era level. By the 1980, and later, census tabulations, substantial increases occurred in the population of Chinese and other Asian Pacific Islanders with the passage of a fairer immigration law in 1965. The origin of these later Chinese immigrants, however, was no longer limited to Guangdong but extended to a much wider area including Taiwan, Hong Kong, and Mainland China.

[94] Chart of data from Campbell Gibson and Kay Jung. "Historical Census Statistics on Population Totals by Race, 1790 to 1990, and by Hispanic Origin, 1970 to 1990, for the United States, Regions, Divisions, and States" (Population Division Working Paper No. 56, Appendix C. Washington, D. C.: U. S. Census Bureau, 2002).

Utah, some Chinese railroad workers stayed in nearby regions in Utah such as Salt Lake City and Ogden. Chinese in Salt Lake City opened grocery and merchandise stores, laundries, and restaurants along Plum Alley, which led to white opposition toward them. In 1902 and 1903 the miners union campaigned to boycott Chinese restaurants and laundries, oppose employment of Chinese, and prohibit the selling and buying of Chinese goods.[95]

Figure 23 Wing Sing Laundry, Tucson c. 1899. Courtesy, Arizona Historical Society/Tucson AHS Photograph H-13.

In Tucson, Arizona, most early Chinese immigrants were brought in as cheap, reliable laborers in the late 1870s to help extend the Southern Pacific Railroad through the desert. Upon completion of this work, as

---

[95] Kate B. Carter, comp. *The Early Chinese of Western United States* (Salt Lake City, UT.: Our Pioneer Heritage, 1958, 10), 478.

Chinese rail laborers in Utah had done earlier, some stayed in the region and opened small businesses during the 1880s in the few areas from which they had not been excluded such as laundries, restaurants, vegetable farming, and other service occupations.

About 2,000 Chinese immigrants came to Butte, Montana as early as 1868 to mine for gold. When they were faced with discriminatory taxes and laws as well as threats of harm to drive them out of mining, many turned to running laundries. This was not a long-term solution for, as will be noted in the next chapter, similar problems arose with their laundries.

Chinese Laundries In The Midwest

Resettling from western states where anti-Chinese feelings were strong, most of the Chinese living in large cities around 1900 worked in laundries, restaurants, or stores that sold imported Chinese products.

A thriving Chinese community that included laundries, grocers, and merchants formed in St. Louis as early as 1870. St. Louis was then a rapidly growing city energized by new industry and manufacturing. Most of the early Chinese in St. Louis did not come there directly when they entered the United States but relocated from ports such as San Francisco or New York. They may have resettled in interior parts of the country such as St. Louis, possibly because of the discrimination and violence that Chinese had experienced in large cities on either coast during the latter part of the 19th century.

The earliest Chinese laundries in St. Louis appeared in city directories around 1873. During the early years up to 1879, the hand laundries clustered near Hop Alley, a downtown area where most of the Chinese stores and grocers were located and formed an ethnic enclave. Over time, more of the laundries were situated widely over residential areas of the city with few located near Hop Alley. By 1900 there were over 100, reaching a peak of 165 in 1929 when Chinese laundries represented 60 percent of all St. Louis laundries.[96] But by the 1960s, there were few laundries left, and the last one closed in 1977.

Similarly in Chicago, the city with the largest Chinese population after San Francisco and New York, hand laundries were a major occupation of Chinese immigrants.[97] A large increase in the number of Chinese laundries occurred between 1870 and 1920 after which they started a gradual decline. In 1880-1881 there were 67 and within a year there were 165 hand laundries. A peak of 704 laundries occurred in 1928, which exceeded the 421 operated by non-Chinese. Initially centered in the downtown business area, as their numbers increased they dispersed into rooming house and apartment neighborhoods throughout the city to minimize competition with each other. Many elderly Chinese ran one-man laundries in slum areas mainly for a place to stay than to make money.

In Minnesota Chinese immigrants began to arrive in large cities such as Minneapolis and St. Paul by the mid-1870s as well as in isolated rural areas. In the 1920 census, the Chinese population in Minnesota reached an exclusion era peak of 385. Many small midwestern towns, as elsewhere, had Chinese laundries, but typically there were only one or two in any small township. Furthermore, there were usually no other Chinese engaged in other work in these towns so they had solitary lives and often suffered racial intolerance for which they had little recourse.

---

[96] Huping Ling, *Chinese St. Louis: From Enclave to Cultural Community* (Philadelphia: Temple University Press, 2004).

[97] Siu. 37-43.

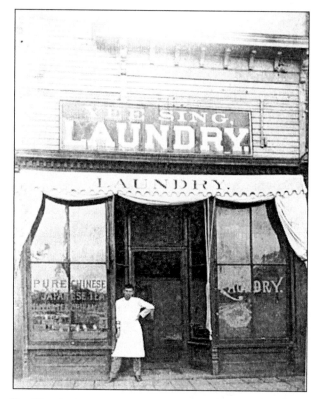

Figure 24 Yee Sing Woo in front of Yee Sing Laundry, Minneapolis, 1895. By permission of Acme View & Advertising Company, Minnesota Historical Society.

Such was true for Sam Ding who operated a laundry in 1919 in Ames, Iowa, where he was the only Chinese (See Figure 25). Similarly, Sam Lee had a laundry in Minonk, Illinois, where there were no other Chinese (See Figure 26). Both men faced problems with their businesses and each abruptly left town, abandoning their stores. A cruel prankster harassed Sam Ding by leaving clothes that contained hidden substances that damaged the clothes of other customers. In Sam Lee's case, some customers suspected that he profited from selling some customer clothes to a second-hand store in Peoria.[98]

---

[98] "Fifth Street Chinese Laundry," http://www.minonktalk.com/fifthst.htm (accessed Dec. 1, 2006).

Figure 25 Sam Ding's Laundry, Ames, Iowa, c. 1919. Courtesy, Farwell T. Brown Photographic Archive, Ames Public Library, Ames, Iowa.

Figure 26 Sam Lee Laundry, Minonk, Il c. 1907. Courtesy, Minonktalk.com

Chinese Laundries in the East

As noted in Chapter 1, in 1870 Chinese from San Francisco replaced Irish women laundry workers in Belleville, New Jersey, who frequently went on strike for higher wages. Before long, the Chinese replacements employed the same tactic as the Irish women. By 1885 all of them had been discharged but it is probable that some of them opened their own laundries in the northeastern U. S. It is likely that some drifted toward the Southern states where they could have new opportunities for laundry work.

In Boston, Chinese primarily worked in laundries in 1892. A few Chinese restaurants also were operating but about 70 percent of the 1,000 Chinese men worked in the 280 Chinese laundries.[99] By 1888, there were about 2,000 Chinese laundries in New York City alone.[100] Over a third of Chinese in New York City were in the laundry business when the number of Chinese laundries was at its peak around 1910.

Chinese Laundries in the South

The growth of Chinese laundries in the South lagged behind the western and eastern states perhaps partly due to the abundant supply of black washerwomen in the region. Racial discrimination confined the job opportunities for black women to domestic work such as laundry, thus reducing opportunities for Chinese to enter the laundry business. In the 1870s, black washerwomen in Galveston, Texas, defended their livelihood by demanding that Chinese laundries close within fifteen days while black women at a power laundry held a strike over their low wages.

In addition, there was less demand for laundry services with the less industrialized South. Still, in 1897, New Orleans had as many as 50 Chinese laundries operating alongside about a dozen stores selling

---

[99] Mary Chapman, "Notes on the Chinese in Boston," *The Journal of American Folklore*, 5, 19 (1892): 321-324.

[100] Wang, "No Tickee, No Shirtee," 35

Chinese goods, and one Chinese restaurant. Most of the laundries were located in or near the French Quarter of New Orleans, according to insurance maps.[101]

City Chinese Laundry,

CHARLEY ONG LUNG, Prop'r.

Only First Class Hand Work. Look here Collars, &c. Cuffs per pair, &c., and everything else at remarkably low prices. You will find me on Jackson Street, next to Defiance Engine House. Give me a call. I guarantee satisfaction

Figure 27 Ad for Chinese laundry, Albany (Ga.) Journal Herald, March 25, 1893.

Laundries versus Grocery Stores

Another important reason for fewer laundries among Chinese in the South is that they had other work opportunities not available to them in the eastern states. Many Chinese in the South operated grocery stores serving mostly customers in black neighborhoods in small towns like Greenville, Mississippi and Augusta, Georgia,[102] as well as in larger cities in Texas like Houston and San Antonio.[103]

---

[101] "New Orleans in 1897. Underwriters Inspection Bureau of New Orleans Street Rate Slips," http://nutrias.org/info/louinfo/1897/chinese.htm (accessed June 12, 2006).

[102] James W. Loewen, *The Mississippi Chinese: Between Black and White,* (Cambridge, MA.: Harvard University Press, 1971). Sally Ken, "The Chinese Community In Augusta, Georgia from 1873-1971." *Richmond County History,* 4, no 1 (1972): 51-60.

[103] Edward C. M. Chen and Fred R. Von Der Mehden. "The Chinese in Houston," http://www.houstonhistory.com/erhnic/history1chin.htm (accessed Aug. 30, 2006); Mel Brown., *Chinese Heart of Texas: The San Antonio Community 1875-1975.* (Austin, Tx: Lily On The Water Publishing, 2005).

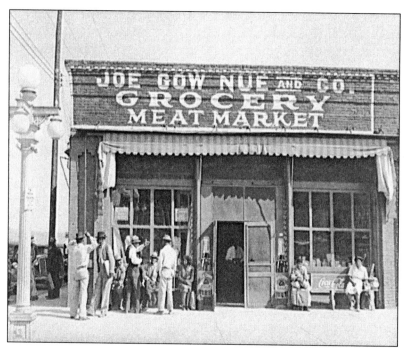

Figure 28 A Chinese grocery store in Mississippi, 1939. [104] Courtesy, Library of Congress LC-USF34-052450-D

The Chinese grocers were more flexible than white-owned stores in doing business with blacks. Unlike white grocery stores that required cash payment, the Chinese extended credit to blacks allowing them to settle their accounts at the end of the month. This arrangement was mutually beneficial because most black customers did not always have money when they needed food while the small Chinese grocers could not compete with the large white stores on a price basis or large selection of goods. This informality also often led to customers hanging out in and around the stores, which served as neighborhood centers for socializing, as shown in Figure 28.

---

[104] Thanks to Roland Chow and Carolyn Chan for correctly placing the store's location in Greenville, Ms. where they grew up and not in Leland, Ms. as recorded by the Library of Congress.

As in the case of Chinese laundries, these stores were family-run businesses. Children played and worked in and around the stores to help their parents. In some cases, like laundry families, the grocer and his family lived in the back of their stores for convenience and to save money.

Racial Issues

Racial prejudice was prevalent throughout the South, and often blatant, especially against blacks during the pre-Civil rights era. However, Chinese were not treated as badly as blacks, and in fact were afforded many white privileges such as access to white theaters and restaurants. In Georgia, Chinese children could attend white schools before the 1940s although not in Mississippi until more than a decade later.

Still, a few Chinese were victims of assault, robbery, and even homicide. Although some of these incidents may not have been racially motivated, it was not surprising that the laundrymen generally regarded them as further evidence of prejudice against them as they were not fairly treated by whites in many daily interactions both in and beyond the laundry. Some laundry customers, white and black as well, were at times rude, demanding, and arrogant in their demeanor.

The longstanding white domination of blacks in the South prior to the Civil rights activism in the mid 20th century was a lesson that was not lost on the laundrymen. They realized that whites regarded Chinese as just one step or two above the blacks. Lacking any power to demand respect, Chinese found it prudent to defer to whites and passively endure racial prejudice. When they were unfairly treated or subjected to verbal taunts, the laundrymen were not shocked because that kind of behavior only confirmed their expectations.

Although they realized that racial oppression had led to the low income, education, and social standing of blacks, the laundrymen privately felt superior. However, since many of their customers and all of their workers, aside from family members, were black, they behaved respectfully toward blacks because the success of their laundries depended on it. Because there were so few Chinese in the Southeast, they were not viewed to be as much of an economic threat as those in areas with large Chinese populations. Consequently, even though they were still regarded as foreigners, Chinese in southern towns and communities may have been better treated than those in regions on either coast.

Chinese Laundries in Small Towns

In addition to regional differences, important differences also existed between Chinese laundries in large cities and small towns. When Chinese began their flight from western regions, thousands of laundrymen ended in remote and small communities with few, if any other Chinese. Their experiences differed markedly in many ways from those of laundrymen in cities with large Chinese populations like Chicago, New York, and Pittsburgh, the sites for three of the most authoritative studies of Chinese hand laundries. [105]

---

[105] Siu, This rich study of the bachelor Chinese who ran hand laundries in Chicago was a PhD dissertation started in the 1930s but not published until 1987. It provides an accurate depiction of the isolated lives of these laundrymen in the early 20th century. He described the physical layout of laundries, work demands, living space within their stores, and relationship to other laundrymen. Siu, himself, was brought from China by his father to help in his laundry, so his insider perspectives enabled him to understand the plight of Chinese laundrymen. As a sales representative for laundry suppliers he visited many laundries where he was accepted and trusted because he shared many of their experiences and could speak Chinese. Nonetheless, "The Chinese Laundryman" was limited to interviews with and observations of bachelor laundrymen in Chicago during the 1930s and 1940s. His work failed to include laundrymen with families. Moreover, it did not examine the many isolated Chinese in small towns across the country with no contact with Chinese communities and social networks.

In contrast to laundrymen in cities that had sizable Chinese populations, those laboring in small towns were culturally isolated with no easy access to a Chinese community where they could participate in cultural practices or recreational activities. They also suffered from social isolation as they had little or no common interests with either blacks or whites nor did most have adequate English speaking skills or familiarity with American ways needed for socializing with them.

The number of isolated and solitary Chinese laundries across the country was substantial. As one example, consider the situation in one part of the Midwest. According to the 1900 census listings, Iowa had 75 China-born Chinese men, mostly between ages of 16 and 60. All but one, a student, operated a hand laundry. These laundries were located in 50 of Iowa's 99 counties, with only one, and in a few cases, two laundries in any one township. These laundry owners typically worked alone, or with only one or two partners in a few instances. Only one had a wife living with him.

By 1910, according to the census, Iowa had fewer Chinese immigrants, 54, but aside from 3 restaurant owners, one student, one prison inmate, and one secretary, all worked in laundries that were spread over 26 of Iowa's 99 counties. Most laundries were still operated by one man, and a few, by two men.

Wang, *"No Tickee, No Shirtee'* This PhD dissertation is much broader than Siu's scope. It goes beyond Chinese laundries and provides a detailed history of the relationship between Chinese and white-owned laundries to show the social context, especially in Pittsburgh.

Renqui Yu, *To Save China, To Save Ourselves.* This work deals only with Chinese hand laundries in New York and focuses on the history of the Chinese Hand Laundry Alliance formed in 1933 to fight for their economic survival against white wet wash plants and to unify in support of China against Japan in World War II.

There was substantial change between 1900 and 1910, due to diverse factors including deaths, retirements, closures, ownership changes, immigration, and migration. Of the 50 Iowa counties that had at least one Chinese laundry in 1900, 31 no longer had one in 1910. Seven counties without a Chinese laundry in 1900 had at least one by 1910. Only three of the 75 men operating laundries in 1900 were still listed as laundrymen in the 1910 census. Only one laundryman had a wife, but it was not the same married laundryman listed in 1900. By 1920, the number of Chinese immigrants more than doubled to 132.[106] Most still ran laundries spread across 39 counties, but a few opened restaurants. In Des Moines about a third of the 33 Chinese were in the restaurant business working as owners, cooks, and waiters.

The situation was similar in many other states during these years. In Kentucky, for example, there were fewer Chinese, about 30 at each census over the same period, and they were isolated and scattered over from 8 to 12 counties. All were involved in laundry work in 1900, as were almost all of them in 1910. In 1920, laundries still dominated, but Chinese had opened 2 restaurants in Louisville that provided work for 15 Chinese as owners, waiters, and cooks. Most laundries were one-man operations, with a few having from 2 to 4 partners or helpers. Only one Chinese, a restaurant owner, had a wife. She was white, and they had a son and a daughter.

One eastern state, Delaware, had only 32 Chinese in 1900, a drop to 18 in 1910, and a rise to 30 in 1920. As in Iowa and Kentucky, in

---

[106] Chinese were such a rarity that when the first Chinese baby was born in Davenport, Iowa in 1926, it made the front page of the local newspaper which also noted that he was named Calvin, in honor of President Coolidge. John Willard, "Chinese Baby Made Q-C History in 1926," www.qctimes.com/articles/2003/01/28/faces/export48825prt (accessed Oct. 25, 2006).

smaller towns, where typically only one Chinese lived, all operated laundries. Laundry work also dominated in Wilmington, the largest city in the state and where most Delaware Chinese lived. Aside from one student and two restaurant owners, one in 1910 and another one in 1920, all Chinese in Wilmington during these years worked in laundries, either alone or with one partner.

The picture found in these three states from different regions was not unusual. Equally isolated circumstances existed for many laundrymen across the country. In the Southeast region, aside from Atlanta and Augusta,[107] most Chinese settled in small communities where they were either the only, or one of very few Chinese. Opportunities for laundrymen and their families, for those fortunate enough to have them living with them, to interact with other Chinese was virtually absent for these isolated Chinese.[108]

It is remarkable that these laundrymen that lived in extreme isolation from other Chinese in small towns all over the country were able to survive with their limited knowledge of English. Unlike Chinese in communities with many other Chinese to turn to for advice and

---

[107] Augusta, Georgia had the largest Chinese population in the southeast. The presence of more families allowed the formation of a Chinese community with active Chinese churches gave more opportunities for Chinese to socialize with each other than in other southern cities. Rather than working in laundries, which were very few, most Augusta Chinese operated small neighborhood grocery stores in mostly black neighborhoods.

[108] Many Chinese toiled in laundries all over the country in areas where they, and their families, if any, were the only Chinese in town. Among the countless isolated laundrymen, listed with their ages and locales, were: Yee Gin, 55, Athens, Ohio, 1900, Charley Lum, 36, Darlington, South Carolina, 1910, Frank Jung, 30, Macon, Georgia, 1930, You Yee Len, 39, Irwin, Pa, 1910, Toy Ock Hing, 27, Benton Harbor, Michigan, 1900, Sing Wong, 30, Moulton, Maine 1900, John Hu, 29, Durham North Carolina, 1900, Chong Yep, 30, Elk Point, South Dakota, 1900, Sam Fong, 52, Albion, Iowa, 1910, Charley Lee, 50, Shenandoah, Va. 1910, Gin Sing, 29, Madison, Fl, J. W. Suey, 33, St. Augustine, Fl, 1910.

information about important business and personal matters, these Chinese had no readily available sources of information. Small town laundrymen had to rely to a greater extent on printed materials and books written in Chinese to help them deal with important topics. Subscriptions to Chinese newspapers from both San Francisco and New York provided their main source of information about world developments and issues pertaining to China. During this period well before the availability of Chinese language radio and television, it was the fastest and most complete means of keeping in touch with China for Chinese living in small towns.[109]

Their limited ability to communicate with white doctors, the absence of Chinese doctors, and their greater familiarity with Chinese medicine led some to rely on Chinese herbal remedies that they learned about from Chinese newspaper advertisements.[110] They obtained medical information and guidance about sex from books written in Chinese like the Ladies Handbook of Household Medicine and the guide to sexual hygiene, both shown in Figure 29, purchased by mail probably from San Francisco or New York.

Like their big city counterparts, small town laundrymen and their families led frugal existences, living in the back, above, or close by their laundries to save on housing costs and travel time. Some did not even have telephones, not so much as to save money, but because there was no one to call. Long distance calls to Chinese in other cities were

---

[109] The impact of the Chinese press extended over the country. In 1936, Leong Gor Yun noted in *Chinatown Inside Out*, "It speaks to the Chinese in a language he understands; it is his only medium for knowing what is happening in his world and the world at large." Quoted by Chen, *"Being Chinese, Becoming Chinese American,"* 5.

[110] Examination of one issue of a 1924 paper showed almost half the space advertised such products. Chen, *Being Chinese, Becoming Chinese American.* 158.

prohibitively expensive in those days and used only for urgent matters. They usually relied on postal mail to contact Chinese in other towns.

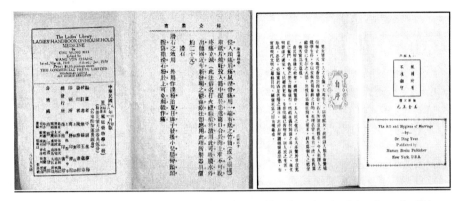

Figure 29 They used medical manuals (lt) or sexual hygiene books (rt) written in Chinese.

Small-town laundrymen made occasional visits to see Chinese living in other towns to have some social life. These trips were limited to one-day visits on Sundays, as they had to work on the other six days unless they had a partner who could keep the laundry operating during a longer absence. Running a laundry involved six, and sometimes, seven days of work for 52 weeks every year. Even though closed on Sundays, the laundrymen often had to spend that day in equipment repair and maintenance. [111]

Studies of Chinese laundry life based on laundries in cities with large Chinese populations are inadequate for the understanding of small town laundrymen experiences. In some respects, small town laundrymen were in a better situation. With little or no competition from other

---

[111] My observations about small town Chinese laundry life come from many conversations of Chinese laundrymen I heard during occasional day visits with my father to my Uncle's laundry in Atlanta. In addition, I draw on discussions with my parents during childhood as well as in later life, interviews within the past five years with relatives familiar with Chinese laundrymen of the South, and historical documents. Although based on the South, they are likely to be similar for small town Chinese laundrymen all over the country.

Chinese laundries, there was no need, or mechanism, for them to regulate or govern their operations, locations, and prices, as was the case in cities with many competing Chinese laundries. Chinese in small towns were generally able to locate their laundries in the central business districts, allowing them closer contact with the community.

In contrast, laundrymen in large cities needed to spread out across town to avoid competing with other Chinese laundries with many of them isolated in residential areas far from the main part of town. Also, unlike many Chinese laundries in New York and other large cities that only did finishing work after clothes were washed by large wet wash laundry 'factories,' small-town Chinese laundries may have been more profitable as they both washed and ironed the clothes.

4. Challenges To Chinese Laundries

American laws, more ferocious than tigers:
Many are the people jailed inside wooden walls,
Detained, interrogated, tortured,
Like birds plunged into an open trap—
  What suffering!
To whom can I complain of the tragedy?
I shout to Heaven, but there is no way out!
Had I only known such difficulty in passing
  the Golden Gate . . .
Fed up with this treatment, I regret my journey here.[112]

As Chinese continued to expand their presence in the laundry trade in the late 19th century, whites became increasingly alarmed that 'hordes of Mongols' would take over the country. Newspaper editorials pointed out and condemned the Chinese monopoly on laundries. They frequently denounced washhouses as "public nuisances," where the "filthy practices of the Chinese in allowing pools of dirty and stinking water to accumulate around their laundries produce breeding places of disease which it is most wise to guard against." Opposition to Chinese laundries emphasized their dangers to public health.

Labor organizations such as the Anti-Chinese and Workingmen's Protective Laundry Association were formed in 1876 in San Jose, California, to protect employment of white men and women. They opposed the Chinese washhouses, which with their low prices, competed

---

[112] Hom, 84.

well against white-owned laundries. These organizations pushed for discriminatory ordinances that placed Chinese hand laundries at a disadvantage with the aim of driving the Chinese out. For example, an 1870 ordinance in San Francisco forbade the carrying of laundry on horizontal poles, a common procedure used only by Chinese laundrymen when they picked up and delivered laundry.

Contesting Laws Biased Against Chinese Laundries

Chinese laundry owners in larger cities unified to fight unfair ordinances. In San Francisco during the 1880s, they formed a laundry guild, *Tung Hing Tong*. Funded by $30 annual dues, it defended members against laws favoring white laundries. It also devised rules to govern competition and settle disputes among Chinese laundries regarding location and pricing. In other cities, similar guilds were formed but their membership was based on which district in Guangdong the laundrymen came from, a factor that later led to conflict and sometimes violent warfare among rival factions or tongs.[113]

Ban on Laundries in Wood Buildings

In San Francisco, a landmark court decision involved an 1880 ordinance that prohibited laundries in wooden buildings because of the fire hazard. Laundries of that period used heated coals for drying of clothes. Laundries located in wooden buildings were in fact less safe from fire than brick buildings. None of the Chinese laundries in wood buildings received permits, while only one non-Chinese owner was denied a permit.

---

[113] Wang, "No Tickee, No Shirtee," 297-302. Laundry guild memberships declined during the depression of the 1930s when many laundrymen could not afford dues so Chinese family associations took over many of these functions.

The *Tung Hing Tong* contested this law in a historic 1886 court case.[114] They hired an attorney to assist one laundryman, Yick Wo, in filing a writ of *habeas corpus* when he was imprisoned for refusing to pay a $10 fine for operating his laundry in a wooden building.[115] The city defended the action as within its police powers to protect the health and safety of citizens even though Yick Wo's laundry had met local sanitary and fire standards. The city argued that wood buildings are a fire hazard, and since laundries burn coals to dry clothes, such a law is in the public interest.

However, Yick Wo's attorney argued that a law prohibiting laundries in wood buildings was discriminatory in that only Chinese laundries occupied wood buildings. Inasmuch as all Chinese laundries were in wood buildings, this law was unfair because it violated the 14th Amendment of Equal Protection. The case against him was eventually overruled by the State Supreme Court in 1886.[116] After the Yick Wo decision in his favor, arrests and convictions of Chinese laundrymen for violating laundry ordinances decreased substantially.

Limits on Hours of Operation

In the 1880s, Chinese laundrymen typically worked from ten to sixteen hours per day. Actually some Chinese laundries operated twenty-four hours a day as two different laundries often shared a facility, working in shifts, to split the costs of rent. In 1882, San Francisco tried to end

---

[114] *Yick Wo v. Hopkins* 118 U.S. 356, 370.

[115] Laurene Wu McClain. "From victims to victors; A Chinese contribution to American law: Yick Wo versus Hopkins," *Chinese America: History and Perspectives* (2003): 53-62.

[116] Ibid.

that practice by passing an ordinance that prohibited the laundering of clothes between 10:00 p.m. and 6:00 a.m.

However, in California, courts ruled that these laws were "an unreasonable interference with the liberty of the citizen in the prosecution of his occupation" and laundries are "a perfectly legitimate, harmless, and necessary business," and not a danger to public health or safety. They concluded that restricting the hours of launderers only, and no other workers was an "unreasonable restriction upon the rights of laundry owners."[117]

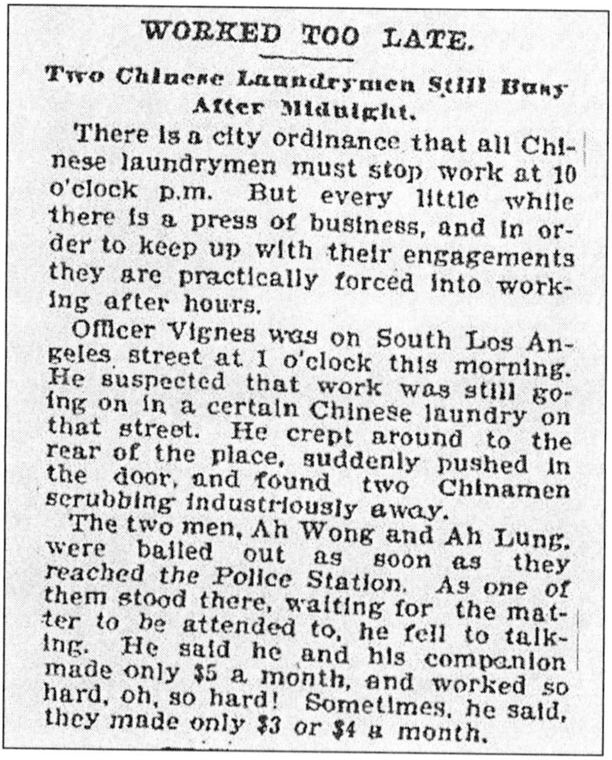

WORKED TOO LATE.

Two Chinese Laundrymen Still Busy After Midnight.

There is a city ordinance that all Chinese laundrymen must stop work at 10 o'clock p.m. But every little while there is a press of business, and in order to keep up with their engagements they are practically forced into working after hours.

Officer Vignes was on South Los Angeles street at 1 o'clock this morning. He suspected that work was still going on in a certain Chinese laundry on that street. He crept around to the rear of the place, suddenly pushed in the door, and found two Chinamen scrubbing industriously away.

The two men, Ah Wong and Ah Lung, were bailed out as soon as they reached the Police Station. As one of them stood there, waiting for the matter to be attended to, he fell to talking. He said he and his companion made only $5 a month, and worked so hard, oh, so hard! Sometimes, he said, they made only $3 or $4 a month.

Figure 30 Two Chinese laundrymen arrested for working past 10 p.m. Los Angeles Times, April 7, 1896, 8.

---

[117] David E. Bernstein, "Lessons from the Judicial Reaction to the Regulation of Chinese Laundries, 1860s to 1930s" (January 1999). Available at SSRN: http://ssrn.com/abstract=146952 or DOI: 10.2139/ssrn.146952.

Later, San Francisco enacted an ordinance in 1912 prohibiting a broad range of laundry-related activities, including washing, ironing, and delivering clothes between 6:00 p.m. and 7:00 a.m. Similar laws were passed in other cities (See Figure 30), but courts generally did not uphold these laws and gave rulings favorable to the Chinese.

Laundry Taxes: 1860s-1870s

Many communities throughout the west imposed taxes on laundries that were specifically applicable only to the Chinese.[118] In 1869, Montana subjected Chinese laundrymen to a harsh laundry tax that was equal to one fourth of their gross earnings. The law appeared neutral, but its intent "was obviously discriminatory." After an adverse court ruling, the Montana Territory ceased enforcing the tax.

In 1873, San Francisco passed an ordinance requiring laundries employing one horse-drawn vehicle to pay $2 per quarter, those employing two such vehicles to pay $4 per quarter, and those employing none to pay $15 per quarter. Since almost all of the Chinese laundries came under the third classification, it was a discriminatory law. In Los Angeles, the Chinese dominated the laundry industry throughout the 1870s. The city council passed a $5 per month tax that applied to all businesses in the city but was actually enforced only against Chinese laundrymen. In 1879, the city council, dominated by the anti-Chinese Workingmen's Party, increased the tax on laundries to $25 per month.

Phoenix required a quarterly license tax "from every Chinese wash-house within the limits of said city." There were at least three cases of Chinese laundrymen indicted in public nuisance cases in Arizona

---

[118] Ibid.

during the 1880s and early 1890s because of the offensive stench from dirty water and laundry waste disposal.[119]

During the 1890s when Chinese laundries proliferated in Montana, whites tried to prevent their growth by passing laws requiring laundry workers to pay license fees. In 1908, Montana inaugurated a tax on laundries starting at $10 per quarter for those with no employees and at $25 for those with one or more employees. Like an earlier law, the statute applied solely to Chinese laundrymen and exempted steam laundries and self-employed laundresses.

The story of how the Chinese laundrymen in Montana in the late 1800s contested the laws against them illustrates the complex maze of legal maneuvering by both the Chinese and their attorneys and their adversaries who wanted to drive them out.[120] One Chinese laundryman, Yot Sang, filed suit after he was arrested in 1896 for not paying the license fee. A Montana court held that the law was unconstitutional, and ordered his release because it involved "class" discrimination that gave different rights to similarly situated people, i.e., steam and hand laundry owners.

Another laundryman, Quong Wing, paid under protest, but filed a complaint in Montana District Court to recover the $10. He won, but the Montana Supreme Court overturned the decision. Undaunted, his attorney took his case to the U. S. Supreme Court pleading that the tax law was unequal class legislation. It unreasonably and unconstitutionally discriminated against male-owned hand laundries in favor of steam

---

[119] Andrea Pugsley, " 'As I Kill This Chicken So May I Be Punished If I Tell An Untruth:' Chinese Opposition To Legal Discrimination In Arizona Territory" *Journal of Arizona History*, Summer (2003): 170-190.

[120] David E. Bernstein, "Two Asian Laundry Cases," *Journal of Supreme Court History*, 24, (1999): 95.

laundries and women-owned hand laundries. After more state hearings, Quong Wing won as the court declared the law unconstitutional.[121]

In 1933, the New York city council proposed an ordinance that would have required all public laundries pay a license fee of $25 per year and post a $1,000 security bond, but aliens were ineligible. Many Chinese laundry owners could not afford the fees and those who could were ineligible as Chinese could not become naturalized. Unable to garner the support of the traditional Chinese merchant leaders to fight this unfair law, the Chinese laundrymen organized to form the Chinese Hand Laundry Association[122] to oppose the proposed ordinance. They succeeded in getting the license fee reduced to $10 and the bond to $100, and an exemption for "Orientals" from the citizenship requirement. In 1946, this alliance also fought for small hand laundries to block large Chinese laundries that did the washing from unfairly raising prices.[123]

Zoning Laws

As Chinese laundries spread throughout the city, and began moving into white residential areas, opposition increased because the Chinese laundry workers and owners often lived on the laundry sites. In 1880, the board of supervisors passed a law that required consent of the

---

[121] As an alternative strategy to licensing laws, three steam laundries and labor unions in Butte, Montana, launched a boycott of Chinese businesses, basing the action on cultural and racial inferiority of the Chinese. They also argued that because of the Chinese, unemployed white girls could find jobs only as prostitutes. The boycotts failed and Chinese obtained an injunction to end them. In 1908 Montana turned to a new $10 quarterly tax on all persons engaged in laundry work, a tax that exempted steam laundries, and applied only to Chinese.

[122] Yu, 31-36.

[123] Other cities had owner alliances when many Chinese laundries existed. In Los Angeles, the Chinese Laundry Business Alliance met monthly to solve problems such as landlord conflicts, customer disputes over damaged laundry, business license issues, and laundry or dry cleaning procedure updates. Personal communication, Donna Wong, Sept. 15, 2006.

board for anyone to "establish, maintain or carry on a laundry" in the area where most Chinese laundries were located.

A Chinese laundryman, Sam Kee, was arrested for violating a Napa, California ordinance that forbade the maintenance of public laundries in a section of the city where his laundry had operated for twenty years. However, a judge ruled that the ordinance abridged the liberty of the owner to select his own occupation and his own methods in the pursuit of happiness, and thereby deprived him of equal protection of the laws secured to every person by the constitution of the United States. In 1886 a federal district judge made a similar ruling after police arrested every Chinese laundry owner in Stockton, California for violating an ordinance that required them to move to a largely uninhabited part of the city.[124]

Despite the reluctance of federal courts to uphold them, anti-Chinese laundry zoning laws continued to proliferate in California. In 1892, Chico, California passed an ordinance requiring a written permit from the town's board of directors before an individual could open a public laundry outside two designated areas. In one violation of this law, the California Supreme Court sided with the defendant, Sing Lee, by noting that a laundry is not offensive or dangerous to the health of those living within its vicinity. Despite this setback in the attempt to restrict Chinese laundry locations, Los Angeles passed a zoning ordinance in 1911 that prohibited conducting and maintaining "works and factories," including laundries, in residential districts over most of the city.

In proposing these laws aimed at the Chinese laundrymen, local authorities justified them as the exercise of police powers to protect the

---

[124] In re Tie Loy (The Stockton Laundry Case), 26 F. 611 (C.C.D. Cal. 1886).

health and well being of the community. Thus, fires are a real danger to the community so laws that reduce the likelihood of fires such as banning laundries in wooden buildings were defended as being in the public interest, and were not racially motivated. Similarly, a law that limited the number of hours that a laundry could operate protected the workers from being overworked by their employers.

Laws to Harass Chinese Laundrymen

Laws of all sorts containing penalties that ranged from fines to jail time were passed against Chinese laundries with the intent of harassment rather than of protecting public health. For example, in 1899 a New York Assemblyman proposed fines for Chinese laundries if they did not issue receipts written in English to customers for their laundry.[125]

> "His measure provides that every laundryman shall furnish a receipt to patrons which shall specify in English the kind and number of good delivered. Violation is punishable by $10 fine for the first offense, $20 for the second, and $50 for each subsequent violation."

Another New York law in 1933 required that Chinese laundrymen be fingerprinted when applying for a license. The Chinese objected and took the issue to the New York Supreme Court, which gave no relief.

> Objections by Chinese laundrymen to a recent order by James A. Geraghty, Commissioner of Licenses, requiring applicants for laundry permits to be fingerprinted came before the Supreme Court yesterday when Justice Schmuck reserved decision in a suit by Low Mark, one of the 2,000 members of the Chinese Hand Laundry Alliance, Inc.
> In asking that Commissioner Geraghty be compelled to issue licenses without fingerprinting the applicants, Mark declared

---

[125] "A Blow at Chinese Laundries," *New York Times*, Jan. 20, 1899, 4.

that to compel him to be fingerprinted was degrading and in violation of his constitutional rights to purse a livelihood.[126]

Chinese challenged many of these laws aimed against their laundries. They learned to seek justice by demanding judicial review. While local and state courts generally upheld these laws, judges in federal courts often repealed them on the grounds that they were veiled discriminatory laws that harmed the Chinese laundrymen. The ban on laundries in wood buildings and the limit on work hours were considered discriminatory violations of the 14th Amendment since the Chinese, but not the white, laundries were adversely affected.[127]

Similar campaigns were waged against Chinese and their laundries in Canada such as the Toronto Police Board of Commissioners ruling in 1902 requiring that laundries have licenses to insure "improved sanitary conditions, less danger from infection, prevention of gambling, opium smoking, etc," The specific laws varied in detail, but they were thinly veiled directives against Chinese laundries that closely paralleled those enacted in the United States.

The battle between the white-owned steam laundries and Chinese hand laundries led to organized efforts on both sides to gain dominance. In 1890, the Chinese Six Companies, an organization of Chinese community leaders planned to raise a million and a half dollars to buy

---

[126] "Laundry Protest Heard. Court Reserves Decision on Chinese Objection to Fingerprinting," *New York Times*, July 4, 1933, 20.

[127] A similar and influential case involved a Supreme Court ruling that a limit of bakers' hours infringed their right to choose. *Lochner vs. U. S.* involved a law that appeared to be protecting the health of workers, but the Court ruled that it violated their rights. Judges hearing laundry cases in the 1890s were not sympathetic to the Chinese but their "perceptions of their institutional obligations" to uphold the Constitution compelled them to treat the Chinese fairly.

outright the 3 or 4 largest steam laundries in New York to reduce the competition.

In retaliation, the Master Laundrymen's Association, a trade group of white power laundry operators, raised a war chest of $500,000 to fund a crusade to "remove every laundry run by Mongolians" in New York, Brooklyn, and New Jersey. Their plan, described in Figure 31, was to attempt to outbid the Chinese for the lease for any property occupied by a Chinese laundry, arguing that the presence of the Chinese in this country "is greatly to the detriment of the white population, morally and socially," and concluding that "it is the duty of every man and woman…not to give any work or trade whatsoever to this heathen race."

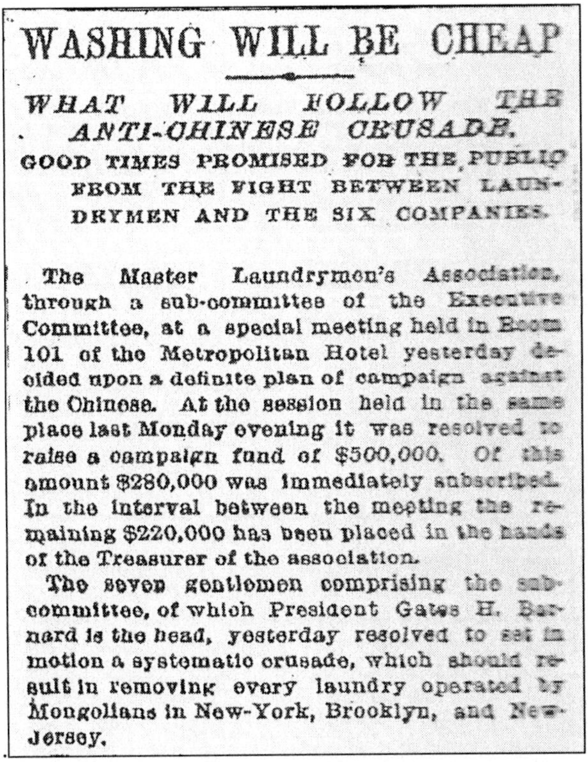

WASHING WILL BE CHEAP

WHAT WILL FOLLOW THE ANTI-CHINESE CRUSADE.

GOOD TIMES PROMISED FOR THE PUBLIC FROM THE FIGHT BETWEEN LAUNDRYMEN AND THE SIX COMPANIES.

The Master Laundrymen's Association, through a sub-committee of the Executive Committee, at a special meeting held in Room 101 of the Metropolitan Hotel yesterday decided upon a definite plan of campaign against the Chinese. At the session held in the same place last Monday evening it was resolved to raise a campaign fund of $500,000. Of this amount $280,000 was immediately subscribed. In the interval between the meeting the remaining $220,000 has been placed in the hands of the Treasurer of the association.

The seven gentlemen comprising the sub-committee, of which President Gates H. Barnard is the head, yesterday resolved to set in motion a systematic crusade, which should result in removing every laundry operated by Mongolians in New-York, Brooklyn, and New-Jersey.

Figure 31 A battle for control of N. Y. laundries. *New York Times*, March 21, 1890, 8.

Competition Between White and Chinese Laundries

Steam laundries, owned by whites initially, had to convince people to use them when they tried to expand. The public did not easily abandon the old ways of washing laundry by hand. Many customers preferred Chinese hand laundries, which were viewed as less likely to damage clothes and felt that the quality of finished laundry was better if done by hand. The steam laundry industry maintained such views were old prejudices and promoted the belief that work done on modern laundry machines was as good as any done by hand laundries (See Figure 32).

THE PASSING OF A PREJUDICE.

It is one of the good signs of the times that the public generally has nearly gotten over the old prejudice against steam laundries. The people have come to understand that the premature destruction of shirts, collars and cuffs in the steam laundry is more imaginary than real, and that goods done by hand do not last any longer than those turned out by machinery.

Laundry processes as conducted in well regulated laundries do not injure the fabric, neither washing by machine or drying over a steam coil, nor starching by a machine or ironing by a machine is any way more destructive than the corresponding hand process. Ironing by machinery very closely resembles the same work done by hand. In the latter case there is a hot metal surface, flat or nearly flat, and there is an ironing board or table covered with cloths; in the machine there is a heated roll and a padded roll, or, in other words, a collar, for example, is ironed between two cylindrical surfaces instead of two flat surfaces. That is the only difference.

The machine, moreover, has its advantages over hand-ironing. It moves quicker, and maintains a uniform heat and uniform compression, things which the hand can never succeed in accomplishing. In fact there is no question but that it is simply a matter of experience.

Figure 32 Laundry industry promotion of advantages of power laundries. The Laundry Manual, Chicago: National Laundry Journal, 1898, 14.

Steam laundries also had to counter the public fear that contagious diseases were transmitted when the laundry of many customers was mingled in large washing machines. They maintained that power laundries actually were more sanitary than hand laundries.

Their argument was that the much higher water temperatures used in power laundries would be more effective in killing germs than the lower temperatures tolerable to workers scrubbing clothes by hand. Steam laundries touted the technological aspects of their machinery as a masculine approach to laundry that was superior to the primitive methods of Chinese hand laundries that followed the domestic methods used by women.[128]

Propaganda emphasizing health hazards accompanied legislative attempts to drive Chinese laundries out of business. White-owned steam laundries published advertisements (See Figure 33) with vivid images of Chinese laundrymen 'spitting' on clothes to moisten them for ironing to emphasize the health risks of using Chinese laundries.

Do away with this. Patronize a white laundry. White labor only at

Pioneer Laundry. Phone 118

Figure 33 A white-owned laundry ad in Canada invoked image of unhygienic spitting on clothes by a Chinese laundryman. Daily News, Prince Rupert, B.C. May 19, 1911

Some whites objected to such tactics, and viewed them as unfair methods used by whites wanting to scare customers from using Chinese laundries, as one 1885 newspaper editorial comment indicated. Yet, at the

---

[128] Joan Siow-Huey Wang, "Gender, Race and Civilization: The Competition between American Power Laundries and Chinese Steam Laundries, 1870s - 1920s," *American Studies International*, 40, (2002): 52-74.

same time, the editorial showed other biases against Chinese laundrymen.[129]

> An enterprising laundry firm in Washington composed of members of the superior race has been detected in circulating a local paper with an article describing the Chinese laundries as the centres of propagation and distribution of infectious disease. The object is supposed to have been to wrest from the loathsome Orientals the profits of washing the department towels. The worst that can be said of most Chinese washermen, we believe, is that their charges are high and that their work is destructive, and the native or adopted citizens who cannot compete with them have, it would seem, mistaken their calling. The particular competitors in this case have resorted to a trick that is quite as mean and rather more cowardly than the Wyoming method.

Figure 34 Safety of Chinese and white laundries. *New York Times*, Feb 18, 1917, 17.

---

[129] Editorial, Untitled. *New York Times*, Sept. 28, 1885, 4. The 'Wyoming method' was a thinly veiled reference to the Rock Springs massacre against Chinese miners in 1885.

A different approach was to emphasize how unfair the Chinese monopoly on laundry services was and how it deprived white women employment opportunities. In Texas, the headline of an article in a Dallas newspaper urged readers to avoid use of inferior Chinese laundries in favor of white laundries.[130]

> The white laundries of Dallas are complaining that the patronage of many of the people who can afford to patronize institutions giving work to white labor, is sent to the twenty-two inferior Chinese laundries of this city, The people should give the white laundries a chance. They are perfectly safe in doing this, as all of them use the best and clearest of artesian water and the most thorough general system of cleansing, which is not the fact with the Chinese and outside concerns.

How Chinese Laundries Managed To Compete

Chinese hand laundries initially focused on men's clothes such as shirts, handkerchiefs, cuffs, and collars. In New York City in 1898, the prices were 10 cents a shirt, two cents for a collar and a pair of cuffs, and two cents for each handkerchief.[131] By contrast, in 1908 some non-Chinese hand laundries charged anywhere from 25 to 50 cents per shirt, a markup of from 15 to 40 cents per shirt from the wholesale cost of 10 cents each that white power laundries charged for wet wash services.[132]

For almost one hundred years, from the 1820s to the 1920s, businessmen and gentlemen wore the same shirt for several days, replacing the detachable high stiff collars and cuffs to send to the laundry.

---

[130] "Dallas Customers Cannot Be Too Careful Where They Send Their Soiled Clothing," *Dallas Daily Times Herald*, May 11, 1894, 5.

[131] Louis Beck. *New York's Chinatown: A Historical Presentation of Its People and Places* (New York: Bohemia Publishers, 1898), 59.

[132] "The City of Churches," *National Laundry Journal* 59, no. 1 (1908): 25a.

Washing businessmen's shirt collars was not much different from doing other laundry items, but to starch, dampen, and iron them correctly required considerable skill and experience. The laundryman used a hot iron to apply raw starch presses to the detached collars, which produced a glossy appearance.

The early hand laundries used eight-pound solid irons that were heated to a very high temperature over hot coals. The temperature of the irons was not easy to regulate, and sometimes they got too hot. To avoid scorching clothes, they were quickly dipped in and out of a container of water to reduce the temperature before being applied onto clothing.

The laundryman also blew through a tube of a water-filled can to spray a mist onto the clothes to dampen them for ironing. There was public concern that this procedure was unsanitary as it was thought that all laundrymen "spit" directly onto clothes to dampen them.[133]

This task of ironing shirts was difficult to do at home so wives preferred to send their husband's shirts to Chinese laundries or other commercial laundries. Although the detached collar was obsolete by the late 1920s, a clean white shirt with a starched and stiff collar maintained its popularity with businessmen even in summer. In addition, newer fabrics of shirts needed more attention to achieve a tailored appearance. These factors helped maintain growth in the hand laundry business during this period.[134]

---

[133] Siu, 66-67. See also "Chinese Laundry in California." *The Barre Patriot*, Oct. 10, 1852 for a description of how Chinese laundrymen filled their mouths with water from a bowl and then emitted a misty spray to dampen clothes for ironing. The account noted that in ordinary (white?) laundries the same effect is achieved by dipping fingers into the water and then snapping them over the clothes.

[134] Wang, "No Tickee, No Shirtee," 137-138.

Chinese competed well during the early 1900s against steam laundries.[135] White laundries had many costly labor disputes with its workforce of women who worked long hours for low pay in factory-like environs. In Troy, New York, home of the first commercial laundries in the U. S, Kate Mullany organized an all-female union that went on strike in 1864 to gain better pay and working conditions.[136]

> This problem was minimal among Chinese laundries, which usually involved small partnerships. The owner or head of the small hand laundry did not hire employees but worked in collaboration with family members, or in many cases, partners that were not relatives.[137] This arrangement avoided labor-management disputes, cut costs, and allowed lower prices that helped their laundries compete against their larger white laundry rivals.

Malicious Acts Toward Chinese Laundrymen

In addition to the attempts to harm the Chinese laundry business through discriminatory laws, laundrymen were targets of many acts with harmful intent and consequences, ranging from pranks to robbery to homicide.

When laundrymen hung wash on outside clotheslines to dry, it was common all over the country for malicious children to throw dirt at

---

[135] The distinction between Chinese and white laundries was so firmly entrenched that some City Business Directories listed Chinese laundries as a separate category from laundries as late as 1930.

[136] Carole Tubin, *Working Women of Collar City: Gender, Class, and Community in Troy, New York, 1864-1886* (Urbana and Chicago: University of Illinois Press, 1978).

[137] Shehong Chen, *Being Chinese, Becoming Chinese American* (Urbana, Il.: University of Illinois Press, 2002), 133, Peter S. Li, "Ethnic Business among Chinese in the U. S.," *Journal of Ethnic Studies*, (1976): 35-41, Siu, 77-79.

the clothes, requiring the items to be rewashed.   As one observer in Sonoma County, California, noted: [138]

> Rocks were thrown at Chinamen on the streets, sometimes when delivering clothes they would be assaulted and the clean clothes scattered in the dirt; of course the poor Chinaman would have to take them back and do them all over again or pay for those damaged beyond repair.

> At other times gangs of young men would collect a flock of ancient eggs, rotten vegetables, or some other obnoxious substance. After darkness fell, they would gather in front of a laundry, have one of their number rap on the door, run out of range so that when the Chinaman opened the door the rest of the mob would give him a volley of garbage, much of which would get inside and foul up everything it contacted.

Another common problem for laundrymen was that young boys would toss rocks to break windows of their storefronts, as reported in an 1883 incident (See Figure 35). Yee Lee, one of the victims, witnessed the vandalism and requested a policeman who also was a witness to arrest the Irish lad who broke his windows. The policeman declined, claiming he could not catch the youth.   The article concluded with Yee Lee's resignation and inference that the policeman was probably also Irish.

These mischievous pranks against Chinese were widespread. One especially malicious and cruel incident mentioned briefly in the preceding chapter that harmed the work of a Chinese laundryman occurred in Ames, Iowa in 1919. An unknown person left a parcel of shirts with dye capsules embedded in the collars. When the shirts were soaked in water, these capsules released a brown substance that deeply stained all of the clothing of other customers.

---

[138] William C. Shipley, *Tales of Sonoma County Reflections on A Golden Age* (Charleston, S.C.: Arcadia Publishing, 2000), 52.

> ## THE THEORY OF YEE LEE.
>
> There are three Chinese laundrymen in Greenwich-street, between Liberty and John. One of them inhabits a shy and secluded cellar on the east side of the street. The other two have laundries on the ground floor and on the west side. One of them is Hong Wing, or syllables to that effect, and the other is Yee Lee. The hoodlums of the neighborhood are in the habit of vindicating the superiority of a Caucasian civilization by smashing the windows of these laundries whenever they feel jolly or there is any public event which seems to stand in need of celebration. It is alleged that the windows have been smashed four or five times since New-Year's Day. They were last smashed last Thursday night by way of commemorating the opening of the Brooklyn bridge. Hong Wing had four large panes shattered, having already boarded up the lower half of the principal sash. He looked melancholy, but showed no ability to give an explanation of the disaster when a TIMES reporter made him a visit of condolence last evening.
>
> Yee Lee, whose windows had suffered equally, was more conversable and less melancholy. Yes, the windows had been smashed on Thursday night. They were always smashed at night. He had complained to Pleece Captain, but Pleece Captain say he have no men, not at 1 o'clock at night. Yee Lee saw boy, Ilish boy, smashing glass Thursday night. Pleeceman saw boy, too, Ilish pleeceman. "Pleeceman stand light over there," indicating the corner diagonally opposite and in plain view, "I lan out and told pleeceman allest boy. Pleeceman say he no can catch boy. I tlink lat Ilish pleeceman know lat Ilish boy. You tlink so?"
>
> The establishment of Yee Lee is in Capt. Caffrey's precinct.

Figure 35 "The Theory of Yee Lee," *New York Times,* May 10, 1883, 2.

Sam Ding, the victimized laundryman, had to rewash all of the clothes at least six times. A short while later, he received another package of shirts left on his doorstep for washing. Sam first cautiously isolated and soaked its contents in a bucket of cold water and when the brown substance was released as on the previous occasion, it did not contaminate an entire load of wash.

According to a local newspaper,[139] shortly after this episode Sam Ding simply shuttered the doors of his laundry and disappeared one day, but not without first thoughtfully leaving a note on the door to inform

---

[139] "Cunning Chinaman Catches Clothes Coloring Culprit," *Ames Tri-weekly Tribune*, May 21, 1919.

customers where they could claim their laundry. No one knows the exact reasons he left, but these hostile actions by his unknown tormentor may have convinced him to move on.

Robbery of Chinese Laundrymen

Laundrymen were tempting targets for robbery and assault because many of them worked alone, often late at night. They kept cash in their stores, many of which were located in dangerous parts of town. They preferred to hide cash savings inside the store rather than depositing it in banks.[140] Incidents of robbery and assault committed against Chinese laundrymen were frequently reported in American newspapers.

An account[141] in a New York paper in 1882, illustrates how vulnerable laundrymen were to being victims of such crimes. The article reported the arrest of two members of the "Short Tall" Gang that had terrorized several 'celestial washermen,' as the paper identified them, in several crimes over a short period. The ruffians had "sacked one Chinese laundry in Williamsburg and stole $250," attacked another laundryman on Spring Street who was "knocked down and robbed of $40 in his laundry," entered a laundry on Forsyth Street and after tying up two laundrymen, "menaced them with pistols, and stole $75," and committed still "another robbery with violence" at a Chatham Street laundry.

The newspaper report indicated that police had been rather lax in protecting the Chinese laundrymen as two officers were being charged for not arresting the suspects even though a witness had identified them for the police at the scene. This indication of unwillingness of authorities to

---

[140] Wang, "No Tickee, No Shirtee," 95.

[141] "Plundering Chinese Laundries. Arrests of Ruffians Who Have Robbed the Celestial Washermen," *New York Times*, Oct. 30, 1882, 1.

take action to protect Chinese served to confirm their belief and fear that they could not receive justice. They felt that when contesting offenses against them committed by whites, courts almost always sided with whites. Chinese language newspapers reported these numerous attacks and similar incidents involving laundries.[142] Awareness of these crimes reinforced concerns of Chinese laundrymen all over the country that they might be similarly victimized.

Laundrymen Homicides

Chinese language newspapers publicized incidents of Chinese murdered by whites or blacks. These homicides often involved robberies, but some also involved racial hatred. Of course, not all cases involved laundrymen as the victims but anxieties about being racial targets of violence were heightened among laundrymen by reports of the murder of any Chinese.[143]

Two examples of such homicides can illustrate why laundrymen were apprehensive about their safety. In 1889, Joe Lee, a Chinese laundryman in Rome, Georgia died several days after he was ambushed one night behind his laundry and bludgeoned with a blow to the back of his head with the back of an ax handle. The assailant, a black youth, then

---

142 Wang, "No Tickee, No Shirtee," 86-87.

143 Actually, the majority of Chinese homicide victims in large cities died at the hands of other Chinese. These incidents usually involved disputes among business partners or territorial conflict among rival tongs or gangs. A rash of killings of laundrymen by Chinese tong members occurred during the 1920s. From 1900 to 1930, 25 of 33 Chinese homicide cases in Chicago with identified killers involved other Chinese. "1916 Chicago's First Conviction of a White Man for Murdering a Chinese," http://www.ccamuseum.org/Research-2.html#anchor 125 (accessed Aug. 1, 2006).

entered his laundry and stole money from under the unfortunate laundryman's pillow.[144]

In Philadelphia, youthful ruffians brutally murdered Chang Ah You without any provocation by him in the Sam Wah Laundry in 1883. The newspaper report (See Figure 36) made light of the crime, directing attention to the pidgin English of the Chinese witnesses in their attempts to describe the crime. The account went on to emphasize that this funeral represented the first time that a pagan, Chang, had received a Christian burial but it did not comment on the outrageousness of the crime.

A CHINAMAN'S FUNERAL.

AN IMPRESSIVE SCENE IN A PHILADELPHIA CHURCH—AH YOU'S MURDERERS.

PHILADELPHIA, March 6.—John B. Clark, as principal, and Samuel H. Brough and Thomas B. Lyons as accessories, were committed to prison without bail by the Coroner to-day charged with the murder of Chang Ah You, a young Chinaman who was employed in the laundry of Sam Wah, at No. 844 South Second-street. The evidence before the Coroner showed that the three young men entered Sam Wah's laundry on Feb. 22, and, without provocation, assaulted the inmates, Clark striking Chang Ah You a blow over the eye with a pair of brass knuckles, which fractured his skull, and from which he died on Sunday last. At the inquest this morning Charles Sing, an American-ized Mongolian, acted as interpreter. When the Chinese witnesses, in describing the attack, became excited and lapsed into pigeon English, the specta-tors laughed aloud.

Figure 36 Part of newspaper report of funeral of Ah You, homicide victim. "A Chinaman's Funeral." *New York Times,* **March 7, 1883, 1.**

The tone of the article was typical of newspaper coverage of incidents involving Chinese, often showing a mix of amusement and contempt for the Chinese beliefs, customs, and practices. It described the

---

[144] Roger D. Aycock, *All Roads to Rome* (Roswell, Ga.: W. H. Wolfe Associates, 1981), 230-233.

funeral as having, "… nothing of the scenes with which all Chinamen are familiar … There were no idols standing in the corners; there was no burning of incense. Even the little idol which Ah You at one time deemed his most precious treasure was absent. To some extent Ah You had given up the religion of Confucius." [145]

Exactly how many Chinese, laundrymen or others, were actually attacked or killed by whites or blacks is not known. But the actual incidence rates were not important because even a few cases created a high level of fear and vigilance. Concern about possible assaults and robberies may have been stronger among laundrymen as their stores were often located in dangerous neighborhoods and operated by only one or two men.

In some laundries, they installed a fence of vertical iron bars spaced about 10 inches apart that arose above the entire front counter to protect themselves against unwanted customer intrusions into the workspace. An opening in the fence at the counter level was large enough only to receive or return laundry packages. Another security precaution taken in Chinese laundries was the use of a cash drawer attached securely under a shelf or counter that could not be opened without pulling the right combination of several levers under it to release a locking mechanism. [146]

---

[145] A balanced account should acknowledge that Chinese also killed whites, although sometimes after being provoked in racial confrontations. In one such tragic incident in 1887, Charlie Jim clubbed a 13-year old boy in retaliation for vandalism and harassment. Although the laundryman probably did not intend to kill the boy, unfortunately he died from the blows inflicted to his head. "Charlie Jim's Victim. A Chinese Laundryman Retaliates on His Tormentors," *New York Times*, Aug. 19, 1887, 8.

[146] For a similar description of these and other physical features common to Chinese laundries, see Siu., 56-68.

Demeaning Images of Chinese and their Laundries

Chinese laundrymen were also victims of negative images directed against all Chinese in popular forms of entertainment. These depictions harmed their standing in society, emphasizing their inferior status to whites. Minstrel show entertainers portrayed the Chinese with the unflattering character of John Chinaman just as they used Jim Crow and Zip Coon characters to demean blacks. Whereas their depictions of blacks emphasized lack of culture and refinement, the portrayal of John Chinaman showed he was "forever foreign." He spoke 'pidgin English,' to the delight of white laborers, mocking the singsong sounds of the Cantonese language. He had clothing that differed from western styles and he wore his hair in a pigtail queue, subjecting him to more ridicule.[147]

Silent motion pictures presented stereotypical negative images of Chinese men as emasculated or asexual beings, adding to society's unfavorable image of them. Biograph Films made several such silent films with Chinese characters, often laundrymen. By portraying the laundrymen as ludicrous buffoons, the films created stereotypes that made them targets of ridicule for the white audiences in contrast to other films focusing on evil Chinese dope fiends who entice young white women and schoolgirls into their opium dens.[148]

"*In a Chinese Laundry,*" a laundryman makes amorous advances, unsuccessfully, to a white girl in the store to pick up her laundry. The 1897 film ridiculed the laundryman's sexual incompetence, contradicting

---

[147] Robert G. Lee, "*Orientals: Asian Americans in Popular Culture*"

[148] John Haddon, "The Laundry Man's Got A Knife," *Chinese America: History and Perspectives*, (2001): 31-47.

the reality that some Chinese laundrymen actually married white women, a situation that was not socially acceptable at the time. White audiences, probably felt less anxiety over interracial sex after viewing this film with its portrayal of the laundryman's failure.[149]

A theatrical melodrama, "The Queen of Chinatown," produced by Joseph Jarrow in 1899, portrayed negative images of Chinese that pandered to many of the worst fears that whites held. Although laundrymen were not specifically depicted in this show, the negative feelings it aroused easily extended to all Chinese. Posters for the show (See Figure 37) featured opium-smoking Oriental men enticing or coercing white women into their dens or parading arm in arm with them on city streets. Performed on Broadway only twice, these vivid images both reflected and increased societal fears that Chinese might foster opium use by white women as well as be a sexual threat to white men by marrying or having sexual relations with white women.[150]

In addition to these visual images, popular American writers created images of evil, clever, and cunning Chinese villains, epitomized by Sax Rohmer's 1913 sinister Dr. Fu Manchu, described as "the yellow peril

---

[149] In another Biograph film, "*The Heathen Chinese and the Sunday School Teacher*" (1904), three white women invite Chinese workers from the Sam Kee Laundry to attend Sunday school. The 'plot' is not entirely fanciful. White women in Sunday schools in many towns did occasionally invite Chinese laundrymen to teach them English or try to convert them to Christianity. Insofar as Chinese laundrymen lived in a bachelor society, it is not difficult to see why some of them might become romantically or sexually attracted to white women teachers, a situation that no one spoke about openly but one that provoked anxiety among whites. In the film, the women find the Chinese men attractive, and by the third scene they are corting with them in no less than an opium den. Eventually police arrive to arrest the Chinese just in time. The Sunday school teachers, undaunted, try without success to bail out their Chinese paramours as the film ends.

[150] Thomas Allston Brown, *A History of the New York Stage: From The First Performance in 1732 to 1901* (New York: Dodd, Mead, 1903), 341.

incarnate in one man." This evil mastermind plotted against whites to take control of the world. These sinister stereotypes, dramatized in movies and on radio programs, generated suspicion of Chinese among whites who reacted with hostility toward these exotic demons.

Figure 37   Posters for an 1899 Broadway show, Queen of Chinatown by Joseph Jarrow.

Even when a fictional Chinese such as Earl Derr Bigger's master detective, Charlie Chan, cleverly solved crimes of murder, he was still depicted with a touch of derision. These stories written between 1925 and 1932, and later made into B movies were intended to counteract the typical stories of Chinese as evil villains. Although Chan is bestowed with admirable qualities of intelligence and moral integrity, he is saddled with inscrutable aphorisms uttered in pidgin English,[151] not unlike those mocking gems of wisdom misattributed to Confucius, such as:

---

[151] One critic noted, "In this respect, Charlie's flowery and slippery speech resonates with the poisonous devil's tongue of Dr. Fu Manchu.. What these two creations helped to fashion and substantiate in the early decades of this century was a stereotype of the racial Other's language and, more important, a stigmatization of the race." Yunte Huang, *Transpacific Displacement: Ethnography, Translation, and Intertextual Travel in Twentieth-Century American Literature* (Berkeley: University Of California Press, 2002), 116-118.

Way to find rabbit's residence is to turn rabbit loose and watch.
Some heads, like hard nuts, much better if cracked.
Too late to dig well after honorable house is on fire.
Mind like parachute—only function when open.

Together, these media images fostered powerful negative images that reinforced popular beliefs that Chinese men were of an inferior race and undesirable members of society. These attitudes served to justify mistreatment and even exclusion of these foreigners. And, even though there was no laundryman depicted in many of these demeaning depictions, these images adversely affected the laundrymen because of the strong association in the public view between "Chinese" and "laundry." Thus, some whites who had never dealt with Chinese laundrymen still held firm negative ideas about them. Some parents tried to chasten their children with frightening warnings that bad boys are kidnapped by laundrymen who chase them with red-hot irons, as excerpts of interviews with several youth conducted in the early 1930s demonstrate.

> "Now I had heard all sorts of weird stories about "Chinamen" and was rather afraid. I had heard that they chased boys with a red hot iron and did all kinds of mysterious and sinister things in their back rooms. I also knew that they acted and talked "funny" and you couldn't know what to expect from them."

> "The only time I recall my parents saying anything about them was one time when I walked past the store with them and said that the Chinaman's store was real spooky. One of my parents then said, "Look out or he will cut your head off. ...When I was ten I saw a movie in which the Chinese were the spooky crooks or bad guys... They didn't say anything, but they were always doing murders, stealing, importing, or being smuggled across the border half dead, inside of crates full of straw. I never hated them because in real life I never met any."

> "... her opinion...was formed entirely from the vivid motion pictures she saw involving Chinamen in villainous roles...When R. S. had occasion to pass a Chinese laundry, she walked hurriedly by

or crossed the street… R. S. was extremely surprised upon entering high school and making the acquaintance of a young Chinaman and discovering that the Chinese are as law-abiding as any other American citizens."

The strange language, clothing, and hair, of these little yellow men all add to the mystery surrounding laundrymen who seem to work all day ironing shirts. The American public accepts them in the role as laundrymen, but they know little else about them and their families, content that they perform a job befitting a member of what they regard as an inferior race. As one interviewee argued,[152]

> "I don't mind them working in the laundry business, but they should not go any higher than that. After all, there are not enough jobs for us whites, without them butting in. Besides, we could never compete with them. They naturally work harder, and for much less pay."

Fears of Sexual Relations Between Chinese Men and White Women

Part of the hostility against Chinese, and other minorities, stemmed from white fears that some might enter into marriage or sexual liaisons with white women. This concern was heightened by the low availability of Chinese women here. Media images reinforced the pressure for laws in many states against whites marrying nonwhites.[153] When a 16-year old white girl wanted to marry a laundryman in Brooklyn in 1900, they had to go into hiding as the mother, father, and brothers threatened to kill the couple. The parents filed a search warrant, vowing to find her and put her into a home until she came of age, proclaiming, "We would

---

[152] Siu, 22.

[153] Many states passed anti-miscegenation laws mainly directed against black-white sexual relationships but they often applied to Chinese too. Hrishi Karthikeyan and Gabriel J. Chin, "Preserving Racial Identity: Population Patterns and the Application of Anti-miscegenation Statutes to Asian Americans, 1910-1950," *Asian Law Journal*, 1-39, (2002): 1-40.

rather see her dead than married to that Chinaman. If we could get ahold of him we would kill him." [154]

Some whites worried that Chinese laundrymen might prey on white school-age girls. In 1889, a Milwaukee newspaper alleged that two middle-aged Chinese laundrymen had imposed sexual relations with several under-aged white girls in their store. A riot involving a mob of over 2,000 ensued that demolished one Chinese laundry and in the melee anyone who 'looked Chinese' was likely to be attacked.' The laundrymen were jailed but later released as evidence suggested that the girls had been willing participants over several months. [155] [156]

In contrast to the prevalent negative and demeaning stereotypes of Chinese laundrymen, in the context of laundering Chinese were sometimes portrayed in seemingly benign or even positive terms. As early as 1852 a laundry product named 'Nelson's Premium Chinese Washing Fluid' claimed to have miraculous cleaning capability (See Figure 38) as if the product would have more commercial success by associating it with

---

[154] "Maggie Mark Not Found. She and Chinese Sweetheart Still In Hiding," *New York Times*, Aug. 11, 1900, 12.

[155] Victor Jew, " 'Chinese Demons': The Violent Articulation of Chinese Otherness and Interracial Sexuality in the U.S. Midwest, 1885-1889," *Journal of Social History*, 37 no. 2 (2003): 389-410.

[156] In 1902, Samuel Gompers, the leader of a national labor union, pandered to these fears of Chinese men enticing young white girls into sexual relations.
"Time was when little girls no older than 12 years were found in Chinese laundries under the influence of opium. What other crimes were committed in those dark and fetid places when these little innocent victims of the Chinamen's wiles were under the influence of the drug are almost too horrible to imagine." American Federation of Labor, *Some Reasons for Chinese Exclusion. Meat vs. Rice. American Manhood against Asiatic Coolieism .Which Shall Survive?* Senate Doc. No. 137, 57th Congress, 1st Session (Washington D. C.: Government Printing Office, 1902).

the Chinese who were noted for their laundering expertise.[157] Still, a pernicious adverse effect of this dubious positive image was that it fostered the public perception that Chinese were capable only in domestic work.[158]

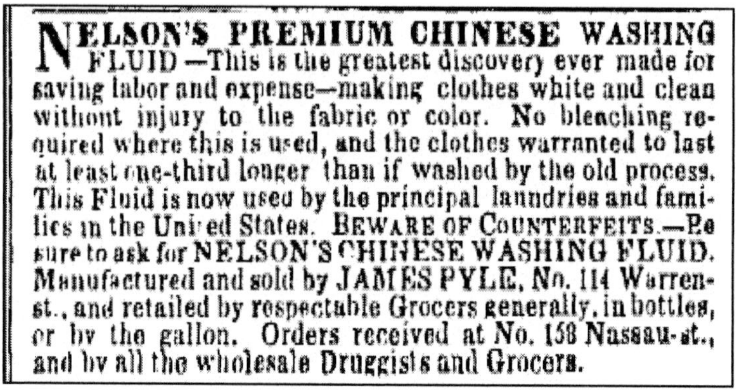

NELSON'S PREMIUM CHINESE WASHING FLUID.—This is the greatest discovery ever made for saving labor and expense—making clothes white and clean without injury to the fabric or color. No bleaching required where this is used, and the clothes warranted to last at least one-third longer than if washed by the old process. This Fluid is now used by the principal laundries and families in the United States. BEWARE OF COUNTERFEITS.—Be sure to ask for NELSON'S CHINESE WASHING FLUID. Manufactured and sold by JAMES PYLE, No. 114 Warren-st., and retailed by respectable Grocers generally, in bottles, or by the gallon. Orders received at No. 158 Nassau-st., and by all the wholesale Druggists and Grocers.

Figure 38 Ad for a laundry product employs 'Chinese' as part of its name to imply superior cleaning properties. *New York Daily Times*, Oct. 4, 1852, p. 6.

The Chinese laundryman was even employed as the target of intended humor. The illustration on the sheet music cover in Figure 39 for the song, 'No Wash-ee To-tay,' portrays a very relaxed and smiling Chinese laundryman, which suggests that he is celebrating his decision to take the day off from his usual labor at the 'Long Sing' Laundry. Given that Chinese laundrymen were notoriously hard workers for many hours

---

157 That Chinese were noted for laundry skills in New York by 1852 casts doubt on the claim cited in Chapter 1 that the *first* Chinese laundry opened in 1851 in San Francisco.

158 Similarly, in a Calgon water softener ad that appeared as late as 1972 a white customer enthusiastically asks the Chinese laundryman how he gets clothes so clean. The laundryman proudly but slyly proclaims, "ancient Chinese secret," capitalizing on popular images that Chinese ways are part of a mysterious and ancient culture. Only in doing laundry, are the Chinese ascribed these powerful abilities. By invoking this stereotype, whites keep the Chinese in their place in society as providers of domestic services. Only at the end of the advertisement, does the announcer voiceover disclose that it is actually Calgon, an American product, and no Chinese secret, that is really responsible for the clean clothes.

daily, and that customers would be unlikely to tolerate their laundryman taking a day off, the sentiment expressed in the title is highly unrealistic.

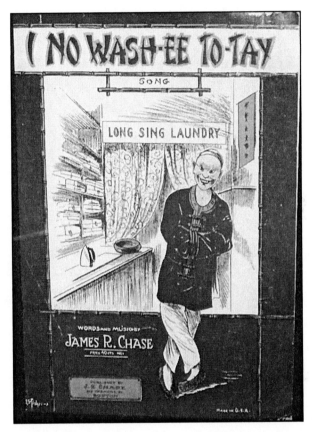

Figure 39 Sheet music cover for "No Wash-ee To-tay," mocks a Chinese laundryman.

The fact that many Chinese were laundrymen led the public to form a strong association between laundries and Chinese as laundry bags provided at one hotel show. A guest wanting laundry service placed items outside their rooms in bags that bore a caricature of a Chinese man on the outside (See Figure 40).[159]

---

[159] A sales pitch for a laundry bag in 2006, touted it as a "Most honorable laundry bag," and proclaims, "No one knows laundry better than the Chinese. They've even perfected the bag."

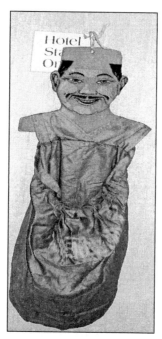

Figure 40 Chinese laundryman image on hotel laundry bags. Courtesy, Steven Doi.

These associations between Chinese and laundry were clever and at one level, humorous. However, given the history of anti-Chinese sentiment, they not only reflected but also served to foster and maintain society's condescending and disrespectful attitude toward them.

5. Chain Migration of Laundrymen

The Chinese laundryman, as Americans see him, is not a person, but a thing.[160]

Studies of Chinese laundries typically have examined the lives of individual laundrymen. They provide useful general depictions of how they arrived here, became laundrymen, and what their work involved. However, these accounts reveal nothing about the important interconnections among these laundrymen without which newcomers could not have survived. Chinese working in the U. S., and Canada, commonly helped male relatives come from China in a chain of migration to work in family-run businesses such as laundries, and later, in restaurants and grocery stores. Many laundrymen within a geographic region were related to each other even though they bore different surnames because many had to abandon their true names to assume the fake or "paper-son" identities on documents their sponsoring kin purchased for them.[161]

This chapter focuses on the Chinese in the American South during the first half of the 20th century as a case study of chain migration.[162] Such a study is more difficult in a region with a large Chinese

---

[160] Siu, 23.

[161] The use of paper names also meant that men with the *same* surname were not necessarily relatives.

[162] According to U. S. census data, few Chinese, mostly male, lived in the South during the Exclusion law years, with the peak between 1900 and 1920. The highest counts were 166 Chinese in Georgia in 1900, 135 in Florida in 1910, and 211 in Mississippi in 1920. In Mississippi, the Chinese clustered in the Delta region where most operated family grocery stores serving a black

population whereas the South, with its handful of Chinese until after World War II, is better suited for identifying the members of a migration chain, tracing its temporal sequence, and examining the interpersonal interactions.

The nature of this important but infrequently studied process may well have varied in different regions. Despite this uncertain comparability across regions, this case study may provide insights that further our understanding of how kinship ties functioned in making chain migration possible among laundrymen as well as for other Chinese.

Fun Fai's 19 Chinese Laundries of The Deep South

Although Fun Fai[163] and his sons never set foot in the U.S., at least 19 of his descendants did. Three of his grandsons emigrated as paper sons from the Hoiping district to Gold Mountain. They would spend most of the rest of their lives operating laundries in the Deep South, a region fabled for its hospitality, but not to people of color. Even if it cannot be entirely corroborated, this account of their journey to the South is a plausible one. Using personal experience, observation, and archival evidence, this analysis identifies the members of the chain, describes the temporal and geographical aspects of their migration, and analyses how these men assisted each other.

These laundrymen worked hard to survive, sent money home to support their parents, and in some cases, wives and children back in China. Some were able later, with much difficulty, to bring their families

---

clientele, which was often ill treated by white businesses. In contrast, most Chinese in Florida and Georgia, with the exception of Augusta where small grocers prevailed, ran laundries

[163] His clan name is omitted to respect concerns of some relatives who do not want it disclosed that they have paper names. There were about seven different surnames among Fun Fai's 19 male descendants in the South. This chapter is based on a presentation by the author at the Association of Asian American Studies Conference, Atlanta, Georgia, March 28, 2006.

to the South. Others who were more fortunate had their wives and children with them, living in the backs of their laundries and helping with the work. The stories of how they made their way to the South and entered the laundry business are similar in many respects.

A familial network of hand laundries, as shown in Figure 41, involved chain migration of 16 male kin (See Figure 42) of Fun Fai from Guangdong province starting in the late 1800s. Three other descendants, born in the South, also ran laundries and as of 2007, a great, great, great grandson in Atlanta still operates a Chinese laundry.

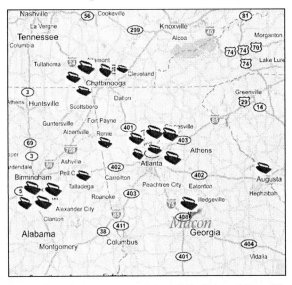

Figure 41 Map of Southern locations of the 19 laundries of Fun Fai.

These men came from villages in Guangdong that for generations had fostered strong cooperation and loyalty among clan members. Decisions to immigrate were group, rather than individual, choices.[164] Upon arriving in San Francisco, they benefited from the aid of *huiguans*, or

---

[164] Haiming Lui, "The Social Origins Of Early Chinese Immigrants," In *The Chinese in America: A History from Gold Mountain to the New Millennium*, Susie L. Cassel, ed. (Walnut Creek, Ca.: Alta Mira Press, 2002), 21-36.

mutual aid organizations, established by immigrants who came from districts that shared a regional dialect. This assistance was vital to help their adjustment to a new country by providing short-term lodging and help in finding work or locating relatives.[165]

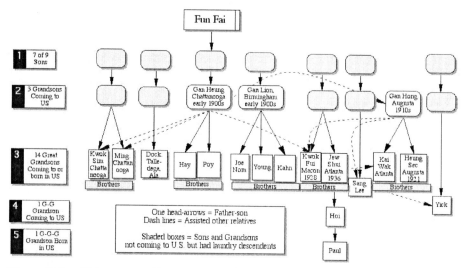

Figure 42 Familial network of laundrymen descendants of Fun Fai in the American South.

The First Wave of Fun Fai's Descendants in the South

Exactly why or how the first of Fun Fai's descendants settled in the American South, so far from San Francisco, the port of entry for most Chinese, is unknown. It is likely that he knew someone from his village already in the South who helped him find work. That three of Fun Fai's grandsons from China settled in the South where they would spend the rest of their working lives operating laundries does not seem likely to have been coincidental.

---

[165] Him Mark Lai, *Becoming Chinese American: A History of Communities and Institutions* (Walnut Creek, Ca.: Alta Mira Press, 2004), 40-48.

These grandsons, Gan Heung, Gan Lion and, Gan Hong, came to the U. S. between 1900 and 1920 approximately and started a chain of migration by assisting their younger relatives in following their path to the South. They purchased immigration documents for brothers, sons, and nephews and provided travel expenses, lodging, and work experience to help them save enough to eventually start their own laundries.

Gan Heung

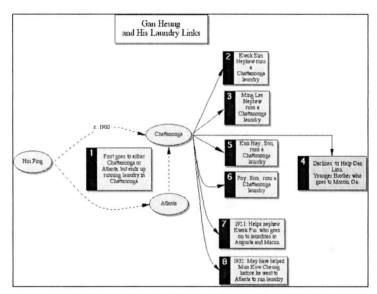

Figure 43 Gan Heung's travels and links to laundrymen kin coming to the South.

Gan Heung was born around 1882. He was a grandson who came to the U. S. around 1900, undoubtedly as a paper son (See Figure 43), leaving his wife and sons behind in the village. Gan Heung may have first apprenticed in a Chinese laundry in Atlanta,[166] which then had the most Chinese laundries in the region, about 40 at its peak in 1919. Then, after

---

[166] Alternatively, he may have known someone who worked in the region in construction, either on the Augusta canal started in 1873 or on the construction of Alabama & Chattanooga railroad, and stayed in the South when that work was completed.

establishing his own laundry business in Chattanooga, Tennessee, Gan Heung sent for his two sons, Kuo Hay and Poy to come work with him. Both of them later also operated laundries in Chattanooga. Gan Heung also helped two sons of an older brother in China, Gan Shim, start their laundries in Chattanooga.

Gan Lion

Gan Lion,[167] another of Fun Fai's grandsons came over from Hoiping at age 18 in 1906 to seek work, leaving his new wife behind. He went first to Mexico, and from there he entered the U. S. Although he had no identity papers, he persuaded authorities that he had lost them (See Figure 44). This explanation worked since many official records had been destroyed by the 1906 S. F. earthquake and fire. Gan Lion traveled by train from San Francisco to seek assistance from his older brother, Gan Heung, in Chattanooga. However, he became dehydrated during the long journey because he was afraid to drink the water and was hospitalized in Atlanta. His older brother, summoned to him in the hospital, not only refused him assistance, but also chastised him for coming to America and being a burden to him. Gan Lion then learned of an opportunity to work for an older Chinese in a laundry in Macon, Georgia. Eventually he saved enough to buy the laundry, which he later sold when he returned for a visit to China around 1910 to start a family. After the birth of his first two sons in China, he returned to the U. S. in 1922 accompanied by his wife and family this time.

Their plan was to return to Georgia to buy another laundry. However, en route from California they stopped in Birmingham,

---

[167] Interview with Young Quan by John Jung, Oct. 16, 2005

Alabama, where Gan Lion had relatives who ran a restaurant, which was not doing well. He decided to settle there and open a hand laundry. Later three of his sons, two born in Alabama, also operated laundries in the area.

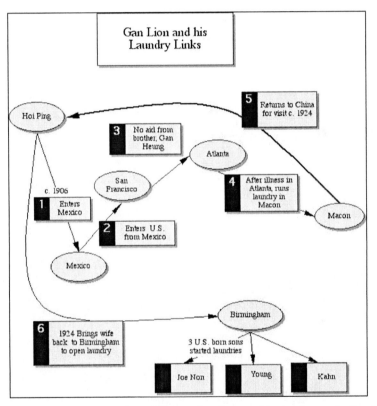

Figure 44 Gan Lion's travels and links to laundrymen kin coming to the South.

Gan Hong

Gan Hong,[168] another grandson, was the older of twin sons born sometime in the 1880s to Fun Fai's sixth son (See Figure 45). Gan Hong

---

[168] Interview with Kim Sheung by John Jung, August 25, 2004 and with Grace Lo, 2004-2005.

immigrated to the United States about 1900, leaving his wife and 5 children in China, and entered at New York falsely using a diplomat's visa.

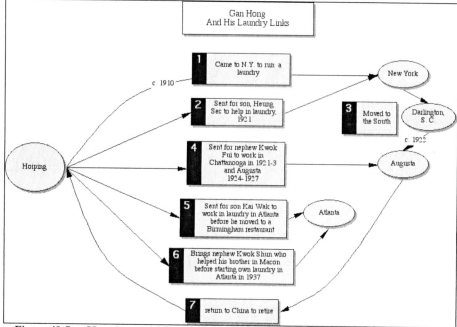

Figure 45 Gan Hong's travels and links to laundrymen kin coming to the South.

He first worked in New York in a laundry. Then in 1921 he sent for his 16-year old son, Heung Sec, to come from China to help him in the laundry. A few years later they moved to Darlington, South Carolina to work briefly in a laundry there before settling in Augusta, Georgia. They purchased a laundry in the business area, one of the few in Augusta. Most Chinese opened small family grocery stores like one shown in Figure 46. Augusta grocers, and their families, lived in or near their small stores, which were spread over black neighborhoods, as was true for Mississippi Chinese, as described earlier.

Gan Hong became a community leader and co-founder of the local Chinese Consolidated Benevolent Association in 1927, and his son, Heung Sec, was an active member. After helping his son come over, Gan

Hong also purchased papers to assist his older son, Kai Wok, and two nephews, Kwok Fui and Jew Shiu, in coming to Georgia. When Gan Hong retired, he returned to China leaving Heung Sec to run the laundry.

Figure 46 Many Chinese in the South operated small family run grocery stores to serve black communities such as this one in Augusta, Ga.

The Second Wave of Fun Fai's Descendents
Heung Sec

About 1934, Heung Sec returned to China to marry in an arranged match (See Figure 47). His wife preferred staying in China, so he left her, a son, and a daughter behind and returned to Augusta around 1937 just before the Japan-China conflict escalated into full-scale war. Unfortunately, his wife died at an early age from kidney problems and his son also died young from a medical condition.

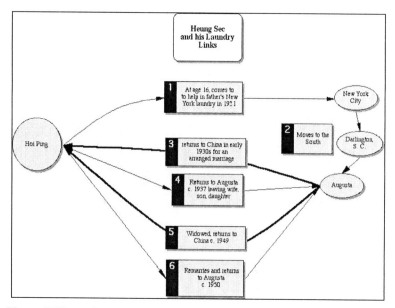

Figure 47 Heung Sec's travels and links to laundrymen kin in the South.

After World War II, Heung Sec was able to return to China to visit his daughter and while he was there, he met and married June in 1950. They returned to Augusta and operated the Kam Lee Laundry (See Figure 48) in downtown Augusta, the only Chinese laundry left in Augusta after World War II and it continued to operate well into the 1970s.

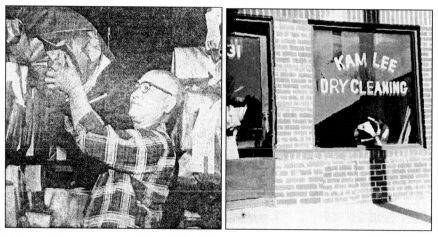

Figure 48 Kam Lee (aka Heung Sec) shortly before his retirement in 1967 (lt) and his laundry store on Seventh Street in Augusta, Georgia (rt). Courtesy, June Loo.

Kwok Fui

When Kwok Fui[169] first arrived in the U. S. in 1921, he worked in Chattanooga, Tennessee, for a few years with his uncle, Gan Heung, in his laundry, as shown in Figure 49. Then in 1924 he moved to work in Augusta, Georgia, with his uncle Gan Hong for several years in his laundry.[170] He purchased a partnership in a Chinese store in Augusta to establish himself as a merchant before he returned to Guangdong in 1927 to marry in an arranged match. Returning the next year, his partnership with the Augusta merchant permitted him to enter with his bride, Quan Shee. He purchased a laundry (See Figure 50) from another laundryman in Macon, Georgia, and operated it with his family for almost 30 years.

Kwok Fui and his family were the only Chinese in the city. The nearest Chinese were other laundrymen and their families in Atlanta, 100 miles to the north. Due to their isolation from other Chinese, when the older children entered adolescence, he began to think of moving his family to San Francisco to enable them to have social and cultural contact with other Chinese of their own age.

In the early 1950s he was able to afford to move his family. He sent his wife to acquire a residence before the children moved. Kwok Fui remained alone in Macon for four years to operate the laundry to provide income for his family in California before he could retire and join them.

---

[169] Kwok Fui was my father, and he adopted an American name, Frank Jung, as Jung Ben was his paper name.

[170] A different account is that his uncle, Gan Hong, helped him come to work in N.Y. and then in Augusta for several years between 1924 and 1927 before he got his own laundry in Macon, Georgia. The documented facts favor Kwok Fui's version but it is possible that both versions have some truth, since Kwok Fui did work in both Chattanooga and Augusta even if the details of the two accounts may conflict.

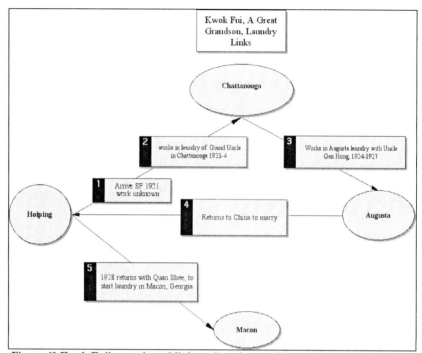

Figure 49 Kwok Fui's travels and links to laundrymen kin coming to the South.

Figure 50 Kwok Fui reads Chinese newspaper during smoke break (lt) in his Sam Lee   Laundry in Macon, Georgia (rt), 1953.

Jew Shui

When Jew Shui arrived as a paper son in 1936, he was denied entry. His papers indicated that he grew up in Hong Kong, but he failed to answer many questions about that city's surroundings and recent history. He appealed and gained entry after a month of detention on Angel Island.[171]

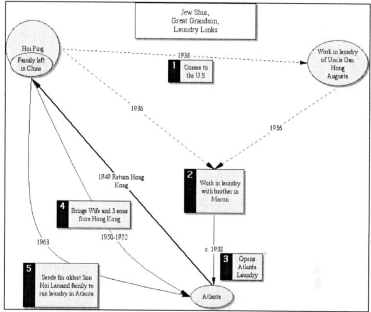

Figure 51 Jew Shui's travels and links to laundrymen kin coming to the South.

He first worked for a year with his older brother, Kwok Fui, in Macon before moving to Atlanta to start his own laundry (See Figure 51). With a cousin, Kai Wok, he ran two laundries, the Loo Ling Laundry on Georgia Avenue and Joe's Laundry on Capitol Avenue, during the 1940s.

After World War II but before the communist takeover of China in 1949, he had another laundryman run his store while he returned to

---

[171] Record Group 85 File 36330/8-5 *Immigration and Naturalization Service*, San Francisco.

Guangdong to be with his family for about one year.[172]   In 1950 he succeeded in bringing his wife and the two youngest of his four sons to live with him in Atlanta (See Figure 52).

Figure 52 Jew Shui was able to bring his wife, Thay Woy, and two of his sons, William and Henry Jew, from Hong Kong. Courtesy, Henry Jew.

His laundry on Capitol Avenue was appropriated in the mid 1960s to provide parking for the Fulton County baseball stadium built in 1966 for the Atlanta Braves team. Luckily, he was able to find another location right around the corner at 56 Georgia Avenue only a few blocks from where his family resided. By then his oldest son, Hoi Lam, had come from Hong Kong to Atlanta with his wife and five children as refugees.

---

[172] Laundrymen covered for each other when one had to be absent for as much as a year or two. If there were more than one Chinese working at one laundry, one of them would take over the management of the laundry so that owner could go back to China. In an extreme case, several men took turns covering the laundry of one man in Alabama who was having reentry problems that lasted about a decade. Kwok Fui had his 16-year old nephew cover his laundry while he visited his family in California.

They worked together for a few years running Joe's Laundry.[173]

After his father retired, Hoi Lam operated the laundry until about 2004. A grandson of Jew Shui, Paul, now runs the laundry. Ironically, the laundry, displaced from its original location by the stadium in 1966, outlasted it, which itself was replaced by Turner Field in 1996.

Mun Kow

Mun Kow (aka Loo Sang), another great grandson of Fun Fai, left his impoverished village at age 15 around 1910. First, as Figure 53 shows, he went to the Philippines where he learned carpentry skills and worked on boat building. He became a cabin boy on a ship traveling to Europe and the east coast of the U. S. where he jumped ship in New York and found work in Albany, N. Y., earning 20 cents a day. Later he got to Chattanooga where he worked at the "Oriental Restaurant." He eventually worked his way west all the way to California, where he got hired on a ship to go back to China in 1927.

Before returning to China, Mun Kow first wisely made a $550 investment in a partnership in a Chinese store with 3 other Chinese in Oxnard, California. This act established him as a merchant, a step that would permit him to return later with a wife. In 1930 at age 35, he reentered the U.S. using a paper son identity with Ng Shee, his bride from an arranged match. He worked in Oxnard for about a year until after his first child was born.

Then, he moved his family to the South, working with his uncle Gan Heung in Chattanooga. For a short period he had a laundry in Rome,

---

[173] Confused by his surname, Jew, customers assumed his name was 'Joe,' hence the unusual name for his Chinese laundry.

Ga., before starting one in Atlanta.[174] His family of five children grew up in the back of the laundry and helped with the work. He then sold the laundry, and moved to Gaston, Alabama, where he hoped to run a department store with a friend but it did not work out. He was able to repurchase his Atlanta laundry where he worked until retirement.

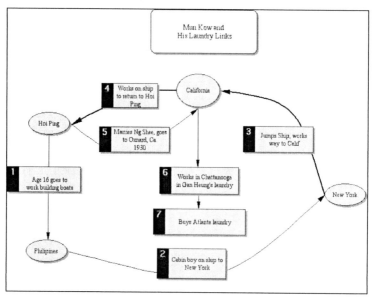

Figure 53 Mun Kow's travels and links to laundrymen kin coming to the South.

Maintaining Contact with China

Even though they spent most of their working years in the South, the China-born laundrymen never felt they fit. They maintained strong ties to China. All but three made return visits when possible. Kwok Fui and Heung Sec both returned in the late 1920s to marry in arranged matches; Kwok Fui was able to return with his bride but Heung Sec was

---

[174] The immigration file indicated that Mun Kow arrived in 1911 in San Francisco as a one-year old with his mother, Lum Ah Hong who was not eligible to bring a child into the U. S. The Secretary of Commerce and Labor granted an exception. It is likely that the Mun Kow who came as a baby in 1911 and the newly married man who came in 1930 with the same name were *not* the same person. The first Mun Kow may have returned to China and sold his identity paper sometime before 1927 to Loo Sang who entered in 1930 using his name.

not. Jew Shui made one trip back in the late 1930s to visit his wife and sons that he had not been able to bring when he first came. But with the outbreak of hostilities with Japan in World War II, he was unable to make another visit until 1949. During this trip he finally succeeded in bringing his wife and two of his sons over from Hong Kong where they had fled to during the war. Another laundryman in Alabama, an adopted son of one of Fun Fai's grandsons, had the misfortune of going to China in the early 1940s and getting stranded there for about a decade because he was denied reentry due to inadequate documents. Several kin from nearby cities came to his aid, rotating turns operating his laundry for him during his prolonged absence.

The descendants of Fun Fai who left families behind in China sent regular remittances from their laundry earnings to support them. Many patriotically contributed funds to help support Chiang Kai Shek's forces against the invading Japanese armies. At social gatherings, many expressed wishes and hopes of returning to China after they made enough money or when they retired.

However, this goal became impossible when the Communists took over China. A more realistic remedy for the cultural isolation that they and their families experienced was to relocate, upon retirement, to places with large Chinese populations such as San Francisco and Los Angeles. There they hoped their children would have better economic and social opportunities, learn more about Chinese customs, and find Chinese marriage partners. Starting in the 1950s, a chain migration from the South to the west coast occurred for the families of Poy and Hay from Chattanooga, Kwok Fui from Macon, and Kahn Quan from Birmingham.

Others, like Heung Sec in Augusta and Young Quan in Birmingham, chose to stay in the South, partly because they still had many productive years left to work in their laundries or because their children were not yet of marriageable age.

A different testament to the strength of the ties of the laundrymen to their Chinese origins and roots is that some of the elderly who died before they could return to China requested burial in a Chinese section of Atlanta's Greenwood cemetery located in a predominantly black neighborhood (See Figure 54). Even though some men died in other towns as far away as Chattanooga, Cordele or Macon, they were buried in Atlanta near deceased Chinese relatives and friends.[175]

Figure 54 Chinese section, Greenwood Cemetery, Atlanta. Courtesy, Daniel Bronstein.

Overview

Although their paths of immigration varied widely, all came with the

[175]"Loo Sing dead from blood poisoning. Chinese laundry operator will be taken to Atlanta." *Cordele (Ga.) Dispatch,* Oct. 17, 1919. "Chinese Funeral." *Los Angeles Times,* Feb. 19, 1895, 2. Obituary of Chung Yow Loo. Chattanooga Times, Oct. 26, 1961. Obituary of Ming Loo Lee. Chattanooga Times, March 31, 1969.

common goal to earn a living and send money back to their impoverished families. Each gained entry as a "paper son" through the aid of an earlier immigrant. Arriving with little knowledge of the English language and American ways, they depended heavily on assistance from one or more earlier arriving relatives. They worked as apprentices in the laundry of a relative for a few years and then acquired their own laundry. In turn, they extended the chain of migration by helping other relatives come.

After a few years, single men returned to China to enter arranged marriages. Some were able to bring their wives, but others returned leaving wives and children behind. Those already married, but who came over alone, returned every few years for short stays but were unable for many years to bring families here. Most, even those located in towns with other Chinese, felt culturally isolated. Plans to return to China after a lifetime of hard work abruptly ended when the Communists assumed control in 1949. Some moved to California but others elected to remain.

These constraints defined the lives of these descendants of Fun Fai in the South. Living in a region with a long history of racial intolerance, they were treated as foreigners and, at best, as objects of curiosity. Neither black nor white, they were stuck between the proverbial 'rock and hard place,' working in a difficult occupation while living in cultural isolation in an often hostile society. Still, they managed to endure, complaining at times, but still able to do what was needed to improve their lives and those of their children.[176]

---

[176] Sons and grandsons of the descendants of Fun Fai that immigrated to America included many successful professionals in fields ranging from engineering to medicine to science including several professors, an astrophysicist, an architect, an oncologist, two dentists, and several pharmacists.

6. The Hard Laundry Life

Toiling in a laundry:
Sweat pours like rain.
Day after day, year after year.
Still stranded in a faraway sojourn.

Toiling in a laundry:
Profits almost nothing.
After putting up a capital sum
When will you break even?

Toiling in a laundry:
You may get a mean lousy customer.
He won't speak a word of reason.
He'd sue you instead! [177]

The difficult life of a Chinese laundryman is clearly summarized in the following depiction of the daily routines involved in their labor:

> … A lifetime spent sorting, soaking, boiling, washing, scrubbing, rinsing, rubbing, starching, drying, ironing, pressing, folding, packaging, collecting and delivering could break the health of even the strongest laundry worker. There was an established process for all laundry. Soiled clothes were marked to identify individual customers. Next, everything was sorted into piles of linens, cottons, whites and coloured fabrics. The laundry was soaked to soften fabrics and loosen dirt. Many items would then be boiled to remove ground-in dirt and stubborn stains. Next came scrubbing, brushing and rubbing to remove grease; rinsing to remove impurities and soap; blueing to whiten garments; and spraying to dampen the dry clothing before it was ironed. Year-in and year-out, day-in and day-out, from dawn to dusk, this repetitive work continued. It required tremendous mental endurance and extreme patience. [178]

---

[177] From: Li Yang, Laundry Trilogy *China Daily News,* Sept. 3, 1940.

[178] Ban Seng Hoe, *"Enduring Hardship: The Chinese Laundry in Canada,"* 19.

The experiences of Lee Chew[179] who came to Gold Mountain before 1900 attest to the struggle for survival that laundrymen faced. Inspired by the success of one laundryman who had returned to his village, Chew obtained steerage passage on a steamer for $50, a considerable amount of money then. He was disappointed for even after he had worked for two years as a servant, he received only $35 a month, part of which he sent back to his parents in China. He was still able to live well and save $410 after two years, which enabled him to open a laundry with an experienced partner in a small town doing laundry for men employed by the railroads.

Work in a laundry started early on Monday morning. One partner washed while the other did the ironing. The man who ironed did not start until Tuesday, as the clothes were not ready for him to begin until then so he had Sundays and Mondays off. The man who did the washing finished Friday night, and so he was off on Saturday and Sunday. Each man worked only five days a week, but from seven in the morning till midnight.

They endured many insults from customers. Some tried to defraud them by trying to pick up laundry that did not belong to them without presenting any claim tickets. They would insist that they had 'lost' their tickets. Some tried to start fights if they did not get what they asked for. Sometimes laundrymen were fined for losing shirts that they had never seen. But even after sending home $3 a week Chew was able to save about $15. Rent cost $10 a month and food nearly $5 a week each.

---

[179] Lee Chew, *"The Biography of a Chinaman,"* (Independent, 15, 19 February 1903, 417–423. Reprinted in The Life Stories of Undistinguished Americans: As Told By Themselves, ed. New York: Hamilton Holt, 1990), 179-181.

Another immigrant described[180] later how in 1914, as a young man, he paid $50 for ship passage and left his wife and children behind to go to Canada where he expected he would earn more money. He worked in laundries in Vancouver, Banff, and Calgary. In Calgary where he worked for twenty years he had to boil water in order to clean clothes. He scrubbed all the clothes with bare hands and developed blisters that bled from prolonged contact with harsh soap and washing-soda.

His financial expectations working in Canadian laundries were not met and for many years he could not afford a radio, telephone, or television. He rarely attended church because he did not have spare change for the collection plate. Ironically, he survived the Great Depression only because his brother in China sent money. Unfortunately some destitute and desperate Chinese in Calgary and elsewhere committed suicide.

King Ho came to Canada in 1918 at age 20, leaving his wife behind in China, to help work in a Winnipeg laundry that his father opened in 1905 with five partners. He earned about $10 a week, which increased slowly up to about $50 a week by the 1940s. He saved money by living in the laundry so he could send money back to his wife who was not able to join him in Canada until 41 years later. During this lifetime of separation, they still created a family from three short return visits he was able to make over this period. Ho, in reflecting about his laundry experiences, summed it up thusly, "Words cannot adequately express how painful the work is."

---

[180] J. Brian Dawson and Nicholas Ting, *The Chinese Experience in Canada Life Stories From the Late 1800s to Today* http://www.abheritage.ca/pasttopresent/settlement/chinese_laundry_owner.html (accessed June 2, 2006).

"To iron the laundry, we fired a potbelly stove that had several metal holders attached around its body. We heated the heavy irons with handles on those holders. That was how we ironed the clothes. There were no electric irons then."

... "I usually worked past midnight or one to two o'clock - almost eighteen or twenty hours daily." Sometimes, when there was plenty of work, he had to continue working until it was all done, in order to meet the promised pickup time for his customers.[181]

In 1934, Tung Pok Chin[182] arrived in Boston at the age of 19 leaving a wife and two young sons behind in China. He used a paper son identity that his father, a laundryman, had purchased for $2000. He got a job working in a laundry at $8 a week and within a year was earning $15 a week. But his father wanted him to take over his laundry in a nearby town, which was not doing very well. He washed and dried clothes in a tiny 10 x 15 foot space where he also cooked and ate.

For a bed, he used a 2 x 6 foot plank that hung from the ceiling by wires. Unable to improve the business he sold it at a loss and went to work for a distant relative for $15 a week in his laundry. He continued to struggle, going from one laundry to another before buying his own laundry that the seller claimed would yield a $70 profit each week. However, he soon learned he had been cheated, as business was so bad that he could barely pay his rent. Then with the start of World War II, he enlisted in the Navy, one of the few Chinese to do so. After discharge, he remarried in Hong Kong and came back with his wife to New York where

---

[181] Hoe, 19-21, 47.

[182] Tung Pok Chin, *Paper Son: One Man's Story* (Philadelphia: Temple University Press, 2000). With Winifred C. Chin.

he opened a laundry. He struggled to earn a living with the laundry while also writing poetry on the side. His wife helped by working long hours as a seamstress in a sewing factory.

The following account of a later New York laundryman emphasized his difficulty of learning how to deal with the unpleasant, and possibly unhealthy task, of handling dirty laundry: [183]

> When I first handled the dirty clothes, I could not take the smell. I almost threw up. Father saw my reaction and comforted me, "Take your time. You know, picking up these clothes is even worse than moving corpses back in China. I never mentioned the unhealthy conditions of the laundry in my letters to China. Knowing those things would not do the family any good back home. Frankly, I was busy from dawn to dusk. How could I find time to write about all these things? I always wrote 'I am well and healthy here. No need to worry.' It didn't matter whether I was well or sick. Being here, you had to endure.

> The irons weighed eight pounds each. When the iron was hot enough, you took it off the stove where it was heated and ironed until it cooled down. Then you heated it up again. After ironing all day, marks would appear on your palm. Blisters would turn to calluses so thick that even if you cut them open with a knife would not bleed...Many Chinese had health problems after only three years of laundry work. Some caught TB while others had ulcers, internal bleeding, or swollen feet. My father never wrote about his bad health to his wife back in China. Laundry work was a difficult life but the Chinese endured it because they wanted to send money back to their homeland.

---

[183] Yeung-Sing Ng, *Life in New York Chinatown*. Translator Vivian Wai-Fun Lee (Hong Kong, 1955). www.archives.nysed.gov/projects/legacies/Yonkers/Y_Chinese/questions/Yon_Ch_Qu6.htm (accessed Aug. 12, 2006).

These personal accounts are invaluable in shedding light on the difficult lives the early laundrymen led.[184] Not surprisingly, some Chinese laundrymen suffered profoundly from depression due to social isolation, lack of family life, and economic failures. Although the circumstances are conjectural, suicides were reported in Macon and Atlanta (See Figure 55) as well as in Mobile, Alabama and Hawkinsville, Georgia.[185]

Figure 55 News reports of two Chinese laundrymen suicides in the South: Lee Quong, *Macon Daily Telegraph,*1, Jan. 17, 1923 and Yee Min, *Atlanta Journal,* April 6, 1922.

---

[184]Artifacts recovered at these sites provide tangible evidence about aspects of these laundrymen's lives that may have been typical in the region at that time. Women's clothing and jewelry as well as children's clothing and toys found in varying amounts at the sites suggest some laundrymen had families with them. Many could read and write because writing implements and inks were excavated in Stockton and Sacramento. Chinese and English books and newspapers were found in the loft of a laundry in Lovelock. Supporting the belief that laundrymen lived in their laundries, containers from foods and herbal medicines, beer, wine, and Chinese liquor, opium pipes, and ceramic dishes were found at all sites. Animal bones remains from meat they ate were found in a trench behind an Oakland laundry. See Mary Praetzellis. "Chinese Oaklanders: Overcoming the Odds." In *Putting The 'There' There: Historical Archaeologies of West Oakland.* I–880 Cypress Freeway Replacement Project, Cypress Replacement Project Interpretive Report No. 2. M. Praetzellis and A. Praetzellis, eds. Rohnert Park, CA: Anthropological Studies Center, Sonoma State University. http://www.sonoma.edu/asc/cypress/finalreport/part3.htm (accessed Sept. 12, 2006).

[185] Madeline Y. Hsu, *Dreaming Of Gold, Dreaming Of Home: Transnationalism and Migration between the United States and South China, 1882–1943* (Stanford: Stanford University Press, 2000). Laundrymen would lose face if relatives in China knew how they earned their living.

Work Space of A Typical Laundry

Chinese laundries all over the country had so many common physical characteristics and appearances that one might think they had been constructed using the same template.

> "The physical set-up of a typical Chinese laundry in North America became a familiar sight everywhere. Usually it was a small place in a modest building in the working-class residential area. A red "Hand Laundry" sign hung outside the premises, or was painted on the window. Inside, a wall-to-wall counter divided the shop into a reception area and a working place. Behind the counter, some brown packages of clean laundry, with Chinese labels to identify the customers, were tucked on several shelves, waiting to be picked up by the clients. On the other side of the shelves, which functioned as partitions as well, was the working and living quarters of the laundry-house. Washing troughs and machines were aligned near the water supply and drainage systems."[186]

Living Space of A Typical Laundry

Most Chinese lived in the back of their laundries for reasons already cited. This description of the living space in one San Francisco laundry around 1970 could easily apply to many other Chinese laundries. A laundryman, his wife, daughter, and her husband, a waiter, helped operate the laundry. All of them, and a young granddaughter, lived in crowded quarters in the back of the store on the street level.[187]

> It's a very small room, shelves on all the walls stacked with brown paper packages of laundry. The room is quite warm. A red upholstered sofa with stuffing bursting from its arms is sunk under the shelves on one wall, covered with a piece of fringed, pink cotton. Hangers with freshly pressed shirts

---

[186] Ban Seng Hoe, *Structural Changes of Two Chinese Communities in Alberta, Canada.* Ottawa: National Museum of Canada, 1976: 349.

[187] Victor G. Nee and Brett de Bary Nee, *Longtime Californ': A Documentary Study of an American Chinatown* (New York: Pantheon, 1972), 144-146.

balance on the arms and back of the couch. A few feet across from it, a counter has been built beneath the shelves on the opposite wall. There is an abacus and scattered slips of pink paper on its green linoleum top.

... We aren't prepared for the smell of the room in the back. It seems to come from the hot, damp air, the damp floor, the sticky plastic tablecloth on the table in the center of the room, the garbage pail, and the garbage in plastic boxes along the wall. We hear the rumble of the boiler... Beside the tank, the only window in the room is screened over and grease and soot block the netting so no light comes in at all...We notice the sink, just inside the door, has only one faucet. The wall next to it is covered with tinfoil. Don says again that his old man is very backward, this is how he keeps the water from leaking through the wall... "And I'm telling you he never had nothing in this house. No nothing. No TV, no radio, no oven, no shower, the toilet's broken so you have to get water from the sink to flush it. ...

There's a series of four gas burners with black skillets and pots hanging above it on the wall. The only other furniture is the table, the folding chairs around it and a fantastic series of splotched card-board and wooden boxes, containing household supplies which fills an entire wall. At the end of the boxes, near the stairs, several crates have been hammered together into a surface for preparing food. There's a bowl of fresh chard leaves standing on the counter and a deep earthenware bowl, covered with an empty egg carton, containing leaves of cabbage pickling in vinegar. ... It's dim up here...We make out the shape of beds on the floor of the loft, one crib, a pile of suitcases. There's another series of cardboard cartons up here, hammered into shelves. They are filled with thin paperback books written in Chinese. There's one bureau beside the bed closest to the stairs. On top of it there is a pressed white lace doily and a wedding photograph in a stand-we recognize the couple downstairs. There's not much else in the loft.

Lives of Laundry Wives

Until after the early 1900s most laundrymen lived lonely lives as bachelors. About half of them came unmarried but there were almost no eligible Chinese women available and laws prohibited marriages to whites. Those who had married in China before leaving were not permitted under immigration laws to bring them over, as was the case for other laborers. Wives typically did not see their husbands for many years. Husbands, if they could afford the expense, visited every few years, staying long enough to sire children before returning to Gold Mountain. Wives lived with their in-laws and were subservient to the mother-in-law's authority, a situation that could be especially intolerable for a wife if she and her mother-in-law did not get along well.

The conditions for women did not improve in China during the early part of the 20th century whereas opportunities for them to work, at least in low paying jobs, increased in the U. S. and Canada. This situation, combined with changing Chinese attitudes that allowed women to immigrate, led more Chinese women, at least among merchant wives, daughters of merchants, and wives of U. S. citizens, to come to the U. S. from around 1900 until 1924.[188]

Wives of laundrymen had a more difficult time in gaining entry because of the exclusion law. First, their husbands had to have enough money to purchase false documents for them so they could claim to be merchant wives. Next they still had to successfully pass the immigration questioning to enter the country. If they gained entry, they then faced

---

[188] Yung, *Unbound Feet*, 56-58. However, the1924 Immigration Act denied entry for Chinese wives of U. S. citizens until Chinese protests led to a 1930 amendment for those married before 1924.

years of hard work laboring in laundries to help their husbands while also raising their children. These tasks were made more demanding because they did not usually know how to speak, read, or write English or know the customs and values of their host country.

Adding to the hardship, many settled in communities with strong anti-Chinese feelings that often led to discriminatory treatment from whites. Coming despite these obstacles, their arrival dramatically changed life for Chinese immigrants as it allowed the reestablishment of family life with the birth of a new generation. These children, born here, would be citizens by right of birthplace.

The story of Helen Hong Wong,[189] illustrates the plight of the few Chinese wives who managed to immigrate during the early 20th century. She was born in Guangdong but moved to Hong Kong when she was 7. At 18 she married a family acquaintance, a Chinese already in his 50s. Since he held merchant status in the U. S., she was eligible to immigrate but she still had to pass the interrogation. She failed, and was denied entry. Upon appeal she later gained entry after detention on Angel Island for several months in 1922.

She and her husband tried to operate a restaurant in Ft. Wayne, Indiana, but business was poor with the onset of the depression years around 1930. Next they worked in a laundry owned by a friend in Anderson, Indiana for about four years. They, and their four small

---

[189] Helen Hong Wong. "I was the only Chinese woman in town:" Reminiscences of a Gold Mountain woman. In *Chinese American Voices: From the Gold Rush to the Present.* Edited by Judy Yung, Gordon Chang and Him Mark Lai. Berkeley: University of California Press, 2006: 157-164.

children, lived with their friend in two small rooms above the laundry. Eventually a nephew of their friend came over from Hong Kong. The crowded conditions strained relationships so they moved and opened a laundry in nearby Kokomo, Indiana. The hours were long, six days a week and if the work was not completed by Saturday, they would have to work on Sunday. There was little free time, and she recalled she barely had time to get a haircut. They washed about 400 shirts a week and earned only about $20, which gradually increased to about $100 a week. Living above the laundry, they saved on rent. They worked there for about four years, but then her husband died and Helen was not able to continue the laundry operation alone. She did not read or speak English. She moved to Chicago and found work in a bakery owned by relatives. She worked ten-hour days for $20 a month for several years between 1943 and 1947 before finding work in a cookie factory. Helen Hong Wong's story was commonplace as conditions for wives of laundrymen were extremely harsh and did not improve much over their lives. Conditions did not improve much for the next generation of women that came over.

A laundryman and his wife would start work early each day and continue late into the evening until the work was completed. Meals were prepared and eaten in the laundry when the workload permitted. It was typical for them and their children, if they had any, to live in the back or above the store to save on expenses. Work was for six days a week, 52 weeks a year, with no time off for vacations or travel. Husbands knew enough English to deal with customers and manage their businesses, but wives usually spoke only Chinese.

Figure 56 A Chinese family at dinner, 1914.[190] Courtesy, Denver Public Library, Western History Collection. Photograph CHS-X3534.

Figure 57 Young wives such as Helen LeeWong helped operate laundries as soon as they arrived here. Courtesy, San Diego Chinese Historical Museum and LeeWong family.

---

[190] It is unknown if this was a laundry family, but note the clothes drying on the line outside.

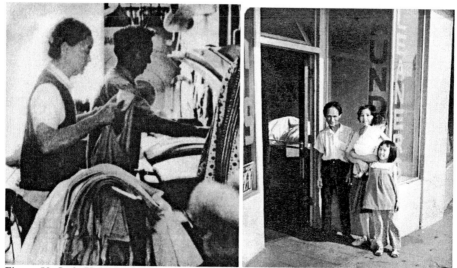

Figure 58   Left: Helen and Ernest LeeWong at work in their San Diego laundry, c. 1970. They lived with their 7 children next door. Courtesy, San Diego Chinese Historical Museum, LeeWong family, and San Diego Reader. Right: Bon and Kim Wong with 2 of their 7 children, Billy and Lucy, at their Hawthorne, Ca. laundry where they lived in the back, 1969. Courtesy, Lucy Wong Leonard.

The wives had difficult and lonely lives, cut off from much social contact with other Chinese women. In addition to bringing up any children, often without assistance from other relatives, wives often were needed to work in the laundry to help make ends meet financially (See Figure 58). Many wives had few other Chinese women nearby; moreover, they had no transportation to make social visits.[191] Their lack of English language skills, far lower than that of their husbands who knew enough to conduct business, limited them to superficial interactions with non-Chinese women.

Interviews with a sample of retired widows of Chinese laundrymen in Montreal provide vivid accounts of some details of the

---

[191] A laundryman's wife in Alabama spent so much time in the laundry that for years she did not even know that a grocery store was next door until one day she was sent to buy some meat. Interview with Young Quan by John Jung, Oct. 16, 2005.

difficult lives of laundry wives.[192] Their accounts could easily represent the experiences of most laundry wives, irrespective of when or where they lived.

In the words of Xu Xiuhua, an 83 year old widow interviewed at a Senior Citizen center:[193]

> "There was not any work to do so he went into the laundry business. He was here for five years and saved up his money to bring his sons over...He bought papers for all of them. After his sons came over, he applied for his uncle...He then bought papers for me...My husband was 20 years old when we were married. We were introduced by matchmakers. He was 27 years old when he came here... We saw each other again when I came over, ten years later...I came here when I was 46, 48 and I have been here since then...I came to help my husband with the laundry... I had to be careful because if we damaged any of the garments, we had to pay for them. I washed everything myself, huge baskets full of clothes. I washed as many as 50 shirts. We just worked in the laundry ourselves. I did the washing, my husband did the ironing...It was very hard money to make. There were no set working hours. When there was more work, we had to stay up and do it. We would work later at night sometimes to eleven o'clock at night. My husband knew a little English. ...The *law-fan* (whites) harassed us all the time...They used to scream, "Chinitown. Chinitown!" whenever we would say anything... Where we worked, there were children who were very bad...they would throw snow at our clothes lines, where the clothes were hung to dry.

Li Defang, a 92-year old Chinatown resident recalled coming to Canada in 1953 to help her husband operate his Montreal laundry. She described the challenges of her difficult and austere existence: [194]

---

[192] Chan Kwok Bun, *Smoke and Fire: The Montreal Chinese*. (Hong Kong: Chinese University Press, 1991).

[193] Ibid. , 47-48.

[194] Ibid., 53-55.

My husband came here first. I came later. When he came to Canada, he started work in a hand laundry...He was five years older than I was. When he was first here, he was 19. He returned to get married when he was 25...He wrote me often...he sent money every month. He came back to China about five times. Each time he stayed one year...I came to Canada in 1953... Our laundry did not do any business with Canadians. Most of us kept business within the Chinese community... We did not hire anyone in our laundry. My husband and I did the work ourselves, we only had twenty dollars of so worth of business a week...We had to pay taxes, rent and expenses. We barely broke even...We had to start work first thing in the morning at six o'clock. We had to go and collect the clothes for various shop-keepers. I had to deliver them to rooming houses. We worked till about nine or ten o'clock at night, we would work till the work was finished... When we came here, there was not much else we could do; we did not have any skills...While we worked, we sent our earnings back to China to help our children and grandchildren. We used to spend all day at the laundry. I made supper for the two of us and we ate there. We worked 7 days a week.

Post World War II Family Reunification

When the Exclusion era ended in the United States in 1943, and a few years later in Canada, laws were passed that placed a priority on reuniting families. The War Brides Act of 1945, its revision in 1946, and the Alien Fiancées and Fiancés Act allowed Chinese men who served in the U. S. Armed Forces to bring wives and fiancées from China

These laws allowed entry of all wives who met the criteria, including those of an unknown number of laundrymen. The overwhelming majority of the wives who came under the provisions of the law were not 'wartime brides' in the sense of marriages formed during the war years. Less than 3 percent who came had been wed within 3 years of the law. The majority had been married for many years but had not been allowed to enter by the exclusion law. Their husbands, both China- and U. S. - born, had returned earlier to China to arranged matches due to the shortage of marriageable Chinese women in the U. S. The War Brides Act made it possible for these wives to apply for entry but they still had to convince immigration authorities of the validity of their marital status.

Unfortunately, those who did succeed in gaining entry soon found that the reunions were not without many painful adjustments for the couples. For one matter, many wives had not realized the poor living and working conditions that their husbands in America endured. Thus, Tenley Chin settled in a small town in Massachusetts in 1948 as a war bride with her husband, David, earning about $60 a week. After expenses, they had only about ten dollars left each week so it was necessary for her to work six days a week for her first six years while raising three children.

> The place that Tenley Chin and her husband had rented for a laundry also served as the family's living quarters. There was neither hot water nor an indoor toilet. What she hated most were the mice, which were "as big as rats." Chiu Chun Ma, who suffered as a child after the death of her mother, had heard many wonderful stories about the Gold Mountain. Her first impression of San Francisco's Chinatown, however, was that it was dirty. Dining in a restaurant her first evening in the United States, she almost became ill when she saw on the table a filthy jar into which customers spit fish bones. While in China, Chiu Chun and her mother had gathered the firewood they needed in the hills. Now, in Burns, Oregon, she was scolded by her husband for using too much firewood for cooking. "How could you make anything boil with so little firewood?" she wondered. [195]

Many wives had suffered much greater physical hardships while in China, so that was not their main problem after coming over. For some, their husbands had become somewhat accustomed to American customs

---

[195] Xiaojian Zhao, *Remaking Chinese America: Immigration, Family, and Community, 1940–1965* (New Brunswick, N. J.: Rutgers University Press, 2002), 137.

during their long separation and found fault with their wives' failure to embrace Western customs. For others, problems stemmed from their husbands having acquired American mistresses during the long years of separation. Reuniting husbands and wives proved more difficult than initially assumed and, in many instances, intensified problems of Chinese immigrants.[196]

Social and Cultural Ties to Chinatowns

Chinese in large cities tended to live close together. "Chinatowns" were initially refuges for Chinese, not the quaint exotic tourist attractions that they would later become. Confinement to this ethnic ghetto provided a sense of security for the early immigrants but it also prevented whites from seeing the Chinese as other than objects of curiosity. The fact that Chinese were not allowed to rent or purchase homes in white areas until many years later reinforced this segregation.

In cities with large Chinese populations, family associations owned meeting halls where Chinese laundrymen gathered with other Chinese men who needed a respite from the drudgery and isolation of daily laundry work. Here they could socialize, and for some, gamble. However, a liability of running Chinese laundries in large cities, as noted earlier, was the long distances of their laundries from Chinatowns. If there were too many laundries in the same area, they risked insufficient business. Laundry guilds in the Chinese community established rules such as the minimum distance that laundries had to be from each other.[197]

---

[196] Bao, *Holding Up More Than Half The Sky*, 50-58.

[197] Wang, "No Tickee, No Shirtee," 297-305.

On Sundays, the only day they closed, laundrymen in large cities would often head to Chinatown to shop, eat in a Chinese restaurant, and socialize. Some indulged in illegal activities such as gambling, smoking opium, or patronizing brothels before returning to their dreary daily lives of strenuous and monotonous laundry work. These respites were, of course, unavailable to the thousands of laundrymen located in small towns across the country without access to a nearby Chinatown. Their Sundays were primarily spent resting for the following workweek.

In contrast to laundries, merchant stores in cities were located in Chinatowns near a cluster of other stores that served mostly Chinese customers. Many Chinatown stores also functioned as rooming houses, and rented sleeping quarters to those laundrymen who did not live in their laundries. Chinatown merchants selling commodities imported from China owed much of their early existence to laundrymen who were their primary customers.[198] Unlike laundrymen, merchants benefited from cultural contacts afforded by their daily proximity to other Chinese. But it also meant competition from rival merchants. In fact, merchants faced risks of failure even though many worked as long and hard as laundrymen did. In fact, some merchants gave up and made more money as working as laundrymen![199]

Adjusting To Their Difficult Life in America

Many laundrymen were obsessed with security, both physical and financial, as they were continually faced with risks of robbery and racist violence as well as fears of not earning enough money to survive or send

---

[198] Ibid., 322.

[199] Dongzheng In Philadelphia, laundrymen had financial success comparable to merchants.

back to China. These views were hardly surprising. Given that they had entered illegally as paper sons, the fear of deportation was ever present. Encounters with racism made them distrust American society, and doubt that Chinese could receive legal justice in any disputes involving whites. At the same time, they felt morally correct, a view that helped them endure mistreatment. They saw whites, or bak goey (white ghosts), as often untrustworthy, unfair, prone to become drunk, and possibly aggressive and violent. Many laundrymen held a stoical and fatalistic attitude about life that may have helped them endure their harsh lives.

Many laundrymen learned enough English to conduct business transactions with customers, but generally preferred to speak Chinese among family members. They acquired enough proficiency with English, or perhaps "Ching-lish," to communicate with their children who grew up as bi-lingual to some extent. They enlisted their children to translate, and even explain, business, financial, and legal documents.

While they adapted in some respects such as wearing Western instead of Chinese clothes, they did not accept many American customs and values. For example, they almost always paid in cash, and never borrowed on credit except for real estate. Distrustful of banks, many kept hidden caches of money in the laundry. Although they rarely, if ever, splurged on themselves, they sometimes indulged their children and grandchildren. Education of their children was highly valued, and they spared no expense to help their children with their school expenses. They were not as poor as they might have appeared, just abstemious, because many of them accumulated sizeable financial assets.

Most of them did not have or need automobiles since they lived in their laundries. Radio, movies, and books and magazines written in

English were not of interest to many of them as sources of entertainment and recreation because of language and cultural barriers. Television, not available until the 1950s, presented the same problems to some extent, although the visual nature of the medium did have some appeal. Some learned more about the customs and culture of the host country from watching television than might be immediately apparent.[200]

They cooked and ate Chinese foods, or food that was cooked Chinese style. Most prepared all of their meals at home, and never or rarely frequented American restaurants. They purchased Chinese ingredients such as spices, sauces, noodles, and preserved vegetables as well as medicines or Chinese liquor through mail orders to Chinese merchants in San Francisco, Chicago, or New York. Some made their own preserved foods and grew their own bitter melon, herbs, and other Chinese vegetables in yards behind their laundries. Those living in areas near Florida ordered fresh Chinese vegetables such as bok choy shipped to them from Chinese farmers there.

Concerns About Marriage for Their Children

A major concern of Chinese parents was that their children marry other Chinese, but with the few eligible Chinese in most regions, this posed a difficulty. Much to the dismay of their Americanized children who valued a romantic conception of courtship and marriage, immigrant parents actively sought to arrange matches between their children and any eligible Chinese. It was not unheard of for parents to try, and sometimes

---

[200] My uncle in Atlanta learned to enjoy, and understand, football, when games were televised. On one occasion when I was visiting him, I observed with surprise, and amusement, that he often second-guessed, in Chinese, the play calling of the Atlanta Falcons. For example, he felt that on third down and long, the quarterback should have called a pass rather than a running play.

succeed, in matching their children with a marriage partner in China, especially since some Chinese were receptive such arrangements for the opportunity to come to the U. S. Similarly, many families with marriage-age children tried to set up meetings for them with any eligible exchange students from China.

Taking Pride in Children's Achievements

Those laundrymen who were fortunate enough to have their families with them wanted their children to have the education that would enable them to escape the laundry and enter prestigious and prosperous occupations and professions. They urged their children to excel in school and were willing and able to support them financially in their education, paying their tuition and educational expenses. Their investment paid off, as many of their children succeeded in many professional fields.

Laundrymen endured the physical hardships and demands of their occupation, financial uncertainty, racial discrimination, and lack of family or family separation for many years. This inner strength of resolve may have come from their experiences with adversity in Guangdong that led them to leave in the first place as well as by their strong sense of obligation and commitment to help their kin back in China who were suffering economically even more than they were.

7. Lives Of Chinese Laundry Children

The Chinese family screened by a wall of steam
Soaks its pride in white bleach
Scrubs the ring around the collar of racial slurs
Rinses with its tears of humiliation
Presses with the starch of its courage[201]

How did the Chinese laundry experience affect the lives of children of laundrymen as they grew up and throughout life? Little attention has been directed toward this topic as past research has examined only the early laundrymen who did not have families living with them. But with the increasing numbers of women coming in the early 1900s, more laundry families were formed during the 1920s and later.

These children of the laundry, like their parents, realized that society viewed laundry work as less than desirable employment. Yet, Chinese were stuck trying to survive a racist society by working on the menial but demanding tasks of cleaning its dirty laundry. Did these experiences of their childhood in the laundry benefit or harm them?

Many children of the laundry rose from such menial beginnings to successful achievement in prestigious and creative professional careers. Perhaps the earliest and one of the best-known persons who had laundry roots was the silent film star, Anna May Wong, who detested her life in her father's Los Angeles laundry. As a child she found her escape from the drudgery of the laundry at the movies where she fantasized about a

---

[201] "Chinese Laundry" © Jocelyne Verret (e-poem) from People From Here and Afar, In memory of Gee Chun, one of the first Chinese laundrymen in Edmonton, *c.* 1895. By permission of author.

more glamorous existence. She went on to become a world-renown celebrated actress in Hollywood, although relegated to roles involving a stereotypical exotic, seductive "Oriental" woman. In the literary arts, the noted writer of fiction and nonfiction, Maxine Hong Kingston grew up in a Chinese laundry in Stockton, California. Her mother fascinated her with many tales of Chinese origins that inspired some of her later stories such as *The Woman Warrior* based on Chinese legends and myth. In public service and government, March Fong Eu was the first elected woman, and Chinese American, Secretary of State in California. Born in the back of her father's laundry in the small Central Valley town of Oakdale, she not only won this office in 1974, but three more times. In 2000, Bill Lann Lee, whose father had a New York laundry, rose to prominence in the U. S. Department of Justice, serving as Assistant on Affirmative Action for the Attorney General during President Clinton's administration. Despite their humble background and obstacles facing Chinese Americans, these, and many other children, who grew up in Chinese laundries accomplished great achievements. To what extent, and how, did their laundry experience provide lessons that helped them achieve their successes?

Around the turn of the twentieth century, self-employed Chinese were primarily laundrymen. In fact, as Chinese ran most hand laundries in North America, it is not surprising that the larger society tended to associate 'Chinese' with 'laundry.' Even when Chinese later became successful in other fields or their educated children entered prestigious professions, society's view of Chinese as laundry operators persisted. This stereotype held by non-Chinese helped perpetuate their condescension toward Chinese who they saw as capable of doing only menial domestic work. This image helped keep the Chinese in a lower social status in the eyes of the general public.

Figure 59 Toy Gow, and two sons in his laundry, Benton Harbor, Mi. c. 1930. Chinese-American Museum of Chicago. Courtesy, Grace Chun.

This laundryman stereotype was also potentially harmful to the children of the Chinese laundry in limiting their own view of their capabilities. Many Chinese children grew up in their parents' laundry (See Figure 59). They saw adult Chinese working only as laundry, grocery, or restaurant workers and had no role models of successful Chinese in prestigious occupations and professions to inspire their ambitions toward similar careers.

What Children Thought About Growing Up in Chinese Laundries

In this chapter, a comparison will be made of some reflections from a small sample of Chinese who grew up in the laundries of their immigrant parents. Of course, not all had the same experiences, or were affected in the same way by similar experiences, and there will be exceptions to any generalizations. Nonetheless, as a point of departure, their memories, views, and reflections shed light on the lives of laundry families. These perspectives on their daily work and living conditions further the understanding of the impact of these experiences on them as they grew up and worked in the family laundry.

The "children of the laundry," three sons, four daughters, and two grandsons, who shared their experiences, were born around the 1940s and 1950s and some are recently retired. The sample, the same number of men and women, comes from different regions of the U. S. and Canada, with three from the East, one from the South, one from the Midwest, and two from the West coast. All but one lived close enough to a Chinatown to allow occasional weekend visits.

No claim is made that these participants are representative of all laundry children but their independently expressed views do ring true as there is considerable consistency across them. All participants have achieved a large measure of success working in diverse fields despite many obstacles they faced as children of immigrants, accomplishments that are a tribute to their determination to transcend discriminatory barriers and to the unrelenting support and encouragement that their parents and families provided.[202]

---

[202] All participants were volunteers who agreed that it is important to share their memories and impressions about their experiences of growing up in laundries. By preserving this part of Chinese American history, they felt they would express their appreciation of the difficult lives their parents had in the laundry life. It is not implied that all children from laundries felt the same or achieved the same levels of success as this sample has done.

> **Elwin Xie** *was born in 1960 and raised in Vancouver's Chinatown. He is a descendant of Head Tax payers.*

My father was born in 1920 on Lulu Island (now called Richmond, a suburb of Vancouver), in a barn on the family pig-farm. He and his nine brothers and sisters attended a predominantly white grade school on Lulu Island. He later studied to be an aircraft maintenance technician in California. There, he had an instructor who could solve complex mathematical equations in his head. His name was Albert Einstein.

What was the reason behind his decision to leave this work? I do recall my father speaking of a near fatal workplace accident. He was working on an airplane when the engine started up without warning. This incident in combination with my mother's arrival may have contributed to his decision to buy a laundry in Chinatown.

At the age of seventeen, my father traveled to Yin-Ping (Enping), China to marry my mother, who was fifteen years old. It was an arranged marriage. Although she was married to a Canadian born Chinese, my mother was not allowed into Canada. The Chinese Exclusion Act of 1923 placed strict limitations on Chinese immigration, virtually cutting off all Chinese immigration to Canada. My father returned to Canada soon after their marriage because the Japanese had captured many of China's coastal cities. The newlyweds were separated for 11 years.

My mother used to recount stories of wartime China during the Japanese invasion. She said villagers would hide in the rice fields or up in the hillsides with the approach of the Japanese soldiers. Immigration restrictions into Canada were lifted in 1947 and my parents were reunited the following year.

Soon after my mother's arrival in Canada, my father and his brother, my Uncle Loy, purchased the Gin Lee Laundry at 274 Union Street on the edge of Vancouver's Chinatown. With the purchase of the laundry, my father ended his career with Canadian Pacific Airlines as an aircraft technician. I do not know why he made this decision, as I am sure my father could have supported the whole family on his salary.

Upon the change of ownership, the laundry was renamed Union Laundry. My family operated the laundry for over 30 years. Many of our customers were from the rooming houses, hotels, and restaurants of what was then known as Skid Road. When the red brick building of the laundry was constructed in the early 1900's, it only extended half way to the property line. In 1962, my parents constructed an addition to the rear, which allowed for the acquisition of modern machinery. Our living quarters were located on the second floor above the laundry. There were three bedrooms: my two sisters shared a room with our maternal grandmother, my parents shared a room with one of my brothers, and I shared a room with two other brothers.

As young children, my brothers and sisters and I started off folding small fluffy items such as towels. As we got older, we were assigned more difficult jobs, such as feeding damp linen into the mangle, a massive flat iron for pressing bed sheets and tablecloths. I spent the bulk of my boyhood folding, packaging, and organizing customers' linen. My time was also spent reconciling the differences between the customers' linen count against the actual count I had in front of me. Creativity and diplomacy was required in order to stave off complaining phone calls from certain sticky customers.

My mother spoke pidgin English when dealing with walk-in white customers. My brothers and sisters and I would help with translation if we happened to be near. Once in awhile, there would be a discrepancy about a missing garment, which would be resolved amicably. On the whole, the relationship between our laundry and its customers was cordial.

In my elementary school years, I figured I was probably the only kid in school who had calluses on the palms of their hands as a result of long hours spent wrapping laundry with sisal twine. One of the tools of the trade was an aluminum ring with a ¾ inch curved blade to cut the twine at the end of the wrap. Even the smallest ring was too big for my young fingers. Consequently, I wrapped this ring with several rotations of white bakery string, thereby enabling the ring to fit. The ring manufacturer obviously never envisioned a young child using their products. Over the years, I became adept at wrapping bundles of laundry with speed and agility. I had the technique down to both an art and science where it almost became a dance with the bundle of laundry. I instinctively knew when to throw my body into the package for weight. This was a dance I could perform blindfolded.

Amongst the four brothers, there would be laundry-bundling races based on speed and quality of finished product. Being the youngest of the four brothers, I never won but had come within seconds of defeating them a few times. At one point, a laundry equipment supplier let us try out a semi-automatic wrapping machine. It was more trouble than it was worth and was quickly returned. Machines cannot compete with the efficiency of a Chinese laundry boy!

I also had pillowcase and towel folding contests with my sisters. There seemed to be a division of labour along gender lines in the laundry. My sisters seemed to get the less physically heavy work. They were not responsible for any of the bookkeeping duties either.

By the time I reached grade seven, I was given the responsibility of the accounts receivables at month's end. It was a job done previously by my brother Wesley, who was now in post-secondary school. I did not look forward to month's end. While I enjoyed the large dollar amounts, I found the job terribly monotonous and I think this experience turned me off numbers altogether later in life.

Sundays may have been a day of rest for many, but for the laundry, it was equipment maintenance and repair day. I was the youngest and smallest of the brothers, so I was naturally the one who had to crawl into small spaces around and within the laundry machinery. I was the "lucky one" to help grease bearings in tough-to-reach locations. My father would routinely have me crawl into the inner cavity burner of the mangle where the flame ports need to be unplugged with a small poker. This was done to prevent uneven heating of the massive round cylinder. I had to twist my body into Houdini-like contortions in order to gain access into the inferno chamber. With a flashlight in my left hand and the small poker in my right hand, my father would issue instructions from outside the inferno cavity: "Okay, Elwin, now move over to the next row. Keep going until you get to the very end. When you're done, we'll make a laundry delivery to a café and get some free eats."

My father made full use of my agility but I have since grown to appreciate things mechanical and electrical. I spent countless hours as a boy staring at welding flashes, as my father was handy with welding and pipefitting. The lighting effects in the laundry were a combination of a fireworks display and strobe lights in a nightclub, complete with a smoky haze.

The laundry was an odd cacophony of sounds. The hiss of leaky steam pipes merged with the noise of an-out-of balance centrifugal extractor ready to fly off its base. The sound of water splashing back and forth in washers was interspersed with the whirling of 2-phase motors in high current startup mode. The concrete floor around the washers was constantly wet due to water cycling out of the washers and there would be wet footprints everywhere, or wheel tracks, if I was wearing roller-skates. In the air was a hint of detergent or bleach, depending on the nature of the load.

My father would collect used cooking grease from restaurants and cafes to make our own laundry detergent. The homemade soap was a concoction of grease, caustic soda, and other chemicals, which was then mixed in a large steam-fed vat that was constantly percolating, much like a witches' brew. My mother would draw from this vat with a saucepan as required.

The laundry was infested with cockroaches and mice. We had two cats, Teeny and Tweety, who always seemed to be pregnant. We would keep the kittens for a month or so after birth.   Then we would let them loose in the nearby Strathcona Park.

I would breed cockroaches by placing male and female cockroaches in a pill bottle.   Once an egg capsule formed, I would gently remove it from the female cockroach and place it in a separate pill bottle.   It would be kept next to the mangle where it was toasty warm to accelerate the incubation process.   I checked on its progress daily and patiently waited for the baby cockroaches to hatch - hundreds of them, milky white.

The laundry was not a safe place to grow up.   Nelson, my eldest brother, was horsing around the hydraulic shirt presses while our mother was pressing collars. With his hands on each of the two "ON" levers, which were spaced apart for safety reasons, he sent the hot 24" x 36" iron clamp down onto our mother's right hand, leaving her hand permanently disfigured.   In another incident, I was doodling with a ballpoint pen on a moving conveyer belt when my hand got caught.   I was able to extract my hand before the ambulance arrived.

Union Laundry was a family business and the family was expected to work.   We were not paid for our labour, but we did look forward to recovering coins that fell out of the pockets of dirty laundry and accumulated on the bottom of the washers.   I was sent down through the hatch into an inner tumbler that was manually rotated by an employee named Jong.   Since the power to the machines was shut off and the belt connecting the motor and driveshaft was disengaged, it was deemed safe.   Looking back, however, this seemed like an exercise in stupidity, all for a handful of coins.

An assortment of items would fall out when we shook dirty tablecloths: loose change (tips not found by waiters), chicken heads, red paper invitations, pieces of wedding cake wrapped in doilies with a silver ribbon - a sure sign that a Chinese wedding banquet had taken place.   We would break out singing, "Here comes the bride, big, fat, and wide!!"

Summers were unbearable in the laundry. The living quarters on the second floor were just as, if not more, hot and humid as the laundry. If butter was left out on the table at breakfast, it would be a pool of yellow liquid before lunch. Laundry work was more tolerable in the cool winter months as we could luxuriate amongst the hot linen, fresh out of the dryers. We would often jump on top of the laundry wagon, piled high with hot towels from a fancy hotel.
Our customers ranged from fancy hotels to skid row rooming houses, full-service restaurants to greasy spoons, and even the Salvation Army Detoxification Centre. As an escape from the drudgery of the laundry, I would accompany my father on deliveries. I think my father used the deliveries as an excuse to get away as well. My mother would often harangue him on our late return. Whether

picking up dirty tablecloths or delivering clean bed sheets, my father would invariably end up "chewing the fat" with the waiters, the cooks, or the on-duty desk clerks.

In addition to working on the shop floor, my mother also prepared meals for our family and staff. We would have about half a dozen workers employed at a time, some Chinese and some not. Most would be day workers and would go home at night.

One employee, a bachelor we called "Lo Woo", lived with our family and slept on an ironing table in the laundry. He kept his life's possessions under his "bed". A second bachelor, Jong, lived in a rooming house nearby but would take his evening meals with our family. He had a gland problem that left him sweating profusely. He always had a hand towel draped around his neck. My father would routinely drive him out to the mental hospital to update his medication. One time he "lost it" and chased my mother around the laundry with a Chinese meat cleaver. A half-inch divot remained on the kitchen table where he slammed down the end of the cleaver. The police were called. Nevertheless, we continued to share our meal times with Jong after the incident.

During my teen years, I took up the trumpet in the school band. After dinner, I would practice my scales and songs for upcoming concerts downstairs in the laundry. I did not have to worry about disturbing the neighbours, as the noise from the laundry machinery would drown out any from my trumpet.

Like other Canadian families, my father purchased a black and white television console in the mid 1950's. The cabinet door to the console came complete with a lock and hasp, which my father kept padlocked as he expected my brothers and sisters and I to be working downstairs in the laundry. To steal a view, I would turn on the television by manipulating the three inch on/off knob with a long stick and then look straight down the crack of the cabinet door at a sharp angle to watch what snow-filled American programming was available.

My mother would sometimes give me money to buy a hamburger and french fries from Sarah at the greasy spoon across the street from the laundry. Sarah was a black woman, whom I later learned was from Jamaica. She was one of a handful of blacks remaining in the neighbourhood. At one time, there were many black families living in the area, then called Hogan's Alley, whose menfolk worked as porters for the railways. The train station was just a few blocks from our laundry.

In the 1950's, my father purchased the house next to our laundry. It was rented out to a group of hippies in a band in the 1960's. Their far-out psychedelic tie-dyed clothes made them stand out in the otherwise staid Chinatown neighbourhood. At one point in their tenancy, they had fallen into arrears. My father made arrangements for one of the hippies to catch-up by working it off in the laundry. Our tenant was not able to complete a full day's work!

During the 1960's, the City of Vancouver, had plans for an urban renewal project that included the construction of a freeway through the residential neighborhood of Strathcona and Chinatown, viewed then as an urban blight. When the mostly Chinese community stopped City Hall in its tracks, urban planners decided instead to construct a viaduct on the edge of Chinatown. Unfortunately, this is where our family laundry stood. The land was expropriated, but not before a fight from my father, who was featured in the local newspaper, vowing to hold off the bulldozers with a shotgun as he resisted forced removal. Accompanying the story is a photograph of my father in our laundry in front of the mangle. With the expropriation funds from the City, my parents purchased a lot across the street from the original laundry and set up operations in 1973.

Our family ran Union Laundry in its second incarnation at its new location at 231 Union Street for a few more years. We sold the laundry in 1979.

While growing up, there were times I was embarrassed to be both Chinese and a laundry kid. I wished my father were anything but a Chinese laundry man, a stereotype I was aware of even at a young age. Rather than folding mounds of towels and bed sheets in a sweltering laundry, I wanted to be outside playing. I wanted to live anywhere but in Chinatown.

In retrospect, my boyhood in a Chinese laundry has left a deep impression on me. The shame I felt as a child is now a sense of pride as an adult. The experience of growing up in a laundry is one I would not trade. At the time, the work was labourious and never ending, but on reflection, it made for an unusual and remarkable childhood. I can now appreciate the fact that my parents "ate bitterness" in order to provide a better life for my brothers and sisters and I.

Bill Eng, *age 64, earned a BSME from New Jersey Institute of Technology and a M.S. Engineering Mgt. from Drexel University. Until he retired in 1999, he was an engineering manager in the International Division of 3M for the last 10 of the 33 years he worked there, extensively assisting 3M subsidiaries in southeast Asia to develop manufacturing facilities.*

My parents came from Taishan in Kwangtung Province (Guhn Au – Chung Lau). Father's English wasn't very good and Mom knew virtually no English. They both spoke the Taishanese dialect with my younger sister and me. My father traveled between China and the U.S. a few times to visit his wife and family for brief visits. They had 3 children born in China but as a laundryman, he was not allowed to bring his family over.

Father purchased our laundry, located only ¼ mile from main business district of Paterson, N.J., from his paternal uncle in the early 40's to earn money to send for his family. Mom was finally able to come in 1941, and I was born the next year. She had to come here pretending to be the wife of someone else (paper identity), leaving their 3 older children behind hoping they could buy identity papers later to bring them over.

I don't think she came to the U.S. through Angel Island. I used to hear the expression "Money Hall" that I think was how she pronounced "Montreal." There was talk of a long train ride, but I don't know where it started, and why it ended in Montreal. She may have crossed Canada and then entered New York or Vermont from Quebec. Finally, many years later in 1963, my older brother emigrated from Hong Kong, bringing his own family, and helped us run the laundry. I was in my 3rd year of engineering school then and this was certainly a blessing.

The building that held the laundry was a converted horse barn about a hundred years old and we lived in very cramped space in the back of the laundry with no clear separation of the work areas from the living quarters. My 'bedroom' was the space where we dried clothes from lines strung across the ceiling during the work hours. We had no heavy equipment in the store, only ironing tables and we sent all clothes out to a wet wash service for washing and most of the shirts to a shirt pressing factory for ironing/folding. Our customer mix was: mostly white (60 percent) and black (35 percent) with only a few Hispanic (5 percent). Father's social circle consisted only of other Chinese in the area. He worked hard and long hours in the store and also endured a self-created hardship, gambling on Sundays at the numerous New York Chinatown gambling halls. He wasn't very lucky at this activity. On several occasions during a police raid, he would be released since I was along. The cops didn't want to drag a nine-year old kid into custody.   He was a proud man and loved his children very much.   I can remember him going out to buy a TV for us to watch in 1950 just because our neighbor would not let us watch his.   This was no small feat due to our economic condition.

Mom did all the daily cooking in traditional village style.   During the holidays (Chinese New Year, Harvest Moon Festival, etc.) she would prepare Chinese cakes and pastries for us and for many of the other Chinese in the area. Some of these people were single men who owned laundries, as well, but, had left their wives back in the village and therefore would have missed out on all of these "goodies" had it not been for my mom's kindness.   Mom knew most of the other Chinese women, some being relatives, in the area and occasionally visited them.   She knew virtually all of these people from days back in the village or Hong Kong.

My parents adopted western dress, but I can say that *my mother's attitudes remained very traditional (very "heong hah" to my wife's dismay)*. Mom had no relationships with non-Chinese (language barrier).

We did all of our Chinese shopping in NY Chinatown (Mott St.) on Sundays. It was a matter of taking the train to Jersey City and then boarding a ferry across the Hudson, all in all about a one hour trip each way. My father generally took me along to give my mother a respite and sometimes the whole family would go if we were invited to a special occasion like a wedding banquet or a baby's first haircut celebration.

Most of the kids I went to grammar school with in a ghetto type lower socioeconomic area were either Blacks or Jewish. Somehow, I managed to fit in quite well with the Jewish population. I also got along with the Blacks, but didn't run around with them as I did with the Jewish crowd. In grammar school, a black art teacher seemed to take pleasure in tormenting me. Nothing I did in her class seemed to be right and on one occasion she had me in tears in front of a class accusing me of something that I didn't do. Perhaps she was putting me in my place, as I had the reputation of being one of the brightest kids in school. How could a little yellow-faced kid be allowed to show up the rest of a school that was over half black? I also had a white phys-ed. instructor who would never let me be a member of the school junior patrol on the pretense that I talked too much in class. It was just plain and simple prejudice.

On the positive side, there was a Jewish music teacher in grammar school who treated me with kindness and respect. She gave me the task of selecting a classical piece of music to play every day at our daily school assembly. I have her to thank for introducing me to classical music and also for allowing me to do something that I was very proud of and making many of the other kids envious of me.

Father passed away in 1952, so Mother and two children (including myself) lived in and operated the laundry. Due to father's death, a large burden fell upon me at a very young age. I wasn't the most obedient child either. I did work in the laundry starting at the age of 10 after my father's passing with some help from cousins and a brother-in-law. After a few years of this outside help, we were on our own and I did work quite a bit more in the store during my teens, although my mom had to chase me around to get things done. Being just a kid, I would shirk my duties at the store so my mother had to do most of the work. Still, she put up with me and did the best that she could to raise us.

Mother kept us together as family in a most crucial period when we were growing up. Her biggest hardship was taking care of a ten-year old son (me) and an eight-year old daughter by herself while learning how to run the laundry at the same time. Fortunately, we did have some help in the beginning years to keep things afloat. I was able to work outside the laundry as a waiter in a local Chinese restaurant and also at the Post Office. I finally moved from the laundry in 1965 after graduating from engineering school and then moved to work in Minnesota.

I didn't really do much dating until my college days. I took a Chinese college student out a few times who worked as a cashier at the same restaurant where I moonlighted as a waiter. Her uncle nixed our relationship because why should she date a person who was only a waiter? Sound familiar? Waiters didn't fare much higher on the social scale than laundry workers even to another Chinese restaurant worker.

I socialized mainly with Caucasian women since the Asian female population was very small in the mid 60's. I was introduced to a Hong Kong girl in 1969 and decided that it was time to settle down. Louisa and I have been happily married now for 36 years and have two children, a girl and boy. I guess that I could have married someone non-Chinese if fate would have led me in that direction, however, my family is much happier with the choice that I made.

During my 3rd year in college (1964), I was a substitute mail carrier for a few summer months. Subbing for vacationing mail carriers, my assignments took me all over the city. One mail route included a Chinese laundry. As I walked in to drop off their mail, the owner and his wife looked at me with curiosity thinking that I looked Chinese, but couldn't accept the notion of a Chinese mail carrier, especially some young person. I said nothing as the owner told his wife that the Post Office doesn't hire Chinese to deliver U.S. mail. This was a job for a real American. The wife agreed. Imagine their surprise when I spoke to them in their own native Taishanese dialect.

I led the high school marching band (1960) to a weekly Saturday football game. The band would march about a mile from the school to the football field, going right past another Chinese laundry. Now, these people knew me and just about fell over when they saw me marching and playing an instrument in the front row. How could a lowly Chinese laundry kid be all decked out in a band uniform and lead a marching band? Wasn't this reserved for a "real" American? There was, of course, another agenda for this particular Chinese family. They also had a son a year older than me whom they always implied was smarter and more likely to succeed than me. Now being in a marching band doesn't make one any smarter, but it did make the point that times were changing and being Chinese wasn't such a liability anymore.

I felt I had some hard lessons early in life that taught me to appreciate all the good things that will come along later. My life in a laundry was a harsh one. Other kids certainly may have had closer to a normal childhood. Despite the economic condition or family dynamic of growing up Chinese, I do feel that we all were a part of a common, but, very localized culture that for the most part started back in some rural village, most likely in Taishan County.

Lucy Wong Leonard, 46, grew up in her family's laundry from 1964 to 1975 in Hawthorne, California. She served in the U. S. Navy and graduated from Southern Illinois University in Health Care Administration and earned a business degree from Webster University. As a Naval Reservist, Lucy was recalled to active duty for Desert Storm.

She lives with her husband, William R. Leonard, a Corpsman she met at Camp Pendleton Marine Base, and three parrots in Lake Havasu City, AZ. She is a life member of the San Diego Chinese Historical Museum and Disabled American Veteran Chapter 27 of Lake Havasu City.

Dirty laundry dominated my youthful years growing up in Hawthorne, California, about 15 miles from Los Angeles, where my oldest brother, sisters and I helped my family run the Victory Chinese Laundry located at 12530 Hawthorne Boulevard from 1964 to 1975. We lived in the back of the laundry until 1967, when we saved enough money for a down payment on a house.

My Dad, Bon Wong, youngest of 13 children, was born in Taishan, Guangdong, China, on April 15, 1923. Unable to provide for the large family, his destitute parents sold him for 100 silver dollars when he was 3 or 4 years old. Some poor families had to resort to this solution and families without sons were eager to adopt. Living with his adopted family, he attended school until he was 14. Then, the Japanese military invaded China. To protect him from the Japanese, his adoptive parents sent him to Los Angeles where he worked in their Chinese laundry. However, his adopted father supported his gambling habit using most of Dad's earnings. At 25, he returned to Guangdong to find a wife. In 1948, he married Louie Kim You, and then they came to California to work in the laundry and start a family. When Dad died in 2003, they had been married for 54 years.

The work demands of the laundry were so heavy that even when the annual city parade every July marched down the main street and right past our laundry, my family could only afford to steal brief glimpses of these festivities before we had to return to our work. I remember once being able to see the actor Chuck Norris when he was a young man during one parade, sitting on the lowered convertible top of a car and waving to everyone in the crowd.

My parents worked long hours every day. We had no vacations, no trips to Disneyland, or any other fun events that the average family took for granted. I remember vividly all the limitations and deprivations that we as a family had to deal with on a daily basis. Every Monday thru Friday, my father opened the laundry from 9 a.m. to 6 p.m., but we were required to be there well before opening, and work till long after closing. On Saturday, my Father opened the laundry at 10 a.m., and even after closing at 5 p.m., he would still be working there past 8 p.m. with my mom and older brother, Phillip. I would know they were still working because my sister Lou Lan and I were at home alone. Lou Lan and I were old enough to look after ourselves: I was 9 and she was 11. For supper, she and I would run to the Safeway grocery to buy TV dinners for ourselves. We had to grow up fast because our parents were working so hard to support the family. Despite our parents' efforts we ended up losing our house. The laundry could not make enough money for the mortgage payments.

On Sundays, my parents did not work in their laundry, but that did not mean that they had the day off. They would spend Sundays delivering large bags of dirty laundry to a Chinese wet-wash laundry in Los Angeles, about 6 miles from our home. The laundry would be washed there and the following Sunday, Dad would pick it up for finishing at our laundry. On Monday, the washed laundry would be pressed, sorted and wrapped. We also took in dry cleaning that we farmed out to a man named Stan Franklin. On our way home, Dad would stop by the grocery. This was the only time we had time to go shopping for groceries so we stocked up for the entire week. Then we would come home to relax the rest of Sunday before getting on the old treadmill again on Monday morning.

I remember how Mom would take her oldest child, Phillip, who was autistic and had been born in China, to learn English at Lawndale Adult Education. We were busy in the laundry, but she would leave with Phillip for night school around 6 p.m. and Dad would look after us while we all continued to work. It was important for Mom and Phillip to learn English, but it added to our difficulty because we could have used their help in the laundry. My four sisters and I would go to school during the day, and then help out with the laundry work after school. During the day, Dad delivered fresh laundry to privately owned cleaners in Redondo Beach, Culver City and Los Angeles, while Phillip ran the laundry. We kids had no social or recreational life because we had no time or opportunity to make outside friends.

When I was in the 4th grade and working late nights, there were scores of parked cars and young people hanging out in the evening across the street in an area called "Island Parking" that was directly across from our store. They scared me a little because we had no security and we were all alone as the other businesses around us closed after 6 p.m. These teens, known as the "Hawthorne Boulevard street racers," lined up their cars on El Segundo Boulevard to cruise from the south to the north ends on Hawthorne Boulevard. Fortunately, they were only interested in their cruising, and never bothered my family.

My sister Suzie and I would collect all the loose change that customers forgot to remove from the pockets of their clothes. Once we had found enough money, I would take it and run down to Taco Tio, to buy greasy tacos and bean burritos for our supper. I remember clearly that they had the best grated cheese and hot sauce which went over the food. Often, Mom would steam us some rice with a little bit of meat, tofu, vegetable, steamed eggs, bits of ham, and set it up in the back of the laundry for our meals. This was a rice bowl and it was appreciated because food was limited. I even taught myself how to make pancakes and waffles. Suzie saved Blue Chip Stamps from our grocery shopping that we eventually redeemed to get a waffle maker. I taught myself how to make these pancakes and waffles. They were inexpensive and filled my tummy up.

I had below average academic abilities growing up because English was not spoken at home. My abilities were low because I could not understand the spoken language in class even though I was born in Los Angeles Chinatown. My parents spoke the dialect called Toishan at home and wrote using Chinese characters. In 6th grade, my teacher asked me if I would make white paper flowers for her wedding. I stayed after school to finish them, so she offered to drive me home. When she arrived at my parent's laundry, she glanced at me to confirm that she was at the right address, but I was too embarrassed to tell her that the laundry was my family's business.

Today, families with financial hardships like ours would be eligible for food stamps or Medicaid, but these programs were not available back when we were struggling to make ends meet. We often did not have healthy and nutritious food, or a sufficient quantity. Dad did his best to provide for us, but he did not know about the important benefits of having a balanced meal. He would buy hamburgers from McDonald's, donuts, and discounted pie pastries. We were unable to afford many things most Americans take for granted, such as a good education, decent clothes, shoes and socks, undergarments, and allowances. We did not have parties to celebrate birthdays because my parents could not afford cakes or take the time away from the laundry. We rarely attended church because my parents still had to deliver laundry on Sunday and fulfill other family responsibilities.

As I grew up we were often confronted with prejudice; I saw how customers harassed my parents. I remember how they called the police because a young Caucasian man lied about paying for his laundry, which he did not. My parent's lack of education, command of the English language and familiarity with American life hurt them in their struggle to earn a living from their laundry.

I have learned to value education in many areas and see its importance. I did become a college graduate not once, but twice. Later after serving in the U. S. military, I even went back to college to take courses to learn more about Chinese language, history and civilization. To be a college graduate is a dream to most, and I know anyone can achieve it. I did not have anyone who supported me while struggling to finish school, but I know anyone can achieve it.

Laura Chin has been a past Executive Director of the Organization of Chinese Americans (OCA), directing the national office of OCA in Washington, D. C. She has also been involved with Asian American rights, working at the level of the federal government with the U.S. Commission on Civil Rights.

My father, born in China, left as a young boy of eight years in the 1930s to come to here alone. Unable to speak any English, he joined one of his uncles who operated a Chinese hand laundry in a Polish neighborhood in Brooklyn, New York. My parents' marriage was arranged, and my sister was born before World War II. (Mother's father was a merchant who operated out of Singapore.) After World War II, father returned to China to bring the family from Shanghai to the U. S. in 1947 and they lived on Elizabeth Street in New York's Chinatown for a few years.

The village where my father was born, near Taishan, is about a 5-hour bus ride from Guangzhou. His father was a landowner, and there were about 8 families working his land and rice fields. Family pictures show a building that was built by my grandfather. The building still stands today and is used for storage by the Chinese Government. The irony here is that my family still has title to the land, but there is no chance that we can claim it.

Coming to the U. S. at age 8, Father essentially grew up in the U.S. so during World War II he was in the American Army in an all-Chinese American Unit and served as a Staff Sergeant. When he left the U.S. Army with $300 in his pocket, he borrowed a few thousand from another village family who had settled in Long Island, New York. With this money he opened up the Dyker Hand Laundry in the Bay Ridge area of Brooklyn, New York in the late 1940s. When this loan was repaid in the late 1950's or early 1960s', I remember that there was an elaborate ceremony between the families to celebrate the repayment of the loan.

In the late 1940s and 1950s, as it still is, Bay Ridge, Brooklyn, New York, was a working class neighborhood. Many residents in Bay Ridge at that time were Swedish, Norwegian, Finnish and Italian. Bay Ridge's population has become quite diverse today, but even today there is still an annual Swedish Day Parade. Our laundry was located on 5th Avenue, between 86th and 87th Street. In the late 40s and early 50s, we were the only Chinese American family in Bay Ridge and my father operated the only Chinese hand laundry in the area. My father spoke excellent English while my mother's was barely passable. However, she managed to speak to the customers when they would drop off their clothes. I remember that his written Chinese and English were lovely. My mother never learned to write English, but learned enough spoken English to pass her citizenship examination.

We lived behind the laundry during the early years. A curtain separated the store from the living quarters. Behind the laundry was a dining room/kitchen area. A narrow hallway led to the bathroom and shower areas. When you walked through the small bathroom area, the large room in the back was partitioned into two bedrooms. My brother, who was born in 1949, shared one of the large rooms with my parents, while my sister and I slept on bunk beds on the other side of the partition. Behind the laundry were a large room that served as the kitchen/eating area, and two other small rooms, with one of the rooms large enough to store many pounds of rice and dried Chinese herbs and vegetables. By the time my sister graduated from high school, and I was in the 4th grade, father had purchased an apartment building across the street that housed five families, with a store front for the hand laundry. We no longer lived behind the laundry, but in a two-bedroom apartment on the third floor.

Both of my parents worked at the Dyker Hand laundry from 7 in the morning until 7 at night, 6 days a week. My mother left the laundry area about 6 pm to start dinner. My parents did not take any vacations, although we did get to go to the Coney Island Amusement Park in Brooklyn during the summer months, and once in a while took a boat ride to Bear Mountain up the Hudson River.

It was during high school that I wanted to help out in the laundry. During the weekends I got to iron handkerchiefs mostly, and I would do occasional touch ups to the shirts, such as ironing the cuffs or collars. I remember these Saturdays quite clearly, for it was a time I could be with me parents during the day, and I could assist by retrieving the packaged laundry for the customers and ringing up the sale on the cash register. At that time, like many laundries, the clothes, mostly shirts, were sent out to a larger laundry service for washing. They would do pickups several times a week. Laundry would be returned and my parents would ring starch in the areas of the collars and cuffs. The shirts were then sent out for pressing. They would come back to the hand laundry pressed, with touch ups to be done by my parents. Shirts and other clothing were then to be sorted, folded and packaged in brown paper with white string for pickup by customers. Eventually, my father also took in dry cleaning and the laundry became the Dyker Hand Laundry and Dry Cleaning.

My father had a mentor, a Mr. Rosen, a school teacher who befriended my father and with whom he kept in touch. He would offer advice to father about his children's education. It was a very good relationship. Father even kept in touch with Mrs. Rosen after Mr. Rosen died.

Generally speaking, I got along with many non-Chinese. My first grade teacher at P.S. 104 took a special interest in me to see that I was disciplined and that I could read.

And I remember, in the early years, going with my mother to buy a fresh 5 lb. pullet for the family dinner on Saturdays. In the early 1950s there was a market that could provide fresh killed chicken, rabbits, and other animals. Looking back, I remember being fascinated by the market, located off the main avenue on 88th Street, and watch them prepare the chickens for customers. In the early 1950s there were also trucks that sold ice and milk on the streets. We always had a freshly made Chinese soup every night accompanied by several Chinese dishes. The only time we went out to eat was on Sunday mornings when we traveled to Chinatown in Manhattan.

My parents would take us to Chinatown every Sunday to have lunch, meet village cousins and other friends, and buy foods that were readily available in Manhattan's Chinatown. The trip by the New York City subway was about a 20-25 minute ride. (I did not eat out in a non-Chinese restaurant until I was in high school, when I had my first green salad. I must admit that I was puzzled when asked what salad dressing I wanted.)

We took New York's BMT "R" Train, transferred to the "N" Train, which went across the Manhattan Bridge to New York's Canal Street Station. We went to Chinatown every Sunday, and had noodles for lunch. I think back fondly to those times when a bowl of wonton noodle soup cost less than a dollar. Being with village cousins and other friends was a regular thing for my parents on Sundays. My father would buy the Chinese newspapers; my mother read them occasionally. I remember going with my parents every weekend, but some time in high school years I felt I did not want to go down; the ritual was getting to me. And there were Sundays that I chose to stay home rather than follow my parents. Of course, it was a time when my parents got dressed up and socialized.

Being a teenager, I did not see the value my parents placed in this ritual. As an adult, I realized it was important for my parents, especially for my father. For my mother, the Sunday ritual did give her a break. Her other relaxation times was when a Cantonese opera troupe came to New York's Chinatown. We would meet my cousin and go to the Sun Sing Theater. My mother would spend hours and sometimes days watching the opera, which performed for almost a week. We also went there to watch Chinese movies with these wonderful actors flying through the space as they fought evil spirits and other worldly beings. I still remember those movies fondly, not that I knew what was said. My father became active in the Kim Lau American Legion Post in Chinatown where he would meet old friends, many of whom served in the same unit during World War II or came to America on the same army transport with their families.

When I was in high school or earlier, my father purchased three properties on 4th Avenue in Brooklyn, about one block away. We kept one of the apartment buildings as our home as the other two buildings were leased. The Dyker Hand

Laundry kept operating. Over my mother's objections, my father sold the buildings that he owned in the mid-1980s, and gave up the hand laundry. He had complained for years about the tiring work of the laundry. By that time, Brooklyn had changed and there were other launderettes in the area and many more Asian Americans.

My parents always urged me to marry a Chinese and made several attempts to set me up with some Chinese men. When I was in college in N. Y. near my parents, they introduced me to a student at Columbia University. We enjoyed a dim sum lunch and our families met, but we had no interest with one another. The same outcome occurred with another Chinese American they had me meet. Anyway, then I left NY for graduate school at George Washington University, and my parents hoped I would marry before I was 25. Someone Chinese American, of course. However, it wasn't until I was 35 that I married, and by then, of course, my parents had no objections at all that my husband was Jewish working as a defense lawyer, and later as a Law Professor at The George Washington University Law School.

Harvey and Jeff (Low) *are brothers who grew up in Toronto and they still live there. They spent many hours around their grandfather's laundry. Harvey, age 44, is the younger brother and works as an urban planner with the City of Toronto. Jeff, age 49, works in Toronto as a marketing manager for a software company.*

Their grandfather, Sam Low, owned a laundry in a residential area at the northern edge of town, far from the Chinese community. Their father came over as a teen in 1949, and worked only a few years in the laundry.

Harvey and Jeff: Sam Low was an interesting man who liked to maintain 'appearances' and feel important. When we were little boys, he would tell us about loans he had made to help other Chinese. I can still remember the details of one loan of $800 to Mr. Wong Sing who ran a very much down-at-heals grocery at Elizabeth Street and Darcy Place, and other loans to people he felt were deserving. He also mentioned that most had never paid him back. His 'nickname' in Chinatown was 'choi-chee low' [Toisanese here -'rich man'] - We heard him addressed many times this way - it gave him no end of pleasure - he never corrected his admirers, and his mood, which was never bad was better for it. He was also treasurer of Kwong Hoy Lun Hop Wai [one of the Chinese fraternal societies]. This role devolved into a legal dispute between him and other members, with him and his associates having long visits in law offices. Then just like the kind of person he was, he must have paid the legal fees himself, as he held the court documents at the time of his death.

The laundry store was always very hot in the summer. The only cooling was the window at the back, a door ajar, and some ceiling and portable fans. No such thing as air-conditioning! The store itself was spartan and devoid of any decorative furnishings – everything was practical. Our store window display was made-up of only a few plants.

When customers brought their laundry into the store, they would be issued a ticket at the front counter. The consecutively numbered tickets were made in store. The ticket was torn in two, and one part was given as a claim check to the customer and the other half stayed with the bundle. The bundles were opened and – and for new customers - each item marked with indelible ink in a location such as inside the shirt collar or inside the trousers so they would not be apparent when the clothes were worn.

The laundry mark system was always a mystery to me. Some customers were known only by their street address number, e.g., '68.' In fact '68' made quite the impression on me – he was a constant pipe smoker. Laundry was sorted into separate washes – white shirts, colored shirts, light towels and dark towels. Elderly gents brought detachable collars and these were tied together – by the owner - through the buttonhole.

By the time, we grandchildren were growing up, there were machines for every task. There was an extractor. The heavy and sodden, rinsed laundry had to be man-handled to lift it into this apparatus that removed excess water by rapidly spinning. There was a specialized press for ironing sheets- another one just for collars. These last two machines were quite elaborate and complicated and must have cost a pretty penny.

The work of ironing shirts was always done by hand. Grandpa got tired of this and contracted it out. The contractor – a middle aged woman, dripping in jade - in turn, paid an 'a-mah' to do the actual work. 'A-mah' was overworked.

A good number of shirts always came back perfectly ironed but razor-slashed. I was concerned but Grandpa wasn't. I asked, 'what will you tell the customer?' Grandpa always laughed this off. He told the customers that their shirts were destroyed by the machinery – and would 'they like some money - in lieu". The customers were always too nice to take the money. But most who experienced this more than twice never came back.

Merchants who sold laundry supplies such as soap, bleach, and wrapping paper had to be dealt with. The bleach suppliers were fellow Chinese. The bleach was progressively thinned out with water. I watched over time as a rich yellow product turn many, many shades lighter. Grandpa asked me to smell it. Eventually it hardly even smelled of bleach. Vast amounts of the adulterated product had to be used to get the same results. I listened to Grandpa's complaints to the supplier who DENIED any thinning. There were also suppliers of coal needed to heat the stove for indoor drying of clothes in the winter. Grandma would watch the unloading and count each bag by setting a wood match aside.

There was a ledger book made from the brown wrapping paper. An old abacus was used to total up the amount to charge for each package of laundry. Grandpa made entries in pencil. I suppose it wouldn't pass an audit today.

We would have to be inventive to amuse ourselves at the laundry store. We had an old iron stove that warmed the basement. As the youngest grandchild, I, would go around with the water squirt bottle grandfather used to moisten clothes before ironing them, and being mischievous, as many little boys tend to be, would wet the wings of insects so they could not fly away so I could catch them and throw them into the burning stove! (Now, as an animal lover, I would never dream of doing anything like that)

After I learned how to work the on-switch on the extractor, a machine that would spin to remove excess water from clothes, I'd put my G. I. Joe action figures in to see what happened to them from the high speed spinning! This prompted Grandfather to warn us kids to never to put our hands in the spin-machine.

We would also play, without Grandfather's permission, in the backyard in the "maze" of bed sheets that hung on rows of clothesline to be dried in the summer. It gave much amusement to my siblings and me. This memory of running up and down, pulling the sheets aside to scare my sister and brother is still vivid, and I can almost hear the squeals of joy that we children made. The scent of fresh laundry today often activates memories of those days as we giggled our way darting through the maze of drying laundry. When the cousins were over, Tag would be the game. All of us would run and jump over the counters in the front of the store – even when there were customers around. I'd also bring my Dinky toy cars and play with them on the bare wood floors amidst the mounds of laundry lying on the floor that I imagined to be mountains and ravines.

Each school day, the youngest grandchild, my brother Harvey, walked back to the store alone to be fed a "Chinese-Canadian" lunch of rice, steamed eggs or pork, and good ole Canadian canned pasta. This menu *never* varied in the 7 years he ate lunch there while in elementary school. Grandma always knew what he liked. She would save the label of the canned pasta so she could bring it with her to the local grocer a few doors away, and point at it with her limited English to indicate she wanted that particular brand.

Grandma was a tough lady. Not that clean, but practical, and always a great cook! Never once saw her get sick or ill – no time when laundry was to be done. No food was ever wasted! Jars of salted fish and other leftovers were left on a side table in the open covered only with paper wrap. Grandma did *all* the cooking.

There was one special routine that was always adhered to: Saturday night dinner in the old basement with all of us crowded around the table seated in an assortment of unmatched chairs. We did not even have a tablecloth as the décor was plain, but the food was delicious. Sunday brunch was always special but grandma did not have to cook as we devoured *dim sum* that my grandfather would pickup occasionally from Chinatown. Afternoon Tea was served promptly each and everyday at 4 p.m. (I guess this was an English tradition that Grandfather adopted).

On special family gatherings, we kids would be entertained as we watched with blood thirsty glee while Grandma slit the necks of live chickens in preparing to cook them for the evening dinner. Grandfather would, to the end of his laundry days, knock off work promptly at 6:00 p.m., especially in summers. He would then bathe, shave and dress – always in gray pants and the most perfectly pressed shirt, and make a trip downtown to Chinatown or to Yorkdale, the newly opened enclosed suburban shopping mall. He also never missed the annual outing to the Canadian National Exhibition each summer – often taking us as youngsters down for some fun at the fair!

Grandpa lived by routines. His favorite chair was by the door so he could see when customers arrived. Watching for customers, he'd sit there smoking with a cigarette in one hand, and a can of Coke in the other. When he was in the mood for a snack, he would give each of us a quarter and more, so we could fetch ice cream for all of us from the nearby store.

Kim Dow, our father, saw that laundry was not in his blood. He last worked full time there in about 1967-69. He came back to the store from a stock boy's position. He left in 1969 and never looked back. Father decided to make the "upward move" with work for Canada Post and later become an investor, eventually acquiring several small apartment properties.

Sam and Yick Hee, our grandparents, continued to operate the laundry until as late as 1976, but by then the laundry business had been in decline for some time. Our shelves of laundry bundles were nearly bare by then. The three tiers of shelves that were always full during my childhood were reduced to much less than one tier. In the final analysis, home washers, coin laundries, and an aggressive expansion by a Toronto laundry and dry cleaning chain – Embassy Cleaners – made the closing of the store a foregone thing. The building that had housed the laundry still stands, but is occupied by a store that sells women's underclothes. The original pressed tin ceiling is still there, as is the original floor, although marred with depressions where the ironers stood for years pressing shirts by hand iron. Today, these physical features are reminders for me of the past history of this family's Chinese laundry.

Eliz Chan, age 65, received a BA from the University of Louisville and obtained a Masters from Southwestern Oklahoma State University. She has worked as a chemist, retail manager, secondary education teacher, computer programmer/analyst, English language instructor, university researcher, and office manager.

Now retired from the U. S. Secret Service where she was a senior staff assistant, she is also the mother of two, and spouse to a career U. S. Air Force officer. Her five laundry siblings all graduated from college and had active professional careers in engineering, accounting, and teaching.

I am the third of six children born to George and Nellie Woo. We lived on the 2nd floor above my dad's hand laundry, the George Woo Laundry, at 227 W. Jefferson St in downtown Louisville, Kentucky.

Both of my parents were immigrants from Guangdong Province, China. My father came over in 1916 as an 8-year old. He was the second son, born of the second wife. His older brother, Uncle Dick, (born of the first wife,) who would inherit the family property, was already in Louisville. My grandfather purchased papers so my father could come as a "paper son" to Louisville to learn a trade and attend American school to learn some English.

Upon reaching adulthood Dad was able to buy his own laundry and later return to China to marry. In Guangdong Mom was already considered an "old Maid" when she married Dad. At 5'3," she was considered way too tall and "too old to marry" in her early twenties. Dad was the same height as Mom (Nellie) and pounds lighter. But the match was made through the local matchmaker and the deal was set. As a laundryman, US law did not allow him to bring a wife or family into the country because he was considered a laborer. This made his mother happy because she now had another pair of hands to labor in her household as an unpaid servant.

I didn't speak that much English when I started kindergarten. At home we spoke in Chinese to each other. We kids did learn a lot of English and American customs from attending Sunday schools at a nearby church but our parents did not belong to the church. By first grade when I was six years old, I could function in English. My older brother Ed did most of the translation for my mom and dad. Later, in 1952 when Ed graduated from Manual High School and was accepted to Purdue University to study Chemical Engineering, Mary K and I did the translations.

Mother talked about these years of separation as being very hard. She grew garlic and sold it at the local village market. Often times there was little to eat until the crops matured. Dad visited when he could and introduced new customs. When he was there, he would have everyone sit down and eat, instead of the older custom of men eating first and the women and children later. Mother wanted to accompany Dad to the U. S. but his own mother wanted to keep Nellie and her grandchild, Edward, at her side. Dad, at the end of his visit home, again asked for his wife to accompany him back to Kentucky. Dad's mother again refused his request. A very disappointed Dad returned to Hong Kong to book a ship for the United States.

Right after father left the village for his return to Kentucky, the Japanese bombed Guangzhou in the "undeclared" war that would eventually be WW II. Everybody was upset and unsure of their futures. Grandmother at long last gave her permission for Nellie and five-year Edward to leave with Dad. Nellie hurried to Hong Kong to catch Dad and make arrangements for their departure. Luckily, she found Dad at a relative's home and was able to purchase papers as a student accompanying a young child on his way to the U. S. Mother used this paper identity to successfully enter the U.S. in the spring of 1939. She was on Angel Island for three weeks while Dad waited for her in San Francisco. Then In the spring of 1939, they took the train east to Louisville, Kentucky.

Dad had his first laundry on Third St. next to Caulfield's Toy and Novelty Store. On the corner was the Courier Journal newspaper. During war time, 1941-1945, business was very good and everybody worked hard. Business was very good and we had lots of soldiers as customers from nearby Ft. Knox, KY. Dad was only two blocks from City Hall and the Jefferson County Court House. After the war Dad moved half a block away to operate a laundry at 227 West Jefferson.

We first lived in back of the store where Dad had his laundry business in the front. Later we lived on the 2nd floor above the laundry. When we were older and Ed was away in college, my parents purchased a large house on the bus line so we could live away from the Chinese laundry. Mother was put in charge of us 5 kids and we moved to the suburbs. Mary K and I wanted to attend Manual High School (downtown) as our brother Ed had and petitioned the school board for permission.

All six of us children helped in the laundry, with our responsibilities varying with age. I remember waiting on customers who dropped off or picked up laundry, folding socks when they had been washed, and operating equipment like the mangle. Workdays were long, and we only had Sundays off. During the WW II, business was very good and we had lots of soldiers on weekends coming to the laundry from Ft. Knox. Mother helped in the laundry as well as raising the children. Mary Katherine was born in 1939, Elizabeth in 1941, Robert in 1943, George in 1945, and Jimmy in 1947. All of us worked in the laundry, with our responsibilities varying with age. The older children waited on customers who dropped off or picked up laundry, folded socks, and operated equipment like the mangle. As the family increased in numbers, she had less time to work in the laundry. Dad had her do the mending and sewing. We ate only Chinese meals so she was in charge of all the food preparations for the family and also provided lunch for the workers. Dad usually had 2 to 4 Chinese employees and five female ironers, usually white women, to hand-finish the shirts.

We were allowed to attend Sunday school with the rest of the neighborhood children and enjoy some of their treats such as Kool-Aid and cookies. We kids learned a lot of English and American customs by attending Sunday school at the downtown Southern Baptist Church. I remember loving to climb up the circular staircase one floor and trying to slide down the banister. We were considered honorary whites for the most part and went where they went. When my sister and I were older, girls at school invited us to attend their slumber parties but mother's strict rules did not allow us to go.

In 1962, the US Immigration Service caught up with my dad's false identity, and he lost his American citizenship. My brother Ed also lost his citizenship since he was born in China. It was not a problem for Dad as he regained his citizenship through a special rider that passed on a congressional bill. Ed lost his job as an engineer on the space program since he was no longer a citizen and thus lost his security clearance. He had to wait five years to reapply for citizenship, which was successful. When the government offered a confession program that would allow Chinese to reclaim their true Chinese surnames, Dad must have been disappointed with his children as we were not willing to take our real name of Woo. We stayed 'Wongs' since all our school records and memories were as 'Wongs.' Mary K and I figured that we would be marrying and changing our names anyhow.

There were several other Chinese laundries in Louisville as well as Chinese restaurants. But there were not enough Chinese to create a Chinese community. There were a larger number of Chinese in Indianapolis, Indiana, about 150 miles north. Father knew some of the Chinese there and would occasionally go there by rail to visit on a Sunday afternoon to socialize. Otherwise my parents did not have much time for social life or recreation, as they did not speak enough English to understand American movies. Our family often spent Sunday afternoon, our one free day, socializing with another Chinese family, the Woo Sangs, that ran a laundry on nearby Fifth Street. In the 1950's we were among the first to get a television set and my parents as well as us kids enjoyed watching daytime programs on it.

We pressured Dad to give up his laundry and enter the restaurant business, as it would be easier on him without traveling back and forth so far to the laundry. He sold his Jefferson Street laundry building and used the money to open the

Golden Dragon Restaurant on Bardstown Road. The first year, I served as his hostess in a red homemade *cheongsam*. We trained the waitresses to take orders for Chinese dinners and to describe our meals to customers, most of whom were unacquainted with Chinese dishes. Everything was so new to all.

Louisville, Kentucky was considered to be the "Gateway to the South." We children didn't feel much of the pressure to integrate as we attended the downtown schools where there where other immigrant families. My best friend in grade school was Jewish and her dad was a policeman. At the dentist's office there were two waiting rooms, one marked "White" and the other "Colored." It was carefully explained to me that I was an "honorary white." In the 60's, back in Louisville, Ky. there were only blacks and whites, but very few Asians. I was in high school when school desegregation began. Suddenly there were a few black kids in class and in the lunchroom. We got along fine and nothing exciting took place. I encountered a few blacks in college and my first Mexican American in college. The Mexican American was a college student, the same as me, also striving for a teaching certification.

Mother did most of the child rearing as father was busy with our laundry all day. She was very strict and traditional with us and we girls were not allowed to leave the laundry or the apartment without permission. Maybe she worried that the whites might mistreat us Chinese. My older sister and I disliked the strict traditional way we were raised. We vowed that we would never raise children the same way our mother raised us. We spent a lot of time with each other and helping to look after our three younger brothers. How I envied my brother Ed who seemingly spent little time at home but was always with his Chinese playmates. On the weekends, Ed made dough balls and went fishing with his cousins. How I wished I were Ed!

My sister and I went to University of Louisville to attend college since my parents insisted that we had to stay at home to attend. My younger brothers got to choose whatever school they wanted. How I wished I were a boy!

Around the 1960s to 1970s business in the laundry started to decline a lot as more people got their own home washer and dryer. Father had offset this loss of business by serving as a drop off station for garments to be dry cleaned, which were farmed out to a dry cleaner. But, sometime in the 1970s father decided it was time to sell the laundry and get into the restaurant business.

I have positive memories of growing up in the laundry. It was hard work, but the fact that I had to contribute to its success was valuable in helping me learn the value of the family working together.

> **Ken Lee,** *age 52, is Professor and Head of the Food Science Department at Ohio State University where he had the honor of giving the Commencement Address for the first graduating class post 9-11, coincidentally on Pearl Harbor Day. He spoke about joining a nation at war, and about his personal experience facing bigotry growing up in a Chinese laundry. He asked graduates that day for their help in making America a safe place to be different.*

My dad came over when he was 10 or 12 from Canton, China. There is confusion about his age since there are both differences in the Chinese and American calendars and outright lying about age for work. My mom was born in Newark, New Jersey, and her mom born in San Francisco, California. Despite being born a U.S. citizen our government deported my grandmother under the blatantly racist Chinese Exclusion Act. Some paperwork was lost, presumably in a San Francisco fire. So my mom was partially raised in China with her dozen brothers and sisters. Only my mom and three uncles survived the Japanese invasion. Grandma sold most of the family jewelry to get everyone out on one of the last boats to leave in the early days of the war.

Dad spent his childhood working in my grandfather's laundry in the Bronx, New York, just under an elevated subway line. Ironing tables were also his bed. It seems all he ever did since he was a kid was work seven days a week in the laundry. Somehow he managed to get a college degree in chemistry from Fordham University in N. Y.

With this high education, why did he put in 30 years of hard labor in a laundry in a Chinese laundry in West Orange, New Jersey? There are vague stories about racial discrimination: whereas blacks were physically thrown from the employment office, Chinese were allowed to apply, but the paper just later trashed. There are resentful stories about a mother-in-law with a vice-grip lock on her daughter, forcing my family into the proximate laundry business. The truth was lost somewhere in the New Jersey meadowlands, a foul urban swamp that we navigated each weekend to stock up in Chinatown, NYC.

It was an arranged marriage. Dad never said much about it. Mom said she was given a choice, and picked him, as he was the best looking. The laundry was something that mom initially ran while dad pursued his dreams and an advanced degree. But racial discrimination and family issues made the laundry his only 'choice.'

As the last of five children raised over a laundry in an all-white town, there was little chance that I was going to learn to speak or write Chinese. They tried to send me to Chinese school, but that was futile.

Dad had a 2B deferment from the army and married mom in 1943. The honeymoon was sad as my uncle, James Eng, the first Chinese American to enlist in the US Air Force, 42nd Quarter Squadron, crashed and died. Dad worked as a chemist for Ballantine Brewery at $65 per week, but that income could not support a family. So with only $200 in the bank they opened a laundry with a $600 no-interest loan from grandma.

My parents lived in a coldwater flat in Montclair, New Jersey, that used kerosene for heat and coal for a potbelly stove. This was dangerous so my mom found a nearby apartment for $100 per month, but the downstairs storefront was part of the package. They decided to use the store to open a laundry. The steam line that ran from the laundry into the upstairs apartment was the family communication pipe. We had no telephone and shared a party line downstairs in the laundry. My mom would tap on the pipe with a can opener, and my code was five taps, for the fifth child. I looked forward to that message as they gave the preschooler mostly trivial errands like going down the street to the hardware store to bring back a bucket of steam.

I was about six years old when my dad put a $100 cash deposit on a real home, where they lived for the next three decades. The family moved out of the upstairs apartment over the laundry, to a place that had grass instead of pavement and neighbors instead of storefronts. My three older sisters and one older brother now lived among the Jews and Italians who were "up the hill" in more affluent suburbia. I admire my parents for their decision to get out of Chinatown to an all-white suburb in New Jersey. Although racism was endemic, so were some encouraging stereotypes of Asians being good at math and art. The synergy of these stereotypes and a community-supported school system enabled me to do well academically.

Our laundry in New Jersey was a very small Chinese island in a sea of Italian American culture. Most of my playmates as a child and many neighbors were of Italian descent. Both shared immigrant status, strong family ties and strong sense of community. Chinese children with Italian first names were common, like Anthony Wong or Lisa Lee. I worked my way through college in an Italian restaurant and found I was quite compatible with the Italian ethic. Here, as in many of my other part time jobs, I gained special favors as the boss assumed I was honest and hard working since I was Chinese. While still a teen as an usher in a theatre, the owner gave me the keys to the place after just two weeks on the job although others had much more seniority. The stereotype of Chinese, like being good at math, worked to my favor as this unearned compliment eventually became self-fulfilling. I hated working in the laundry and was taunted by other kids for it. In retrospect I learned a work ethic that is sometimes called typical of Asians.

The work seemed endless, 11 hour-days, six days a week. I developed great study habits, as I preferred doing homework to the manual labor in the laundry, and it was the only acceptable excuse for not working. Two ironing tables were in constant use, and the third "overload" ironing table was my desk. The empty wooden crates that once contained laundry starch stood on end serving as chairs for both the employees and the family. I would hammer more nails into the crates as they got loose and creaked. This was not altruistic, as a really creaky crate would sometimes pinch your butt and draw blood. So I kept those crates hammered tight.

Asians were tolerated, but Blacks, or Colored as they were called then were not. There were none in town at night. They would arrive in public transportation each day to work and clean houses. We employed four Negro women in our laundry, two operating the shirt presses, and two doing hand-ironing. I and the other preschool neighbor kids knew them as chocolate ladies, who earned a few cents per shirt for their work. One of the chocolate ladies was the mother to a girl who was just one year younger than me. She often marked her daughter's age by asking mine. Her daughter died of scarlet fever while very young, so telling my age was a sad moment. It did not seem right that some kids survived and others did not based on race.

Businesses were divided among ethnic groups. Colored people did not own businesses, but it was acceptable for them to work for others and the laundry employed four colored women. We did the shirts wholesale for several other Chinese laundries in the area. Dry cleaning was a different business owned by Jews, who would subcontract the white cotton shirts to us. The Italians did the actual washing and bulk delivery in a truck with a colored driver. We did the starching, ironing, folding, wrapping and hanging. My dad hired off-duty police (who seemed to lose their ethnic identity in uniform) to drive the delivery van. This gave the laundry some automatic protection.

I was trained to find gas leaks in the boiler room by holding a lit match on the pipe joints. I was in charge of scraping leaky asbestos gaskets from the boiler ports with a screwdriver and wire brush, something that today would require adults in Hazmat decontamination suits. Another one of my jobs was to paint the baseboards around the laundry with chloridane, an EPA-banned insecticide effective against cockroaches. I knew I did not want to inherit this business.

Having purchased the shirt press and boiler with the loan, Dad advertised for wholesale shirt laundering and pressing. A wholesale wet-wash company did the washing while my parents did the sorting, marking, pressing, packaging and deliveries. Our customers were tailors who paid 12 cents a shirt. Dad was fortunate in being able to hire black labor from the south, who were willing to do hard labor since American industries did not hire them.

A Chinese laundry is not a very safe place for small children to play, and I was living proof of that. When I was only four, my hand got locked for just seconds inside the red-hot machine that flattened collars and cuffs on a shirt with the press of a button. The common folklore at the time was to put butter on a burn. I remember the butter melting so fast it seemed to vaporize. I must have been screaming my four-year-old head off, but all can recall is seeing a wad of butter turn to liquid. My dad was operating the machine but to this day, I don't know what he thought about burning and crushing his number two son's right hand. He was so resentful about being stuck in the laundry business it was hard to tell where some issues began and others ended.

It was a long and painful recuperation from a third degree burn. The pediatrician said I was lucky being so young, my bones bent but did not break. My mom later said I hid from her when it was time to change bandages, since it hurt. I don't recall that either. I do remember my sisters were jealous as only I could run around naked in the apartment above the laundry. The graft required tissue from my stomach so I could not wear pants or underwear. Air conditioning was unaffordable, so naked made a lot of sense. The heat from the laundry was great in the winter and was hell in the summer. I suspect the devil may have been in the laundry business before the Chinese.

The actual machinery and parts of the laundry were kid toys. About when I learned to walk, I played with a box full of miscellaneous plumbing parts that were removed from the huge steam boiler needed to keep the shirt presses hot. It seems that nothing, even these spent parts, ever got thrown out. So my toy collection just kept growing. On days when the Colored girls were not working, I could build long tunnels to crawl through from empty cardboard shirt box crates that shipped hundreds of finished shirts at a time. One of my favorite toys was a big electric motor from a washing machine. I could jumper the gearbox solenoids with house current and make it change speeds. Once in a while the motor would shift and sparks would fly making sweet-smelling ozone.

I rejected Chinese culture, as it was unacceptable to be a Chink. Celebrations of diversity were not invented yet. There was only one other Chinese family on the other side of town, and they too owned a laundry. The only Chinese person in popular media was a servant on the stereotypical TV show, "Bonanza." So other kids in my grade school called me Hop Sing (the servant's show name). That was the extent of Chinese role models for ignorant Americans in the sixties. The salvation came later with the broadcast of Kung-Fu. All of a sudden it was acceptable to be Chinese, or at least not a good idea to pick a fight with one. There is some irony in that a white actor, David Carradine, taught a generation of Americans to tolerate Chinese people. While a teen I often was surprised to walk by a storefront window and see a Chinese face in the reflection, as everyone I saw outside the looking glass was white. I was culturally white, but did not look the part. This was euphemistically known as being a banana.

We had a somewhat religious devotion to the Sunday afternoon shopping trip to Chinatown. It was all about sights and smells. We would rumble down a stinky old cobblestone road through the New Jersey meadowlands, then a huge garbage dump, today a protected wetland. The noisy squawking sky would be white with seagulls gorging on trash. I held my breath when we passed pungent places like the pork rendering factory. There were many other factories each with its uniquely toxic smell, and I could only imagine how crappy it would be to grow up in those places. It was said that all the pigs left Secaucus but the smell remains. More choking vapor would cloak us inside the Holland Tunnel. Although there was a tollbooth, the real price of admission to New York City was paid in powerful pollutants every entrant was forced to inhale. Emerging on the New York side was dubious relief as it was not fresh air. Downtown Manhattan had a suspicious odor; a mix of rotting garbage and a sharp metallic stench like overheated electrical equipment. Just past Canal Street, the signature smell of stir-fried, thermally abused peanut oil would mask all other scents, announcing the presence of Chinatown.

One parent would keep the car moving while the other one shopped. It is impossible to park in Chinatown, so the ritual was constant circling or standing until the police said move. Thus much of my view of my ancestral Mecca was through a car window. Constant gridlock made traffic lights irrelevant, and the city acknowledged that fact by installing traffic signals with only two lights, instead of three; so all over Chinatown there were no yellow lights. Through the auto glass I watched whole roast pigs emerging from basement smokehouses to be chopped and hung in grocery windows, and saw endless rows of juicy roast ducks hanging by their necks. Runners with crates of vegetables or trays of cooked foods held high in the air would navigate crowds to restock a store. I saw lots of people who looked like me but were, as Mr. Miyagi said, *"same but different."*

Once in a while I could go in and pick my favorites, including salted preserved plums that most Americans think are absolutely gross. On the rare occasion where a legal parking spot was found we would spend more time, perhaps eating in a restaurant. My parents had a ritual of wiping all the utensils and plates with white paper napkins before they ate. I was amazed at the black residue these napkins revealed. Sometimes we visited people living near Chinatown. I met some of my paper relatives in this way. They were introduced as my Uncle Johnny or some other random American surname. I did not speak Chinese and they did not speak English, so most of the time was spent smiling and eating. My real Uncle Tom's meat market was on Mott Street. He was prosperous, as he owned the whole building and was also a landlord. That entire family lived in a cramped apartment over the meat market that was not tidy as there was never anyplace clear enough to sit down. All my cousins worked as Sunday was their busiest time, so there was not much interaction. My cousin Tommy lost his right hand in a meat grinder in that store. So the laundry business was not the only dangerous place to raise a Chinese family.

My Chinese family attitude toward women is awful. When the polio vaccine first came out, there was much consternation about potential harm, causing, instead of preventing the disease, or worse, being fatal. A serious family meeting preceded the vaccinations. It was decided that the risk of having all five children vaccinated was too great. Instead, they picked my sister Diane to get vaccinated. If she survived without incident, then maybe it was okay to send the older sisters, and then maybe the boys. This, of course, terrified my sister and inflicted psychological damage that none should endure.

For fulfillment of the American dream, the laundry delivered like a Chinese curse in an interesting way. Five children were raised, a suburban home mortgage was paid in full, and each of us entered college on scholarships with help from the parents. But in the traditional Chinese sexist mentality, my parents had no intention of sending any of their three daughters to college, as this was a waste of money. It took the intervention of an exceptional high school guidance councilor to complete the applications, get the scholarships, and get my oldest sister into Douglass College. She later earned graduate degrees in foreign languages. My second oldest sister went to Rutgers Newark, but dropped out to get married and raised two kids. My third oldest sister, who was the polio vaccine guinea pig, earned graduate degrees in art and later in computer sciences. She was the New Jersey teacher of the year in the late 1990's and will retire from public school teaching this year. My older brother attended Cornell University, but the hippie culture was more interesting so he lives under an alias in Hawaii growing marijuana.

I ended up in the Agricultural College at Rutgers, because it had the highest admission standards so it was the first place to apply. I did fine academically and went on to the University of Massachusetts for my doctoral degree. I remain the only one in this family's generation to get a doctorate. Many of my generation have the same or better intellect and work ethic, so I attribute this to my parents' decision to move to a mostly Jewish suburb where education was a cultural exigency.

One of the few letters my dad ever wrote me contained the sentence, "now you can find a nice Chinese girl and move into the house." In his way of speaking, he was offering his fully paid home of 30 years in the New Jersey suburbs as a bribe for a Chinese bride. I think he knew full well that the odds were remote; they raised me in a town with only one other Chinese family, and every girl I ever dated was white. The love of my life and mother of my three daughters is a priceless white Catholic girl from Wisconsin. All three of my sisters married white men.

It seemed like the end of the laundry business happened overnight. Those vast expanses of stacks and stacks of starched white shirts, brightening every horizontal surface, suddenly bloomed in a rainbow of color. White cotton shirts gave way to colored permanent press, and that fabric ended demand for laundry and starch. My dad tried to adapt by opening a dry cleaning establishment next door. I learned carpentry by building the internal structure for the new dry-cleaning store. The dry cleaning dream ended when we busted a doorway through the firewall only to discover an embedded sewer pipe. So my family's laundry tradition literally ended at a wall full of waste.

My mom saw the end coming and got a job as a machinist in a nearby factory. She would work the laundry by day and work a full-time night shift in the factory. That pattern could not be sustained, even for someone with a Chinese work ethic. So eventually my dad began working in the same factory in quality control. They sold the laundry business to a Korean immigrant for $5,000. They helped him get started but I doubt if the new owner ever made it profitable. I got summer and night shift work in the same factory as my parents and sometimes we all commuted in the same car. I remember those were happier times. For my parents, working only forty hours a week with occasional overtime was like being on an extended vacation.

Donna M. Wong, *age 55, is Assistant Dean of Campus Life and Director of the Office of Multicultural Programs and Services at Emory University. She taught as an Instructor at the University of Oregon and served as Outreach Coordinator for a TRIO program that assisted first-generation and non-traditional college students. She is co-author of Making a Difference: University Students of Color Speak Out (2002).*

She and her three siblings all graduated from U.C.L.A. They have professional careers in business, politics, and higher education and are active in mentoring and community service.

In 1949, my father and mother opened the Frank Wong Laundry in Hollywood, California. Opening the new laundry was a "village effort." Arriving in Los Angeles from China in 1949, my parents and sister lived with Bill Lee's family for the first month. Bill Lee, a childhood classmate and friend, scouted potential laundry sites with my father. They chose 6105 Melrose Avenue, a Hollywood storefront that became the life-blood for four children and two adults for the next several decades. The laundry was situated in the middle of a city block of brick buildings in a middle class neighborhood. The neighboring businesses were an advertising agency, a family doctor, a printer, and a grocery store (later, a lighting wholesale office). The John C. Fremont Public Library, a second home for me and my siblings, was on the corner. The rent was $70/month. The two friends spent about $500 for building materials to construct the laundry ironing tables, counters, and a wall that partitioned the business area from the living area. When the Frank Wong Laundry closed in 1984, the rent had risen to $950/month---but the initial primitive homemade furnishings and fixtures remained unchanged over the 35 years. The two people, my parents, who opened the laundry were the two people who closed the laundry---there was never a third employee.

Many of our customers lived in the neighborhood or worked in close-by office buildings related to the movie industry. Some of the neighbors were children that went to the same public schools we did. Some of our teachers knew that we owned the laundry and one teacher was a customer. I remember the embarrassment in thinking that the more affluent students must have labeled me the "laundry girl" who lived in the back of the laundry.

Our family lived in the back of the laundry from 1949 until 1957. The laundry-home was a storefront, long and narrow, approximately 75' x 20'. The laundry business was conducted in the front 40' and the "residence" encompassed the rear 35'. The entire structure had a bare concrete slab floor except for black rubber mats in places where my parents stood and ironed all day. A plywood wall from floor to ceiling, built by my father and his friends, separated the residence and laundry sections. A curtain covered "doorway" provided passage from front to back. The flowered curtain was raised during work hours and lowered after business after hours to provide a small sense of privacy from the passing traffic outside the storefront's floor to ceiling glass window. Behind that curtain, we managed to cook, eat, study, play, and sleep in the open living space that included three beds, radio, one baby crib, storage shelves, a closet area, and another ironing table.

At the rear of the living quarters was the kitchen area with a large sink, a gas stove, a dining table, and refrigerator. My father made most of the furniture--- very basic tables, stools, and shelves. To maximize our living space, we bought folding chairs that could be brought out when needed and then stored away. We had one TV, a small portable radio, a record player, and our bicycles all jammed into this functional living quarter. We did not have a full bathroom, only a tiny toilet room located by the back door. To bathe, we boiled water from the kitchen sink--- the kitchen sink had only one coldwater tap---and poured the boiled water into a big tin washtub for quick sponge baths. My father nailed wooden boards over the rear windows to prevent anyone from peeking through.

Daylight came through a large window framed near the 16' high ceiling at the rear of the building. Overhead commercial fluorescent tube bulbs provided the rest of lighting in the living section. The walls, originally painted white, turned a dingy grey over the years. We never re-painted the walls nor decorated in any other way. I especially remember the very high plaster ceilings because as I lay in my single fold-up bed, I would imagine differently shaped cracks as animals or a multitude of disparate inanimate objects.

My mother cooked, and the children set and cleared the table, and washed and dried the dishes. We four siblings sat near the gas stove and ate our meals together. My father sat and ate his meals at a little table strategically positioned in the doorway between the laundry front and the living space. He'd also sit there on his "breaks" while smoking his cigarettes. From that vantage spot, he could watch for customers. My mother would eat at the ironing table, closer to my father's table in the hallway, after we had been served.

In 1956 my father began looking to purchase a home. Most homeowners in the Hollywood neighborhood near the laundry wouldn't sell to him because of de facto discriminatory housing practices in place at the time. Some explicitly told him they didn't want to sell to Chinese. Consequently, he looked in neighborhoods farther toward downtown Los Angeles and found a home in a racially-mixed area on Normandie Avenue in 1957. The new home had little impact on our daily routines. There was no one other than my father and mother to open the laundry in the morning and greet the customers. We did sleep at "home" but spent most of our waking hours at the laundry. Monday through Saturday we arrived at the laundry at 7:15 a.m. for breakfast and headed home at 8:30 p.m. after having dinner at the laundry (and sometimes later if work required it). The laundry address remained our "official" residence so that we could attend schools in the Hollywood district, which were considered better quality schools than those near our house.

My parents assigned the children daily chores in the laundry. In retrospect, the distributed chores helped develop a strong work ethic and a sense of teamwork and loyalty. We contributed in whatever way we could toward a mutual goal of making a living. Only an excuse of heavy homework could get us out of the work chores. The oldest, Suzi, had to fold pajamas. Eddie folded bath towels. Warren, the youngest child, folded handkerchiefs. I folded pillowcases. By sixth grade, I served the customers and learned how to collect money and make change. I soon became familiar with the customers and their voices. I would run out from back of the wall partition when I saw or heard a nice customer come into the store. Then I would take care of the transactions and sometimes even score a tip---"keep the change, kid." I'd quickly tuck the loose change into my pocket.

All the siblings helped out at the counter to serve customers when we were not studying. We translated for my father if customers gave elaborate requests or inquiries. My mother earned extra money through her sewing skills, such as turning a collar or repairing a tear. Later, while in high school, I learned to do touch up ironing of shirts and earned 3 cents per shirt. I preferred ironing in the back of the laundry so no one would see me doing it.

Initially, we sent incoming laundry out to a larger Chinese laundry to wash all the items, and the same held for the dry cleaning. The clothes were returned to us in clean piles. My parents ironed, pressed, and folded the clean laundry before sorting and wrapping the items into a package for the individual customer.

I recall that my father sang Chinese songs while ironing. The melodies would drift to the rear living quarters. My mother taught us children's songs as we were growing up. Their pleasant singing helped pass the time, transporting them to happy memories of their native country, and setting a peaceful melodic tone in our home. My father smoked cigarettes when he took a short break. One of my fondest memories is my sitting on his lap and him blowing smoke rings for me to burst with my fingers.

Dealing with customers could be challenging though most transactions with customers would be routine, short, and curt:

The customer grunts hello and hands over the laundry ticket; my father walks to the shelves, matches the ticket number and pulls out the blue wrapped laundry package, puts it on the counter, and says the price. Money is handed over, change made, and goodbye, customer.

But at other times transactions were confrontational and challenging, and those were the times I most painfully remember. The customers (predominantly white) could be rude, obnoxious and intimidating. As voices escalated, I would shudder, worried that "something bad" would happen to my father. In retrospect, I realize that complaints typify any service business, but to me, the power dynamic was scary, of David versus Goliath proportions. The outsider 'white ghosts' frightened me.

A laundry complaint would play out something like this:

The customer is handed his package; he rips open the package to examine the ironed shirts. He shakes one out---"Hey, there are still wrinkles here....and here....and, look, right there! NOT GOOD ENOUGH! I'm not going to pay for this!" My father bowing, taking back the shirt...."oh, so solee. We do it again....no chargee. come back tomorrow." Or, another complaining customer yelling, pointing out a stain, "I told you to clean that spot! It's still there. Take that out! I don't want to see that spot again!"

Those interactions sting in my memory. The cranky customers caused my parents to gripe afterwards and feel humiliated in their lowly posts of running a Chinese hand laundry.

As a little girl, I often felt anxious when customers came into the laundry not knowing whether the encounter would be routine, pleasant, or argumentative. I would hide behind the plywood wall partition that separated the front section from the back of the store, crouching to peek out of a tiny carved peephole. I felt safe hidden behind the wall.

The four siblings could always find fun together in the empty parking lots behind the laundry. We played freely unsupervised outdoors while our parents worked inside. We climbed the gas meters and metal pipes and entered imaginary worlds. Other neighborhood kids would sometimes join us in to play tag football or an invented game of basketball, aiming the ball at the rungs of pipes as our target "hoop." Sometimes, we rode our second hand bicycles into the luxurious neighborhoods in the Wilshire District.

We became acquainted with all the neighbor business owners. The printers gave us reams of paper to draw on. The family doctor, Dr. Thomas Daily, whose office was next door to the laundry, took care of our colds for free. A grocery market two stores down the street became a frequent stop for penny candies. A Helms Bakery truck would drive into our rear parking lot and blow a whistle. All the workers would come out of their offices and buy from the trays of pastries. My mom would buy us daily sweets. The exposure to desserts developed a strong sweet tooth as the Helms truck served as a substitute oven that we did not have in the laundry.

Frank Wong Laundry grew as other Chinese laundries in the Hollywood area closed down. Emerging business issues particular to Chinese laundries led my father to join and later become Secretary of the Chinese Laundry Business Alliance, an organization of Los Angeles-area laundrymen who met monthly to discuss and solve common business problems. For instance, landlord problems and pending health site inspections could be addressed, understood, and tackled together. The Alliance served as a networking and support group. The Alliance's annual Chinese New Year's dinner party in a Chinatown restaurant fostered a sense of community among the laundrymen and their families. These gatherings of parents and children affirmed the progress the families were making in American society and gave the adults hope and pride their children would have better opportunities.

I was in junior high school when one day an unexpected tempest rocked the foundation of our lives. That was the day my father told us that he had been living under a false identity. Suddenly, he had a new name and a new birthday. I felt shocked and confused. Perhaps I didn't know my father.

My father, Moon Tung Wong, was born in China, in Taishan (Toisan) province in an area called Bok Hang, Cheng An Li Village. His father owned a bookstore in SiuBu. My mother, Siu Fong Yee Wong, also was born and raised in Taishan province in an area San Ba, Lan Hang village. My father and mother eventually would meet during May 1947 in Taishan. My mother, an elementary school teacher, received a letter from a family friend in Boston about a prospective husband returning from the U.S. to China. A go-between arranged to introduce them at his family's house. After a few dates for dinner, dim sum, and movies, they were engaged and married in June. They married again in Hong Kong in August 1947 because a British marriage license enabled easier immigration to the U.S.

Father first came to the U.S. in 1929 at age 20. He established himself as a "paper son" of a "paper father" with U.S. citizenship by paying $1000 in U.S. money for a false identity, Fook Gooy Wong. His older brother had come to the U.S. several years earlier and helped my father's transition. His brother found my father a job in a Chicago laundry where he gathered the experience he needed for his later business venture. Later my father joined his brother to work in a noodle factory. He worked for a while as a welder in a shipyard during World War II. He studied English in a Methodist church in the evenings. His teacher gave him the American name, Frank, because it had the same first letter as Fook Gooy, his Chinese 'paper' name.

The name Fook Gooy became abandoned several weeks after his false brother confessed his own false identity to the Immigration and Naturalization Service. His false brother had confessed to the INS and implicated my father. An immigration officer tracked the lead to the laundry to confront my father on his identity and false papers. My father confessed and that was the day that he and my mother told us that his name and birthday had changed. He established his true identity and birth name, Moon Tung Wong. We didn't know if the change would affect our enrollment in school or if the news would filter to our teachers.

Since three of us children were born in the U.S., our deportation was not a concern. My parents and older sister were permitted to stay as permanent residents. My father re-applied for U.S. citizenship under his true name and became a citizen again in 1969. My mother also sought citizenship. Preparing for the citizenship oral exam, my mother attended Adult School in 1973 to study English as a Second Language. She would take a bus to the local high school Monday to Thursday evenings, and we would pick her up at 9 p.m. before driving home from the laundry. After she passed the citizenship test in 1973, she did not return to school. She said that there was too much work at the laundry, so she could not continue being an English student. Later in life, we siblings would bring home English textbooks for her to read and study. Although she is not fluent in English, she enjoys picking up some English phrases and looking at magazines. We all speak sai-yup Toisan hwa, a dialect of Cantonese. Although my mother was a teacher in China, she was too busy with work to teach us how to read and write Chinese. Our parents wanted us to become fluent in English and not take time away from our English studies. We siblings would speak English to each other but still speak Toisan to my mother.

Seeking a better future in the United States precipitated the tough realities of estrangement from relatives still in China. After the Communists took over China in 1949, communication between U.S. and China stopped. Exchange of letters was not permitted. Throughout the years, both parents sent money home to support their relatives. Through intermediaries, my parents sent money and notes to Hong Kong, which was then transferred to China. Usually it was twice a year for the birthdays and Chinese New Years. They had to save and sacrifice to send $500-800 each year for both sides of the family.
Communication was sporadic to non-existent---how painful that must have been. Stories of my grandmother, how she lost the farm property and forced to live in a shack spread across the oceans to my parents. Before the Communist take-over, my mother had intended to sponsor and bring her brother to the United States; but the political change made that plan impossible. In 1978, President Nixon and Chinese leaders re-opened U. S. relationships with China, allowing

mail as well as visitation by Americans. My father never returned to China. After the laundry closed in 1984, my mother returned to China with a group of friends in 1985 for one month. She happily reunited with her mother and her brothers. They had not seen or spoken to one-another for more than 35 years.

My parents retained contact with Chinese culture through the years. My parents subscribed to the Chinese newspaper and read it daily. My father also enjoyed writing poetry and submitted poems that were published in the local Chinese newspapers. My father practiced Chinese calligraphy during the workday when customer traffic slowed. Or, if time allowed, he took out watercolor paints and painted landscapes. He saved postcard photos and copied the landscapes onto paper in pencil before painting with a brush. His colorful paintings lined the walls of the laundry like an art gallery. He often handmade the frames, which added a primitive folk art look. He truly enjoyed painting and continued the hobby during retirement. Occasionally Chinese friends would drop by the laundry to visit and bring fruit and doughnuts. Only then would my parents deviate from their work routine to attend to the guests. We children would appreciate these visits as we had an opportunity to see our parents socialize in a relaxed non-business setting.

Better able than my mother to converse in English, my father did most of the shopping and all the banking. Every Sunday, he would go to Chinatown and buy Chinese ingredients and foods. He bought daily groceries at a local Western market (one was two stores down from the laundry) and from a nearby Safeway market. When the laundry first opened, he rode the bus to Chinatown for groceries. After he purchased our first car in May 1950, he drove alone to Chinatown each Sunday. As the children grew older, we stayed at home alone while my parents went together to shop in Chinatown. As my mother's English improved, she walked to the neighborhood Safeway Market for weekday shopping.

My mother cooked most of our meals. She did not allow us to cook because we'd likely get burned from the hot splashing oil. My father, who once cooked in a restaurant, occasionally cooked on Sundays, like a special black bean steamed whole fish. We would enjoy the change and delicious seafood. We normally ate Chinese dishes, usually chicken or pork stir fry and vegetables, and rice at every dinner meal. My mother knew how to steam a yellow Chinese sponge cake that we savor for dessert or snack. Our breakfasts and lunches became more westernized over time, and our favorite lunch meals included bologna or spam sandwiches, Campbell's soup, and Chef Boyardee ravioli. Sometimes my mother cooked pungent Chinese herbs that permeated throughout the back living space and drift to the front laundry section. My parents both used Chinese herbal medicines and practices to rid of aches and flu, so we learned to appreciate those distinct cultural perspectives and aromas.

On Sundays, my father said it was important for all of us to go outdoors and get some healthy fresh air. He'd pile us into the car and drive to Griffith Park, Echo Park, and MacArthur Park for the afternoon to play and listen to a free music concert. On rare occasions, we went to the beach. Every Sunday, my father would go to Chinatown to shop and stop at the Wong Benevolent Family Association. As we got older, he took us to the Methodist Church for Sunday school; but this didn't last more than a few months since we complained and were confused by the church rituals. Both my parents were active with the Wong Family Association, so we interacted with other Chinese families during the Chinese banquet ceremonies and holiday programs.

When we were very young, we never went shopping. My father went by himself, driving to Sears Roebuck to buy all our clothes and shoes. In fact, he would take blue laundry wrapping paper and have us stand on the paper to trace the outline of our feet. He'd then show the shoe salesman the outline drawings and purchase the correctly sized oxford shoes for us. By the time we were in junior high school and high school, we went shopping with him or with our friends to buy our own clothes. We did not have a lot of extra clothing, so we shared clothing when possible and passed items down. We were constantly reminded to be frugal. For the first two years of the business, my parents barely made ends meet. They lived by the Chinese saying, "if you save, you will have" (tieu/you, a Chinese rhyme). They saved money to send home to relatives in China and saved to buy a home. One example stands out: My mother made hand-sewn clothing from the 50-pound rice bags for us girls to wear. Nothing that could be recycled for another use was wasted or thrown out.

For entertainment, we avidly listened to the radio for sports and top 10 music stations. Our parents did not allow us to watch TV, so we'd sit around reading, doing homework, and listening to the radio. They expected us to do well in school and not be distracted by TV. We got along; if we argued in raised voices, we drew our father's attention, and he quickly marched back to whip us all with a bamboo stick feather duster. Ouch! I remember that my parents took us to only a few movies---*The Parent Trap, Mary Poppins, and The Music Man.* They went alone to the Chinese movies only a few times. As we grew older, they allowed us to walk to a local movie theater on Saturdays to watch a double feature. And the more we were allowed to move on our own away from the laundry, the more we interacted with outsiders for friendship and advice.

Several people served as cultural bridges for us through their friendship and mentoring. My best friend Maryon, an upbeat, nice Jewish girl, lived about six blocks away. We met in kindergarten and spent almost every day together. I invited her inside our laundry, and she invited me to her house to eat and play. She was very intrigued by our lifestyle and gave affirmation to the way we worked together as a family unit. She was open to trying our Chinese food and language. Together we went through public schools together and spent time riding our bikes for hours and going to the public swimming pool, birthday parties, and dances. Maryon introduced me to other cultural activities that would not have been accessible, such as music concerts at the Hollywood Bowl, theater plays, and art museums. We remained friends through college (until her early death from cancer).

A few of the laundry customers also noticed us four siblings and treated us with friendly attention. They gave us dolls and American board games. They introduced us to hobbies of stamp collecting and coin collections, which then motivated us to sort through the daily cash box to find pennies, nickels, dimes and quarters minted by year to place in the coin books. A few customers brought in hand-me-down clothing for my older sister and jewelry for my mom. For Christmas, we received a few fruit baskets and fruitcakes. Mrs. Greer, a customer and neighbor around the corner from us, hired me to baby-sit on occasion. There inside her house, I saw a different lifestyle of American living---furniture, kitchen, snack foods, toys spread all over, and children who openly argued and fought.

One customer, Mr. Schaffer, gave my brothers a tennis racket and a few tennis balls, telling them that it was a good sport to learn. We redeemed "Blue Chip' stamps issued by stores for purchases of merchandise to get a second new tennis racquet. Both brothers skillfully played on the high school tennis team. Today, my younger brother Warren teaches and coaches tennis and plays in competition matches. Mr. Schaffer also took my brothers to a Los Angeles Angels vs. New York Yankees baseball game. Another customer who worked at Paramount Studios took us to see the filming of the popular TV show, *Bonanza*. That was a real highlight to see the behind-the-scene action. My older brother Eddie earned an MFA in film at UCLA and became a documentary filmmaker. A woman customer brought us magazines about arts and crafts. When I was in junior high school, she invited me during the summer to her house a few blocks from the laundry and showed me how to do decoupage and other arts and crafts. This experience began my interest in art. I later majored in art at UCLA, completing a focus on printmaking and painting. My etchings became part of an art display that traveled the world to different United States Information Agencies (USIA) in the 1970s.

A significant mentor in my childhood was Miss Marjory Hopper, the children's librarian at the John C. Fremont Library located at the corner, only three stores from the laundry. We went to the library daily to do our homework and to browse for two to three hours a day. The entire library staff treated us kindly. Miss Hopper led story hours during the summer, and she involved all of us acting in the skits, puppetry, and story telling. She taught us how to blow bubble gum and often gave us treats to eat. Most importantly though, she encouraged us in school and motivated us to read all kinds of fiction, try out new authors, and follow our interests with research.

We literally grew up in the library, moving from the children's picture book section to the juvenile literature, and finally over to rooms for adult fiction and non-fiction. As we became older, we read daily newspapers and an assortment of magazines that opened our eyes to American life, politics, and cultural trends. We had access to the latest best sellers. My goal was to read all the fiction books from A-Z. This dedicated exposure to reading strengthened our English language skills since only Cantonese was spoken at home. For escape, I liked to read *Seventeen Fashion Magazine* and *Photoplay* to learn about Hollywood celebrities.

In high school, the library hired me on a part-time basis at the library to shelve and check out books. When I got accepted to UCLA, I even considered becoming a librarian due to Miss Hopper's influence. Miss Hopper belonged to the Hollywood Professional Women's Club and told me stories about their meetings, volunteer service, and group travel. During birthdays, she would take me out to lunch at nice restaurants and teach me how to order from a menu. My parents never took us out to dinner besides the mandatory Chinese holiday banquets in Chinatown. I recently visited her, and she was pleased to learn that I had become a co-author of a book on higher education and students of color.

My parents regarded education as the way to become successful, so it is not surprising that all four of us Wong children strived to be high achieving students. They limited our television viewing time and urged us to study during the summer. One splurge was their purchase of an entire set of the World Book Encyclopedia and Child Craft books so that we would learn more and read on our own. Due to their unfamiliarity with the American culture and educational system, they did not place professional expectations upon us to become doctors or lawyers. They simply urged us to do well and find a livelihood that would provide economic stability. As first generation immigrants, they couldn't provide much detailed advice, so they relied on our schoolteachers and counselors to show us the way to go to college.

The dreams of a better future for family continue through the current generation of the Frank Wong children and grandchildren. My sister, Suzi, the oldest, earned a national merit scholarship and immediately moved away from home her freshman year at U.C.L.A. She later taught English as a Second Language and currently serves as a major gifts officer at a flagship university. We younger three followed her path to U.C.L.A., graduating and moving on to professional careers.

When we graduated college, we all gave our diplomas to our parents, and they proudly mounted them on the walls of our living room.

For my part, much of my professional career has been devoted to helping immigrant and non-traditional, first-generation college students, and students of color. I enjoy meeting students and assisting the younger generation to discover their dreams and achieve their goals. For the 1.5 or second-generation Asian American students, I particularly relate to their issues in negotiating identity and developing personal and professional goals. As an administrator, I have found my voice and place to make a positive difference. I strive to improve policies of access, financial aid, and quality of life for students of color, international students, and fellow staff at the university.

On a personal note, I have come a long ways from being the little girl in the laundry who hid behind the wall, fearful of the outside world. I wish to thank and acknowledge the hard physical work and sacrifice of my parents to enable us children to flourish and attain the American dream of opportunity, free will and transformation. Even though I felt embarrassment as I was growing up regarding my parents' occupation as laundry operators, I now realize that they were extremely smart, successful entrepreneurs who provided security and stability to the family within this unique ethnic occupational niche. I am fortunate and grateful for their perseverance to endure the bitter life so that we children would have a better life and a rich bank of childhood memories.

Overview From These Reflections

The observations of these "children of the Chinese laundry" about the lives of their parents corroborate accounts of work experiences reported by laundrymen of earlier generations presented throughout this book. Additionally, as a whole the experiences the children had growing up in a laundry were remarkably similar. Their reflections on the impact of this life show compelling confirmation in many respects.

As noted earlier, during exclusion, most laundrymen gained entry by purchasing the papers of persons who were exempt such as the sons and daughters of merchants. Many laundrymen also had to resort to 'illegal' documents to bring children and other relatives. A dark shadow always hung over on their future, as the risk of detection of their false identities, and subsequent deportation, was an ever-present fear.

Chinese laundrymen, and the few wives able to come over, did not speak or understand much English. Their American-born children, quite understandably, learned Chinese ways and language at home from their parents before becoming proficient in English when they began to attend school. They then became the translators and interpreters for their parents, one or both of whom, did not know or have any time to learn English.

Growing up in the laundry, young children spent much time playing inside or near the store. The front area as well as the work area of the laundry served as a playground for them. The parents could work and still attend to the needs of young children and monitor their older children. They almost always knew where their children were in marked contrast to working parents that were separated from their children all day. The children may not have always welcomed such close monitoring or their parents' expectation that they help work in the laundry, but it did teach them the importance of discipline, the difficulty of earning a living, an appreciation of the struggles their immigrant parents faced, and a resolve to improve their station in life to avoid becoming laundry operators themselves.[203]

Starting at an early age, children learned to serve customers when they dropped off or picked up their laundry. During slow times, they did their homework in the store but also managed to sneak in play during work breaks. (See Figure 60).

Figure 60 Left: Like many laundry children, Suzi, Eddie, Warren and Donna (l-r), lived in the crowded back of their laundry, 1962. Right: The Wongs placed a priority on education and saved to buy an encyclopedia set for their children. Courtesy, Wong family.

Some children sorted the day's finished laundry to combine items belonging to each customer. Others also prepared packages for customer pickup by wrapping them in bundles but they also squeezed in some play during their work breaks (See Figure 61).

---

[203] Most of these benefits of the hand laundry also held for other small businesses that Chinese families operated such as neighborhood grocery markets and restaurants but the laundries were much more numerous until the early 1900s.

**Figure 61 Left: Some 10 year olds worked, binding laundry bundles. Courtesy, Elwin Xie.
Right: Others, like the author, used work breaks to act out their dreams.**

As children grew older, conflict with parents developed as
confusion and differences inevitably arose over cultural issues. Children,
especially those born and raised here to immigrant parents eventually
faced a clash of cultures and dilemmas choosing between American and
Chinese customs and values. A good example is the conflict created when
children wanted freedom and choice in marriage decisions while their
parents wanted them to have only Chinese partners.

As Chinese, the children encountered varied reactions during
interactions with laundry customers, school classmates and teachers, and
non-Chinese acquaintances. At one extreme, they faced prejudicial
treatment but on the other hand, they also experienced genuine and
consistent attempts by some non-Chinese to reach out, befriend, guide,
and accept them. Some felt embarrassed by their parents' occupation and
did not want their non-Chinese school friends to know about this
background.

Children of laundrymen recognized the importance of education as a key for avoiding low status occupations. Their parents encouraged this attitude and willingly made financial sacrifices to help their children devote maximum time and effort to their schoolwork. As amply illustrated in the small sample here, they took advantage of the opportunities to gain education afforded by the lives of hardship endured by their parents. The sacrifices and unwavering support of laundrymen enabled their children to have better opportunities in life and achieve successes that fulfilled the hopes and dreams denied to them.

A personal observation about my Chinese laundry life:[204]

I also grew up in a Chinese laundry, and I experienced many of the same feelings expressed by the other "children from Chinese laundries."[205]   I shared some of the invaluable lessons that I learned while growing up in my parents' laundry in Macon, Georgia (where we were the only Chinese in the whole town) in a talk in Atlanta to its Asian American community in 2006. Here is a slightly edited version of this talk.

****

Good evening, I am honored to have this opportunity to speak to you tonight on this occasion to celebrate the remarkable achievements of tonight's honorees.

Let me start with what might seem to be a digression. Many of you may not know it, but this past Thursday was "National Take Your Child to Work with You Day." The rationale behind this concept is that children should get a chance to see what their parents do at work, even if just for one day a year.

This is not a bad idea. I know, because I had the chance to watch my parents work when I was growing up. I worked with our parents in our laundry, not just one day a year, but everyday. It got so that I often hated having to work in the laundry, but I now must admit it did teach me some valuable lessons.

1. Work is hard. Ben Franklin, as we all know said… *"Early to Bed, Early to Rise…"*well, he never talked to a Chinese laundryman for even though my parents went to bed early and got up early… six days a week, 52 wks a year. It did not exactly make them any healthier, or wealthier, but perhaps wiser.

2. Murphy's law (If it can go wrong, it will) also applies in the laundry.
When the hired help doesn't come in, the work must still be done.
When machinery breaks down, the work must still be done.

3. The customer always thinks he is right, even when he is wrong Some customers thought we lost clothes that they later admitted they had never brought in… but had misplaced or left at home.

4. Golden Rule: Treat Customers the way you wanted to be treated… this did not always work, but it was a good starting point.

5. Learn how to 'read' or size up customers, I learned how to pick easy to serve customers to wait on, and let father deal with the obnoxious ones.

6. Dealing with many *illiterate* customers, both white and black, quickly taught me the value of being able to read and write and why education is so important.

---

[204] John Jung, "All I Really Needed To Know, I Learned In A Chinese Laundry," Keynote Address, *Who's Who in Asian American Communities in Georgia Awards and Gala.* Omni Hotel, Atlanta, Georgia, April 29, 2006.

[205] Jung, *Southern Fried Rice: Life in A Chinese Laundry in the Deep South*

7. Develop problem-solving skills. For example: Lost tickets were the bane of our existence. By the way, just how the expression, *No tick-ee, no wash-ee,* arose is a mystery to me. We always had to find the laundry, even without a ticket but we had to open, and rewrap, many bundles to find the right clothes

8. Get organized because Time is money: In a laundry, you have to do more than just wash and iron clothes; after that you must sort and reassemble finished items for each customer and to do this efficiently you need to be organized and have a good memory.

9. Money Does Not Grow On Trees, (although it sometimes fell out of clothes). Our parents did not indulge us, *or themselves,* with material items, but they always provided for essential needs especially if it had to do with our schoolwork.

10. Family cooperation is essential for survival… we all had to pitch in and work together in order to make a living.

Now I want to conclude by contrasting two conceptions of the laundry life.

First, the Customer's view, a "romanticized" view (imagine background music: *"Laundryman, My Laundryman," to the tune of 'Chinatown, My Chinatown")*

This view can be illustrated in an old laundry commercial where:

> A white customer asks a Chinese laundryman:
> *How do you get the shirts so white?*
> The laundryman proudly but solemnly answers:
> *ANCIENT CHINESE SECRET!*

In other words, the white ad writer had the laundryman imply *that* Chinese were born with a secret *magical power* to transform dirty, smelly clothes into clean fragrant clothes. This stereotype shows that society saw Chinese as experts, but only in this one area.

But there is a second view, that I will call the "Realistic" Philosophy, which I believe better represents the view that Chinese laundrymen themselves held:

"Children, aspire to something higher in life than doing other people's dirty laundry. You can control your own future with knowledge and education. My dream is that our laundry will provide the finances for you to get this education.

In conclusion, we must recognize that no matter how successful we may be, we did NOT do it alone. We stood on the shoulders and sacrifices of our parents and families, strengths of our Asian cultures that we must pass on to the next generation.

8. Chinese Laundries in Historical Perspective

Soapy white water give you nothing pretty,
Washing clothes not building battleship.
I say too is no great big deal—
Wash yourself in blood washing other man's sweat?
Would you doing that? Would you doing that?[206]

Although Chinese laundries now have become as rare as drive-in movie theaters, at one time they were one of the major, if not the most important, economic engines for the Chinese. The laundry allowed them and their children to survive despite the racist animosity and hostility from white America. The arrival of the Chinese in the last half of the 19th century coincided with the rising demand for commercial laundries that outstripped the supply of laundry services. The expanding industrial revolution was changing the country from an agrarian to an urban society.

Combined with the denial of other work to Chinese, it appeared as if every town and community in the country had at least one Chinese laundry by the early 20th century. One might wonder how Chinese immigrants would have managed under the inhospitable conditions they faced if they had come a century earlier, or later. Had they come a century earlier, there would have been less demand for laundry services for many reasons including a lower value on cleanliness in general and the tradition of wives and mothers doing laundry at home. Had they arrived a

---

[206] From Wen Yiduo *"A Laundryman's Song"* Translator: Hsu Kai-yu, *Harvard Journal of Asiatic Studies* 21, (1958): 147-148.

century later, laundry would have been less viable as a business because technological improvements enabled homes to have hot and cold running water, affordable easy to use home washing, drying, and ironing equipment, better cleaning products, and new fabrics that were easier to clean and maintain.

During the early years of the exclusion era, Chinese were able to survive by accepting 'women's work' such as washing and ironing laundry or cooking meals. Chinese became their own bosses, no longer dependent on whites for jobs as laborers.[207] Owning their own businesses, initially laundries and, to a lesser extent, grocery stores, followed later by neighborhood restaurants, the Chinese were able to earn much more security and higher income than they could working on salaried jobs such as construction, farm, factory, or white collar office jobs. Those who owned laundries would help later newly arriving immigrants learn how the laundry business operated and then assist them with the acquisition of their own laundries.

Public Views of The Chinese Laundryman

Much of the work of many laundrymen was highly visible to the public. As passersby walked past the front window of the laundries, they could readily observe laundry workers ironing shirts. What were the impressions formed by the public about these men who seemingly worked endless hours doing much the same activity over and over?

---

[207] Paul Ong, "An Ethnic Trade: The Chinese Laundries in Early California," *Journal of Ethnic Studies*, 8, no. 4 (1981): 95-112.

Based only on witnessing a laundryman at work in his storefront, one man who had never patronized a Chinese laundry concluded that laundrymen were somewhat odd or incomprehensible, noting:

> They seemed to me to be very small, very expressionless of countenance, and either very hard working or very indifferent to the ordinary pleasures, comforts and interests of life, since they seemed always to be in their shops ironing when other shops were closed and their proprietors elsewhere.[208]

Another man, who was a laundry customer, made this more favorable and sympathetic comment:

> The Chinese laundryman seems to me a small, quiet, and conscientious man. I would trust him to do good work and give honest service. He seems hardly a part of the American community. I have often wondered what he does with his spare time of which he doesn't seem to have much. I don't visualize him as being a mysterious person.[209]

Watching a laundryman's tireless labor sometimes even produced unintended positive influences on observers. Thus, a Yale University graduate student in the late 1950s recalled that the sight of the neighborhood laundryman, Sam Lee, slaving away ironing shirts late every night, served as an inspiring role model of motivation that often helped him and a fellow graduate student survive the rigors of graduate school.[210]

> Whenever late at night I'd grow weary of studying or writing something throughout graduate school at Yale, I'd look out the 2nd-story window beside my desk and there below would be "Sam Lee" ironing some more shirts for 25 cents apiece. I'd tell myself, "If Sam can work such long hard hours for a

---

[208] Siu,16.

[209] Ibid. 17.

[210] Personal communication. Gordon S. Bower, Dec. 24, 2005.

few quarters, I should be able to work at least that hard to get a job as a college professor." I remember feeling a mixture of admiration for him, shame, guilt, and inspiration to live up to his example.[211]

Did Chinese "Invent" The Laundry Business?

White-owned steam commercial laundries existed in the U.S. and England well before the Chinese immigrants opened their hand laundries in the mid 1800s.[212] Yet, for a period it was their hand laundries in small and large communities all over the country that dominated the trade so it could at least be argued that the Chinese 'expanded' the acceptance of the laundry business.

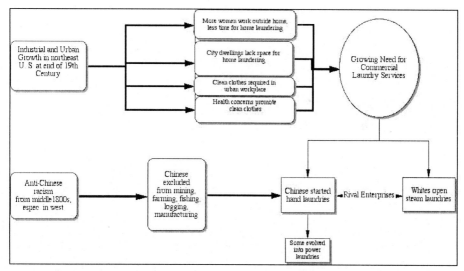

Figure 62 The historical context for Chinese entry into the growing laundry business.

[211] Gordon S. Bower, "Comments at the retirement of Philip Zimbardo, " 2004. http://www.zimbardo.com/downloads/Phils%20Retirement%20Speech.pdf (accessed Dec. 10, 2005). Bower and Zimbardo became two of the leading research psychologists in the world before retiring from Stanford University

[212] Wang, "No Tickee, No Shirtee," 155-158.

An increased demand for laundry service developed in the industrial states of the East from 1870 to 1920, as the lifestyle of a rapidly growing urban middle class needed more commercial providers of household services. More women, especially native-born white women, took jobs outside the home and had less time for domestic chores. This large-scale employment of women outside the home opened commercial opportunities for domestic services, particularly laundry work.[213] Commercial laundries became more feasible with the invention of mechanical washing machines, followed later by electric powered washers and dryers. Demand for laundry services increased with the greater availability of washable fabrics such as cotton. In addition, white middle-class families in urban areas lived in small apartments without adequate space for home laundering equipment.[214]

Chinese Laundries Over The Twentieth Century

Between 1890 and the 1920s, the number of Chinese laundries began to decline noticeably with the extent varying across regions. In other regions such as the East, growing competition from non-Chinese laundries was a major factor. White-owned steam laundries with power equipment gave them advantages of greater capacity. In New York and other large cities, wet wash power laundry plants picked up dirty laundry from small neighborhood laundries such as Chinese hand laundries. They washed and returned the clothes overnight to the small laundries, which

---

[213] Ibid., 160-165.

[214] Joan Shiow Huey Wang, "Race, Gender, and Laundry Work: The Roles of Chinese Laundrymen And American Women in the United States, 1850-1950," *Journal of American Ethnic History*, 24, no. 1 (2004): 58-99.

did the ironing and other hand finishing of the laundry for pickup by customers.

But many customers objected to the garment damage created by machine pressing and preferred the quality of laundry done by hand.[215] Hygiene concerns about contagious diseases also hurt the power laundries, which mingled clothes belonging to other persons in their large washing machines.[216]

However, by the early 1900s the competition from white power laundries, aided by regulations that restricted Chinese laundries, forced some Chinese to close their laundries and switch to other work such as restaurants.

But by the 1920s there was a renewed growth in Chinese hand laundries. In large cities in the east they became 'vertically integrated' by having white-owned wet wash plants pick up clothes for machine washing and return them for the Chinese laundryman to finish by hand.[217] Some Chinese opened wet wash plants, and attracted business from Chinese hand laundries with prices as low as 2.5 cents a pound, about a third lower compared to white-owned rivals although their work quality was often inferior.[218]

During the depressed 1930s, all laundries suffered as many customers could no longer afford their services. It was a turbulent time as

---

[215] Ibid.,254.

[216] Ibid., 259-261., U. S. Health Service. *Public Health Reports*, 32, no. 6 (1917), 230-231.

[217] Wang, 'No Tickee, No Shirtee,' 39.

[218] Ibid., 274, 280.

Chinese laundries and white-owned plants in large cities waged price wars to complete for business. Thus, when a white-owned plant lowered the price of laundering shirts from 15 to 12 cents each, Chinese laundries cut their price to 10 cents. In Chicago a different resolution occurred in 1937, as both Chinese and white laundries agreed to raise prices by several cents.[219] Some Chinese women helped support families working in the sewing factories of the garment industry under sweatshop conditions, one of the few areas for women to work outside of their family businesses. This employment increased when more women immigrated after World War II.[220]

But by the 1940s more Chinese adapted and transformed their hand laundries by adding steam and electric powered equipment that enlarged their productivity.[221] Thus, the Wing Chong Laundry in Alberta, Canada, had installed a washing machine and hot water tank by the 1950s (See Figures 63). During the 1960s, the Union Laundry in Vancouver had the services of a large mangle for ironing sheets (See Figure 64).

Chinese laundries, especially those located near military bases and camps, enjoyed prosperity during the 1940s during World War II because they received substantial patronage from servicemen. The increased profits enabled laundrymen to send money back to help China fight the war against Japan. Many sons of laundrymen were drafted or enlisted in the U. S. Armed Forces, which greatly improved the status of Chinese in

---

[219] Ibid., 228-232.

[220] Bao, "*Holding Up More Than Half the Sky*" 59-61.

[221] Wang, "No Tickee, No Shirtee," 252. The shift from hand laundry was not without problems as machinery occasionally broke down and required repairs and maintenance.

America, but it left some laundries short-handed during this period and many had to close.[222, 223] The exclusion law, which lasted until 1943, also reduced Chinese laundries as it prevented new immigrants coming to replace older laundrymen who died or returned to China.

Figure 63 Interior of Wing Chong Laundry, Alberta, Canada. Courtesy, Glenbow Archives, Photo NA-2979-5.

Adapting their services to the needs of customers, many Chinese laundries added dry cleaning equipment, which yielded a higher profit, and offered mending services.[224] In New York, families that lived in the backs

---

[222] Ibid., 317-319.

[223] After military service, many Chinese men attended college with government assistance. Upon graduation, some were employed in many professions. But others had no choice but to work in their family laundries due to racial discrimination despite having excellent credentials. Kevin Scott Wong, *Americans First: Chinese Americans and the Second World War* (Cambridge: Harvard University Press, 2005).

[224] Wang, "No Tickee, No Shirtee," 294.

of laundries began to seek better housing in residential neighborhoods, freeing space in the laundry to store dry cleaned garments collected from customers to be sent to professional dry cleaning establishments.[225]

But the renewed prosperity was short-lived. The economic prosperity of the 1950s enabled homeowners to purchase improved, affordable home washing and drying machines that were convenient and easy to operate. Self-service laundromats became an alternative to Chinese laundries for people who lived in apartments. Clothing made from new fabrics that were easier to launder became available. All of these factors contributed to the decline of the laundry business.

Figure 64 Harry Yuen and worker using a mangle, 1969. Courtesy, Elwin Xie.

---

[225] Paul Louis Fletcher, SR. "The Chinese wholesale shirt laundries of New York." *Management Research News*, 25, no. 2 (2002): 43.

The Last Remaining Chinese Laundries

In the face of these developments, the remaining days of the Chinese laundry were fast dwindling. Soon their laundries were sold or closed all across the country. The Sam Wah Laundry, started in 1887, had been operated in the Chinese section of St. Louis known as Hop Alley since 1922 by Gee Kee One and Gee Hong, nephews of the original owner. In 1978, this last Chinese laundry in St. Louis, where there had once been 165, was threatened with closure by urban redevelopment. Activists raised funds to gain an agreement to allow these brothers, both then in their 80s with no families and no other place to go, to live in and operate their laundry until they died in the 1980s.[226]

In 2002, the last Chinese laundry in Providence, Rhode Island, Sam Sing Laundry,[227] which had operated for about 90 years, closed its doors. Chinese laundries had existed there as early as in the 1870s. The 1910 Business Directory listed 87 laundries and the 1910 census showed that most of the 272 Chinese worked in laundries. As the Chinese population in Providence dwindled, Chinese laundries closed one by one.

According to the 1885 Norfolk, Virginia city directory, Lee Sing was the first Chinese to open a laundry there. By 1922, there were 30 Chinese laundries in the city but with the later growth of white-operated cleaning and pressing establishments, neighborhood Chinese hand

---

[226] Louisa Lu, "Two Brothers Earn Respect in a Difficult World"
http://www.scanews.com/spot/2002/may/s614/history/story.html (accessed Dec. 1, 2006)
http://www.scanews.com/spot/2002/may/s615/history/story.html (accessed Dec. 1, 2006)

[227] John Eng-Wong "Sam Sing faces closing; laundry business will cease at 121 N. Main after 90 years" *George Street Journal*, March 15, 2002
http://www.brown.edu/Administration/George_Street_Journal/vol26/26GSJ21g.html (accessed Dec. 1, 2006)

laundries became a part of the city's past. The 1995 Norfolk city directory showed only one laundry left, on 35th Street.[228]

Dogon Goon came from China to Portland, Maine about 1914, and opened a laundry in 1918, one of 35 in town. He then returned to marry Toy Goon and brought her over in 1921. After he died in 1940, Toy Len raised their five sons and three daughters while continuing to run the laundry. Later named American Mother of the Year in 1952, she outlasted the laundry, dying at age 98 in 1993.[229]

There are only a few Chinese laundries still in existence such as Joe's Laundry in Atlanta (See back cover), Ching Lee Laundry in San Mateo, Ca., and Chow Keong Hand Laundry in Toronto, Canada (both shown in Figure 65).

Figure 65 Two 2006 Chinese laundries. Left: Ching Lee Laundry, San Mateo, Ca., Courtesy, Mary Gee. Right: Chow Keong Laundry, Toronto, Canada, Courtesy, Jeff Low.

---

[228] George Tucker, "Norfolk's Chinese Heritage Dates Back More than a Century," *Virginian Pilot*, April 2, 1995, J3

[229] Kelley Bouchard, "Chinese Imprint" Portland Press Herald, Feb. 3, 2002. http://pressherald.mainetoday.com/news/immigration/020203chinese.shtml (accessed Nov 24, 2006).

Parallels Between Chinese Laundry And Restaurant Histories

There are interesting similarities in the circumstances surrounding the origins of Chinese laundries and restaurants. Just as Chinese working as domestic servants in the late 19th century acquired experience with laundering many of them also were involved with preparing and cooking meals for families.

Some of them may have later found work as cooks in restaurants or even opened their own restaurants by the end of the 19th century in Chinatowns of mining towns and communities located along major railroad lines.[230] These small restaurants provided meals prepared Chinese style. Their primary customers were other Chinese immigrants, almost all bachelors, who did not have time or facilities to prepare their own meals. Along with the laundry, it was one of the few opportunities for self-employment available to Chinese at the time.

Before 1900, most whites had no interest in Chinese food and disparaged the unfamiliar ingredients in many Chinese dishes. In Virginia City, Nevada, the local newspaper in referring to what Chinese enjoy eating noted, "The long tailed brutes are delighting themselves with worm soup, stewed kitten, roasted puppies, young entrails fried with batter and bird's nest dressing, opium, whiskey, and other favorite viands and drinks."[231] Moreover, since Chinese had been accused of eating rats as well as dogs, their restaurant fare was viewed with suspicion. However,

---

[230] Richard Pillsbury, *From Boarding House to Bistro: The American Restaurant Then and Now* (Boston: Unwin Hyman, 1990), 129-130.

[231] Quoted by Russell M. Magnaghi, "Virginia City's Chinese Community, 1860-1880" In *Chinese on the American Frontier* Edited by Arik Dirlik with the assistance of Malcolm Yeung. (Lanham: Rowman & Littlefield, 2001), 138.

the inexpensive meals served by Chinese restaurants eventually attracted white working-class patrons and by the 1920s many towns all over the country had at least one Chinese restaurant.[232]

Chop suey, a pedestrian dish to many Chinese that was created sometime in the late 1880s, is thought to have created interest in Chinese food among whites. Its exact origins are not clear. One account holds that hungry white laborers went to a Chinese diner late one evening demanding food. There was no food left, so the cook improvised by stir frying some kitchen scraps. The whites found this "chop suey," the Chinese term for "odds and ends" appetizing and hence, it became their favorite Chinese dish.

A more glamorous account is that whites were attracted to chop suey because in 1896 Li Hung Chang, a visiting Chinese diplomat, was served the concoction in a Chinese restaurant. There are many reasons to doubt this version and one view is that Chinese concocted the rumor to generate business.[233] Besides, almost a decade before Chang's visit, Oxford's English dictionary, gave the following 1888 definition: "chow chop svey [sic], a mixture of chickens' livers and gizzards, fungi, bamboo buds, pigs' tripe, and bean sprouts stewed with spices."

Small Family-Run Chinese Restaurants

In running small restaurants to earn a living, as they did with hand laundries, Chinese provided needed services that were in short supply in

---

[232] I examined the manuscript census records for 1910 and 1920 for a sample of cities along the transcontinental rail route: Reno, Elko, Winnemucca, Salt Lake City, Ogden, Cheyenne, Des Moines, and Omaha. There were few Chinese cooks, waiters, or restaurant owners in 1910 but they were numerous in 1920, and in some locations outnumbered laundrymen.

[233] Renqui Yu, "Chop Suey: From Chinese Food to Chinese American Food," *Chinese America: History and Perspectives* (1987): 87-99.

the west during the late 1800s. Work in restaurants, as in laundries, was hard, with long hours for seven days a week. Profits were slim but it offered one of the few ways Chinese could make a living. The typical décor was plain. The small cafes were family-run, with children helping out in food preparation and serving customers. As with laundry families, many restaurant families lived in the back of their stores.

When the Chinese laundry business weakened in the early 1900s in the face of competition from white-owned power laundries, restaurants increasingly took their place as the primary source of self-employment for Chinese.[234] According to the 1930 U. S. census, over 25 percent of Chinese men ran laundries while 15 percent operated restaurants, but by the 1970 census, a complete reversal occurred with less than 2 percent involved in laundries and about 20 percent in restaurant work.[235]

Chinese merchants often combined several businesses at the same location, operating a neighborhood grocery store combined with a small restaurant facility, for example, to serve a limited selection of meals. Some unusual combinations existed such as chop suey and coca cola or a café coupled with a meat market, as illustrated by two examples in Figure 65.

As many whites were suspicious about the ingredients in Chinese dishes, some Chinese restaurants adapted by adding a menu of "American food" such as ham and eggs or broiled chicken to accommodate their

---

[234] Some laundrymen, like Tat Yue did in 1975, switched into the restaurant business. "Switches from Soap to Soup," *Pittsburgh Post-Gazette*, June 10, 1975.

[235] U. S. Census, *1930 General Report, Occupations,* Table 6, 95-97; U. S. Census, *1970 Special Report, Occupational characteristics.* Table 2, 12-37.

tastes.[236] American favorites such as sirloin steak, French fried potatoes, clam chowder, and apple pie appeared on the menu of a 1910 restaurant.[237] A restaurant in Canada featured over a dozen dishes that whites were familiar with, limiting its Chinese offerings to fried rice, chow mein, egg rolls, and chop suey.[238] Successful early "Chinese restaurants" focused on American, and Canadian, fare prepared by Chinese cooks.

Figure 66 Left: Joy Young Café and Market, Augusta, Ga. 1935. Right: Three sons of owner of the New China Café, Santa Rosa, Ca, 1939, Courtesy, Albert Yee.

---

[236] "Chop Suey Resorts: Chinese Dish Now Served in Many Parts of the City," *New York Times*, Nov. 15, 1903, 20.

[237] Shehong. Chen, "Reconstructing the Chinese American Experience in Lowell, Massachusetts, 1870s-1970s." Institute for Asian-American Studies, Boston MA.: University of Massachusetts, Occasional Paper, Jan. 2003.

[238] Sun Grill menu,, Fredericton, New Brunswik, Canada. http://eda.cs.unb.ca/ccanb/ENGLISH/Index/HISTORY/cnbhist/photos.html (accessed Jan. 12, 2007)

Still, some restaurants did not succeed and the owners lost a large investment. In Philadelphia, for example, of the 12 Chinese restaurants listed in 1912, 8 failed by 1915.[239] Some turned to laundry work, just as some laundrymen switched to restaurant operations, each thinking that the other occupation produced a better financial outcome.

However, eventually Chinese restaurants became more successful as Chinese cooks altered their food preparations to appeal to Western tastes. In the 1940s when China became America's ally during World War II, attitudes toward Chinese improved significantly and probably contributed to public acceptance of their restaurants. Chinese food became a popular and inexpensive cuisine for eating out as well as for take-out orders.[240]

Large-scale Chinese Restaurants

Until relatively recent times, families ate most of their meals, prepared by women or by domestic servants, at home. Eating out, in Chinese or other types of restaurants, was not a common practice. The restaurant 'industry' began to thrive with the prosperity of the economic expansion following World War II, and it vigorously promoted frequent dining out more often as a lifestyle, a factor that helped Chinese restaurants grow and prosper. In the 1950s Chinese restaurants become larger, more lavish and stylized, with "Oriental décor" and exotic names

---

[239] Dongzheng 187.

[240] The Chinese stir frying method has also been regarded as healthy but in the 1970s adverse reactions were reported in as many as 25 percent of diners to monosodium glutamate, msg, a common flavor additive used in Chinese cooking, but this finding has not been upheld. See R. A. Kenney, "The Chinese restaurant syndrome: an anecdote revisited" *Food and Chemical Toxicology*. 24 no. 4 (1986): 351-354.

like *Imperial Dynasty, Emperor's Palace,* and *Golden Dragon* to attract the tourist trade, gourmets, and adventuresome diners searching for culinary experiences that differed from their typical fare.

Many dining places in Chinatowns in large cities like Chicago, San Francisco, and New York (See Figure 66) opened to serve this growing clientele. Chinese food was no longer confined to small family cafes serving chop suey, chow mein, and popular American dishes on a few formica-top tables surrounded by bare walls adorned by little else than a Chinese calendar. These cafes, mostly run by new immigrants and their families to serve working class customers, did not compete with the fancier eateries and had its own niche.[241]

The elegant restaurants sought to appeal to the eye as well as the palate of a more sophisticated diner seeking new gastronomic experiences. They offered menus with extensive choices, uniformed waiters, tablecloths and linen napkins, and Chinese art decorations on the walls and in the foyer. The ambiance of the surroundings became an important part of the dining experience. Upscale Chinese restaurants provided an exotic "Oriental" atmosphere in which their food was served. Chefs modified Chinese dishes in ways they thought would please American palates. The food was not always 'authentic' in matching dishes like those served in China, but that was not a flaw as non-Chinese probably would not relish such fare. What was more important was that the food be

---

[241] For accounts of lives of small restaurant families, see: M. Elaine Mar, *Paper Daughter: A Memoir.* (New York: Harper Collins, 1999); Telemaque, *It's Crazy to Stay Chinese in Minnesota.*; William Wong, *American Dream, Chinatown Branch,* (East Bay Express, July 30, 1999). Reprinted in William Wong, *Yellow Journalist: Dispatches From Asian America* (Philadelphia, Temple University Press, 2001), 10-24.

prepared in a style that gave non-Chinese the illusion they were served genuine delicacies.[242]

President Nixon's 'ping pong diplomacy' thawed relationships with Red China by his visit there in 1972. It stimulated greater interest among Americans to seek a wider range of Chinese cuisine beyond the dishes traditionally served in Cantonese restaurants. Popularity of Chinese food continued to grow over the 20th century to become one of the most popular cuisines in most regions of the country.

Figure 67 Port Arthur Chinese Restaurant, N.Y. Courtesy, Library of Congress LC-B2- 5-2

It is ironic that the success of Chinese restaurant cuisine among non-Chinese patrons has been due in part to its exotic features, the same characteristics that racists had used when disparaging Chinese as 'foreign.'

---

[242] Netta Davis, "To Serve the "Other:" Chinese-American Immigrants in the Restaurant Business," *Journal for the Study of Food and Society* 6, no. 1 (2002): 70-81. Shun Lu and Gary Alan Fine, "The Presentation of Ethnic Authenticity: Chinese Food as a Social Accomplishment," *Sociological Quarterly* 36, no. 3 (1995): 535-553.

Another burden for Chinese in the restaurant trade is that patrons expect their prices to be low. Yet, such low prices are only possible by restaurant owners paying workers low wages with no fringe benefits for working long hours under poor conditions that force them to live in crowded and substandard housing. As with Chinese laundries, Chinese restaurants owed much of their success to difficult work for low profit.

Chinese Laundries And Restaurants in Lowell, Mass.

Many aspects of the history of Chinese laundries and restaurant throughout the country between roughly 1870 and 1970 are well reflected in one small industrial New England town, Lowell, Massachusetts.[243] Around 1870 Lowell was a rapidly growing mill city populated by many immigrants, especially Irish and French Canadians. By 1920, it had grown to over 112,000 after which it declined as many textile companies moved to the South where labor was cheaper.

A national depression occurred during the 1870s just about the same time Chinese immigrants arrived there in small numbers, some fleeing the hostility and violence experienced by Chinese in the West. The total number of Chinese in Lowell never exceeded 100, so they were not an economic threat to whites, although in surrounding towns there were some additional Chinese. In nearby towns of Middlesex County, where Lowell was situated, there were as many as 387 Chinese by 1900 but by 1920 their number had dwindled to only 221.

Lowell Chinese Laundry History

In 1900, there were 59 "Mongolians," as they were labeled in the U. S. census record sheets, operating 37 laundries, each typically run by 1 or 2 men. There was a growing need for laundry services in this working

---

[243] Chen, "Reconstructing the Chinese American Experience in Lowell"

class town at this time, with the growth of industry in the town along with an increased national awareness of the important health benefits of hygiene and cleanliness. These conditions offered an opportunity for the Chinese, who were discriminated against in other occupations, to fill this ignored opportunity for self-employed work.

But by 1920, only about half of the town's 79 Chinese still ran laundries as new opportunities arose for Chinese in the newly developing Chinese restaurant business. The decline of Chinese laundries in Lowell, as elsewhere, was due to many factors. Older laundrymen retired or died and there were few replacements due to the Chinese exclusion act that prevented new immigration. Their children benefiting from more education were reluctant to take over the laundries. Furthermore, reduced demand for laundry services stemmed from economic decline in the region during the 1920s from mill closures, and by the Great Depression in the 1930s. By 1950, there were only 12 Chinese laundries left in Lowell, and with the growth of self-service laundromats and home washing equipment after World War II, soon there were none left at all.

Lowell Chinese Restaurant History

The first Chinese restaurant in Lowell opened in 1907 serving Chinese primarily as whites resisted patronizing it. Chinese restaurants adapted their food and décor over the years to attract more non-Chinese customers. By 1920, almost as many Chinese residents were involved in restaurant work as there were in laundries. During the depression of the 1930s, business declined so one restaurant added live music and dancing to attract customers, which enabled it to grow and serve 300 customers at a time by 1937. Acceptance of Chinese cuisine continued to expand, and by the 1970s there were at least 18 Chinese restaurants. In effect, the restaurant replaced the laundry as an economic entry point into business ownership for many Chinese immigrants. As the number of their laundries dwindled, Chinese restaurants increased in Lowell.

Opposite Trends For Chinese Laundries And Restaurants

This relationship between Chinese laundry and restaurant businesses in Lowell was similar in other cities with large Chinese communities. Thus, St. Louis had 165 Chinese laundries in 1929, but only 49 by 1952 and just one by 1980. Figure 68 shows the reverse for Chinese restaurants with only 12 in 1952 but 41 by 1980, and increasing.

Figure 68 The number of Chinese laundries in St. Louis dropped drastically at the same time the number of Chinese restaurants rapidly increased.

The same pattern occurred for Chinese laundries and restaurants in Baltimore. Chinese-owned laundries between 1880 and 1960 listed in the Baltimore City Directory increased from 99 in 1880 to 246 in 1900.[244]

---

[244] "Mapping Chinese-owned Laundries and Restaurants in Baltimore." http://www.law.umaryland.edu/faculty/tbanks/chinatown/image_map.gif (accessed May 26, 2006}.

However, Chinese laundries began to decline after a peak in the early 1900s and only 53 laundries remained by mid-century. In contrast, the first Chinese-owned restaurant was not listed in the Baltimore City Directory until 1900 but the number increased to around 40 or 50 Chinese-owned restaurants over the same time span.

Thus, the restaurant took over the role of the laundry as the main form of self-employment for Chinese immigrants by the middle of the 20th-century. Unlike the hand laundry, which was displaced by home laundries eventually, the Chinese restaurant widened its horizons as it expanded from small greasy spoon diners into palaces of Oriental splendor offering epicurean gastronomic delights for the gourmet as well as all-you can-eat buffets for those with insatiable appetites.

Lessons From The Chinese Laundry

Their laundries are all but gone now, as their services are no longer needed. However, during the years of their existence, these laundries established the first reliable economic pathway for these immigrants and their families to gain admission to a small portion of the Gold Mountain, the goal that originally led them to venture forth to these shores.

Chinese laundrymen did not easily assimilate to American ways. The earliest ones came as sojourners and their hope had been to earn enough to eventually return to their homeland. Strong racial prejudice, long hours of work, poor English language skills, and in many cases, lack of or absence from family, further ensured they would remain foreigners here. Sadly, opportunities for their return to China were greatly diminished when the Communists took control of the country in 1949.

Ben Hecht's 1921 contemplative reflections on the plight of the life of a Chicago laundryman, *"The Soul of Sing Lee"* [245] poetically captured the sense of boredom, frustration, and resignation of the Chinese laundryman. His was a life of monotony and futility day after day, and year after year, trapped in a cycle of cleaning clothes only to have them come back soiled for further cleaning.

> The world of collars, cuffs and shirt fronts does not contain Sing Lee. It contains merely an automaton. The laundry is owned by an automaton named Sing Lee, by nobody else. Now that the day's work is done he will sit like this for an hour, two hours, five hours. Time is not a matter of hours to Sing Lee. Or of days. Or even of years.

> The many wilted collars that come under the lifeless hands of Sing Lee tell him an old story. The story has not varied for thirty-five years. A solution of water, soap and starch makes the collars clean again and stiff. They go back and they return, always wilted and soiled. Sing Lee needs no further corroboration of the fact that the crowds are at work. Doing what? Soiling their linen. That is as final as anything the crowds do. Sing Lee's curiosity does not venture beyond finalities.

But the Sing Lees of the world had a deeper purpose that sustained their unfulfilling and endless work. They endured their lives of drudgery because washing and ironing clothes was not an end in itself but the means toward providing for survival of their families, here or in Guangdong, and giving their children opportunities for a better life.

---

[245] Ben Hecht, "The Soul of Sing Lee," In *A Thousand and One Afternoons in Chicago, 1922-3. Collection of articles from the Chicago Daily News, 1921.* http://www.gutenberg.org/dirs/etext05/8toac10.txt (accessed July 1, 2006).

Bibliography

"1916 Chicago's First Conviction of a White Man for Murdering a Chinese." http://www.ccamuseum.org/Research-2.html#anchor 125 (accessed Aug. 1, 2006).

Aarim-Heriot, Najia. *Chinese Immigrants, African Americans, and Racial Anxiety in the United States, 1848-82*. Urbana: University of Illinois Press, 2006.

"A Blow at Chinese Laundries." New York Times Jan. 20, 1899, 4.

"A Chinaman's Funeral." New York Times, March 7, 1883, 1.

American Federation of Labor. *Report of Proceedings of the Twenty-Fifth Annual Convention*, 1905.

American Federation of Labor. *Some Reasons for Chinese Exclusion. Meat vs. Rice. American Manhood Against Asiatic Coolieism. Which Shall Survive?* Senate Doc. No. 137, 57th Congress, 1st Session. Washington D. C.: Government Printing Office, 1902.

"Asians in the Inland Empire." http://kstephens.topcities.com/soc590/census1880.htm (accessed Aug. 11, 2006).

Aycock, Roger D. *All Roads to Rome*. Roswell, Ga.: W. H. Wolfe Associates, 1981.

Bao, Xiaolan. *Holding Up More Than Half The Sky: Chinese Women Garment Workers in New York City, 1948-92*. Urbana: University of Illinois Press, 2001.

Barde, Robert. "An Alleged Wife. One Immigrant in the Chinese Exclusion Era. Part 2." *Prologue: Quarterly of the National Archives and Records Administration*, 36, no. 1 (2004): 24-35.

Beck, Louis. *New York's Chinatown: A Historical Presentation of Its People and Places*. New York: Bohemia Publishers, 1898.

Bernstein, David E., "Lessons from the Judicial Reaction to the Regulation of Chinese Laundries, 1860s to 1930s" (January 1999). Available at SSRN: http://ssrn.com/abstract=146952 or DOI: 10.2139/ssrn.146952.

_____ "Lochner, Parity, and the Chinese Laundry Cases." *William and Mary Law Review* 41 (1999): 211-294.

_____ "Two Asian Laundry Cases," *Journal of Supreme Court Historical Society*, 24, (1999): 95.

Bouchard, Kelley. "Chinese Imprint" Portland Press Herald, Feb. 3, 2002. http://pressherald.mainetoday.com/news/immigration/020203chinese.shtml (accessed Nov 24,2006).

Bower, Gordon S. "Comments at the retirement of Philip Zimbardo, 2004." http://www.zimbardo.com/downloads/Phils%20Retirement%20Speech.pdf (accessed Dec. 10, 2005).

Bower, Gordon S. Personal communication. Dec. 24, 2005.

Brown, Mel. *Chinese Heart of Texas: The San Antonio Community 1875-1975.* Austin, Texas: Lily On The Water Publishing, 2005.

Brown, Thomas Allston. *A History of the New York Stage: From the First Performance in 1732 to 1901.* New York: Dodd, Mead, 1903.

Bun, Chan Kwok. *Smoke and Fire: The Montreal Chinese.* Hong Kong: Chinese University Press, 1991.

Carter, Kate B. comp. *The Early Chinese of Western United States.* vol.10 Salt Lake City, Utah: Our Pioneer Heritage, 1958.

Chan, Anthony. *Gold Mountain: The Chinese in the New World.* Vancouver, Canada: New Star, 1983.

Chan, Loren. "The Chinese in Nevada: An Historical Survey, 1856-1970." In *Chinese on the American Frontier.* Edited by Arik Dirlik with the assistance of Malcolm Yeung. (Lanham: Rowman & Littlefield, 2001).

Chan, Sucheng. "Against All Odds: Chinese Female Migration and Family Formation on American Soil during the Early Twentieth Century," In Sucheng Chan, ed. *Chinese American Transnationalism: The Flow of People, Resources, and Ideas Between China and America During The Exclusion Era.* Philadelphia: Temple University Press, 2006: 72-73.

_____ *Asian Americans: An Interpretive History.* Boston: Twyane Publishing, 1991.

_____ *This Bittersweet Soil: The Chinese in California Agriculture, 1860-1910.* Berkeley: University of California Press, 1987.

_____ "The Exclusion of Chinese Women, 1870-1943." In Sucheng Chan, ed. *Entry Denied: Exclusion nd the Chinese Community in America, 1882-1943.* Philadelphia: Temple University Press, 1991: 94-146.

Chapman, Mary. "Notes on the Chinese in Boston." The Journal Of American Folklore, 5, 19 (1892): 321-324.

"Charlie Jim's Victim. A Chinese Laundryman Retaliates on His Tormentors."
New York Times, Aug. 19, 1887, 8.

Chen, David Te-Chao . Acculturation of the Chinese in the United States: A Philadelphia
Story. Ph.D. diss., University of Pennsylvania, 1948.

Chen, Edward C. M. and Fred R. Von Der Mehden. "The Chinese in Houston."
http://www.houstonhistory.com/erhnic/history1chin.htm (accessed Aug. 30, 2006).

Chen, Shehong. *Being Chinese, Becoming Chinese American.* Urbana, Il.: University of Illinois
Press, 2002.

_____ *Reconstructing the Chinese American Experience in Lowell, Massachusetts,
1870s-1970s.* Institute for Asian-American Studies, Boston, MA.: University of
Massachusetts, Occasional Paper, Jan. 2003.

Chen, Yong. *San Francisco Chinese: 1850-1943: A Trans-Pacific Community.* Stanford.:
Stanford University Press, 2000.

Cheung, Harry. Interviews with John Jung on 10/20/05 and in 2004.

Chew, Lee. "The Biography of a Chinaman." (Independent, 15, 19 February 1903), 417–
423. Reprinted in *The Life Stories of Undistinguished Americans: As Told By Themselves*, ed.
New York: Hamilton Holt, 1990, 179-181.

"Chicago Workingmen Resolve." *Los Angeles Times*, March 20, 1882, 1.

Chin, Tung Pok. *Paper Son: One Man's Story.* Philadelphia: Temple University
Press, 2000. With Winifred C. Chin.

"Chinese Funeral." *Los Angeles Times*, Feb. 19, 1895, 2.

"Chinese Laundry in California." *The Barre Patriot*, Oct. 10, 1852.

"Chop Suey Resorts: Chinese Dish Now Served in Many Parts of the City."
New York Times, Nov. 15, 1903, 20.

"City Chinese Laundry." *Albany Journal Herald*, March 25, 1893.

"Cunning Chinaman Catches Clothes Coloring Culprit" *Ames Tri-weekly Tribune*,
21 May 1919.

"Dallas Customers Cannot Be Too Careful Where They Send Their Soiled Clothing."
Dallas Daily Times Herald, May 11, 1894, 5.

Davis, Netta."To Serve the "Other": Chinese-American Immigrants in the Restaurant

Business." *Journal for the Study of Food and Society*, 6, no. 1 (2002): 70-81.

Dawson, J. Brian and Nicholas Ting. *The Chinese Experience in Canada Life Stories From the Late 1800s to Today*. http://www.abheritage.ca/pasttopresent/settlement/chinese_laundry_owner.html (accessed June 2, 2006).

Editorial untitled. *New York Times, Sept. 28, 1885*, 4.

Eng-Wong, John. "Sam Sing faces closing; laundry business will cease at 121 N. Main after 90 years." *George Street Journal*, March 15, 2002 http://www.brown.edu/Administration/George_Street_Journal/vol26/26GSJ21g.html (accessed Dec. 1, 2006)

"Find Health Peril in City's Laundries." *New York Times*, Feb. 18, 1917, 17.

Fletcher, Paul Louis SR. "The Chinese wholesale shirt laundries of New York." *Management Research News*, 25, no. 2 (2002): 1-63.

Gibson, Campbell and Kay Jung. "Historical Census Statistics on Population Totals by Race, 1790 To 1990, and by Hispanic Origin, 1970 to 1990, for the United States, Regions, Divisions, and States." *Population Division Working Paper No. 56, Appendix C.* Washington, D. C.: U. S. Census Bureau, 2002.

"Gong/Din Family Immigration Records and History." http://www.tonaidin.net/Bios/Gong-Din_history/history.htm (accessed Aug 15, 2006).

Gong Yuen Tim. "A Gold Mountain Man's Memoirs." Translator: Marlon K. Hom. *Chinese America: History and Perspectives* (1992): 211-237.

Griffith, Sarah M. "Border Crossings: Race, Class, and Smuggling in Pacific Coast Chinese Immigrant Society." http://www.historycooperative.org/journals/whq/35.4/griffith.html (accessed Aug. 6, 2006).

Gyory, Andrew. *Closing The Gate: Race, Politics, and the Chinese Exclusion Act.* Chapel Hill, N.C.: University of North Carolina Press, 1998.

Haddon, John. "The Laundry Man's Got A Knife." *Chinese America: History and Perspectives* (2001): 31-47.

Hecht, Ben. "The Soul of Sing Lee." In *A Thousand and One Afternoons in Chicago, 1922-3. Collection of articles from the Chicago Daily News, 1921.* http://www.gutenberg.org/dirs/etext05/8toac10.txt (accessed July 1, 2006).

Hoe, Ban Seng. *Enduring Hardship: The Chinese Laundry in Canada.* Gatineau, QC: Canadian Museum of Civilization. 2003.

Hoe, Ban Seng *Structural Changes of Two Chinese Communities in Alberta, Canada.* Ottawa: National Museum of Canada, 1976: 349.

Hom, Marlon Kau. *Songs Of Gold Mountain: Cantonese Rhymes from San Francisco Chinatown.* Berkeley: University of California Press, 1987.

"How the Chinese Came to Wales." www.bbc.co.uk/.webloc . www.sacu.org/britishchin#14A8A7, (accessed Dec. 17, 2006).

Hsu, Madeline Y. *Dreaming of Gold, Dreaming of Home: Transnationalism and Migration between the United States and South China, 1882–1943.* Stanford: Stanford University Press, 2000.

Huang,Yunte. *Transpacific Displacement: Ethnography, Translation, and Intertextual Travel in Twentieth-Century American Literature.* Berkeley and Los Angeles: University of California Press, 2002.

Hunter, Tera W. *To Joy My Freedom: Southern Black Women's Lives and Labors After the Civil War.* Cambridge: Harvard University Press, 1997.

James, Ronald M., Adkins, Richard D. and Hartigan, Rachel J. "Competition and Coexistence in the Laundry: A View of the Comstock." *The Western Historical Quarterly*, 25, no. 2 (1994): 164-184.

Jew, Victor. "'Chinese Demons': The Violent Articulation Of Chinese Otherness and Interracial Sexuality in the U.S. Midwest, 1885-1889." *Journal of Social History*, 37 no. 2 (2003): 389-410.

Jin, Dongzheng. "The Sojourners' Story: Philadelphia's Chinese Immigrants, 1900-1925." PhD diss., Temple University, 1997.

Jung, John. "All I Really Needed to Know, I Learned in a Chinese Laundry," Keynote Address, *Who's Who in Asian American Communities in Georgia Awards and Gala.* Omni Hotel, Atlanta, Georgia, April 29, 2006.

Jung, John. *Southern Fried Rice: Life in a Chinese Laundry in the Deep South.* Cypress, Ca.: Yin and Yang Press, 2005.

Karthikeyan, Hrishi and Gabriel J. Chin. Preserving Racial Identity: Population Patterns and the Application of Anti-miscegenation Statutes to Asian Americans, 1910-1950, *Asian Law Journal*, 9 (2002): 1-40.

Ken, Sally. "The Chinese Community in Augusta, Georgia from 1873-1971." *Richmond County History*, 4, no. 1 (1972): 51-60.

Kenney, R. A. "The Chinese restaurant syndrome: an anecdote revisited." *Food and Chemical Toxicology.* 24 no. 4 (1986): 351-354.
Lai, Him Mark. *Becoming Chinese American: A History of Communities and Institutions.* Walnut Creek, CA.: Alta Mira Press, 2004.

"Laundry Protest Heard. Court Reserves Decision on Chinese Objection to Fingerprinting." *New York Times,* July 4, 1933, 20.

"Lee Quong, Chinaman, Commits Suicide Here." *Macon Daily Telegraph,* 1, Jan. 17, 1923.

Lee, Erika. *At America's Gates: Chinese Immigration during the Exclusion Era, 1882-1943.* Chapel Hill: University of North Carolina Press, 2003.

_____ "Defying Exclusion: Chinese Immigrants and their Strategies during the Exclusion Era," in *Chinese American Transnationalism: The Flow of People, Resources, and Ideas Between China and America during the Exclusion Era.* Edited by Sucheng Chan. Philadelphia: Temple University Press, 2006, 1-21.

Lee, Robert G. *Orientals: Asian Americans in Popular Culture.* Philadelphia: Temple University Press, 1999.

Lee, Sharon M. "Asian Immigration and American Race Relations from Exclusion to Acceptance." *Ethnic And Racial Studies,* 12, no. 3 (1989): 369-390.

Li, Peter S. "Ethnic Business among Chinese in the U. S." *Journal of Ethnic Studies,* (1976): 35-41.

"Li Hong, (1899-1962)." http://www.legacy1.net/d_hong.html (accessed Jan. 12, 2006).

Light, Ivan. *Ethnic Enterprise in America: Business and Welfare among Chinese, Japanese, and Blacks* Berkeley: University of California Press, 1972.

Ling, Huping. *Chinese St. Louis: From Enclave to Cultural Community.* Philadelphia: Temple University Press, 2004.

_____ *Surviving on the Gold Mountain: A History of Chinese American Women and Their Lives.* Albany, N. Y.: State University of New York Press, 1998.

Lo, Grace, Interviews with John Jung in 2004-2005.

Loewen, James W. *The Mississippi Chinese: Between Black and White.* Cambridge, MA.: Harvard University Press, 1971.

"Loo Sing Dead from Blood Poisoning. Chinese Laundry Operator Will Be Taken to Atlanta." *Cordele (Ga.) Dispatch,* Oct. 17, 1919.

Lowe, Pardee. *Father and Glorious Descendant.* Boston: Little, Brown, 1943, 244.

Lu, Louisa. "Two Brothers Earn Respect in a Difficult World."
http://www.scanews.com/spot/2002/may/s614/history/story.html (accessed Dec. 1, 2006)
http://www.scanews.com/spot/2002/may/s615/history/story.html (accessed Dec. 1, 2006)

Lu, Shun and Fine, Gary Alan. "The Presentation of Ethnic Authenticity: Chinese Food as a Social Accomplishment." *Sociological Quarterly* 36, no. 3 (1995): 535-553.

Lui, Haiming "The Social Origins of Early Chinese Immigrants." In Susie L. Cassel, ed. *The Chinese in America: A History from Gold Mountain to The New Millennium.* Walnut Creek, CA.: Alta Mira Press, 2002, 21-36.

Lyman, Stanford M. *Chinese Americans.* New York: Random House, 1974.

"Maggie Mark Not Found. She and Chinese Sweetheart Still in Hiding." *New York Times,* Aug. 11, 1900, 12.

Magnaghi, Russell M. "Virginia City's Chinese Community, 1860-1880." In *Chinese on the American Frontier.* Edited by Arik Dirlik with the assistance of Malcolm Yeung. (Lanham: Rowman & Littlefield, 2001).

"Mapping Chinese-owned Laundries and Restaurants in Baltimore."
http://www.law.umaryland.edu/faculty/tbanks/chinatown/image_map.gif (accessed May 26, 2006).

Mar, M. Elaine. *Paper Daughter: A Memoir.* New York: Harper Collins, 1999.

McClain, Charles J. *In Search of Equality: The Chinese Struggle Against Discrimination in Nineteenth-Century America.* Berkeley: University of California Press, 1994.

McClain, Laurene Wu. "From Victims to Victors; A Chinese Contribution to American Law: Yick Wo versus Hopkins." *Chinese America: History and Perspectives* (2003): 53-62.

McKeown, Adam. "Ritualization of Regulation: The Enforcement of Chinese Exclusion 1898-1924." *American Historical Review,* 108, (2003): 377- 403.

Miller, Stuart Creighton. *The Unwelcome Immigrant: The American Image of the Chinese, 1785-1882.* Berkeley: University of California Press, 1969.

Mohun, Arwen P. *Steam Laundries: Gender, Technology, and Work in the United States and Great Britain.* Baltimore, MD.: Johns Hopkins University Press, 1999.

Mun Kow Cheung. Immigration file 1011/199. No. 10657-A Siberia 12/7/11. NARA Laguna Niguel.

Nee, Victor G. and Nee, Brett de Bary. *Longtime Californ': A Documentary Study of an American Chinatown.* New York: Pantheon, 1972.

"New Orleans in 1897. Underwriters Inspection Bureau of New Orleans Street Rate Slips." http://nutrias.org/info/louinfo/1897/chinese.htm (accessed June 12 2006).

"No Laundries in China." *National Laundry Journal* (1905): 41.

Ng, James. "A laundry Background" http://www.stevenyoung.co.nz/chinesevoice/history/lanundrymay03.htm, (accessed June 1, 2006).

Ng, Yeung-Sing. "Life in New York Chinatown." Translator: Vivian Wai-Fun Lee (Hong Kong, 1955). http://www.archives.nysed.gov/projects/legacies/Yonkers/Y_Chinese/questions/Yon_Ch_Qu6.htm (accessed Aug. 12, 2006).

Obituary of Chung Yow Loo. *Chattanooga Times,* Oct. 26, 1961.

Obituary of Ming Loo Lee. *Chattanooga Times,* March 31, 1969.

Ong, Paul "An Ethnic Trade: The Chinese Laundries in Early California," *Journal of Ethnic Studies,* 8, no. 4 (1981): 95-112.

Peffer, George A. *If They Don't Bring Their Women Here: Chinese Female Immigration Before Exclusion.* Urbana: University of Illinois Press, 1999.

Pillsbury, Richard. *From Boarding House to Bistro: The American Restaurant Then and Now.* (1990) Boston: Unwin Hyman.

Pfaezler, Jean. *Driven Out: The Forgotten Was Against Chinese Americans.* New York: Random House, 2007.

"Police Investigate Mysterious Death of Chinese Laundryman." *Atlanta Journal,* April 6, 1922.

"Plundering Chinese Laundries. Arrests of Ruffians Who Have Robbed the Celestial Washermen" *New York Times,* Oct. 30, 1882, 1.

Praetzellis, Mary. "Chinese Oaklanders: Overcoming the Odds." In *Putting the 'There' There: Historical Archaeologies of West Oakland. I–880 Cypress Freeway Replacement Project,* Cypress Replacement Project Interpretive Report No. 2. Eds. Mary Praetzellis and Anthony Praetzellis. Rohnert Park, CA: Anthropological Studies Center, Sonoma State

University. http://www.sonoma.edu/asc/cypress/finalreport/part3.htm (accessed Sept. 12, 2006).

Pugsley, Andrea " 'As I Kill This Chicken So May I Be Punished If I Tell An Untruth:' Chinese Opposition To Legal Discrimination In Arizona Territory" *Journal of Arizona History*, (Summer 2003): 170-190.

Quan, Young, Interview with John Jung, Oct. 16, 2005.

Record Group 85 File 36330/8-5 Immigration and Naturalization Service-San Francisco.

Record Group 85: Records of the Immigration and Naturalization Service, 1787 – 1998 NARA's Pacific Alaska Region (Seattle), Seattle, WA. ARC Identifier: 298983.

Record Group 85: Records of the Immigration and Naturalization Service, 1787 – 1998 NARA's Pacific Alaska Region (Seattle), Seattle, WA. ARC Identifier: 298993.

Rhoads, Edward J. M. "Asian Pioneers in the Eastern United States: Chinese Cutlery Workers in Beaver Falls, Pennsylvania, in the 1870s." *Journal of Asian American Studies*, 2 (1999): 119-155.

Riis, Jacob A. *How The Other Half Lives: A Study among the New York Tenements.* New York: Charles Scribner's, 1890.

Ryo, Emil "Through the Back Door: Applying Theories of Legal Compliance to Illegal Immigration during the Chinese Exclusion Era." *Law and Social Inquiry*, 31, no. 1 (2006): 107-108.

Salyer, Lucy E. *Laws Harsh as Tigers: Chinese Immigrants and the Shaping of Modern Immigration Law.* Chapel Hill.: University of North Carolina Press, 1995.

Sandmeyer, Elmer Clarence *The Anti-Chinese Movement in California.* Urbana: University of Illinois Press, 1939.

Sheung, Kim. Interview with John Jung, August 25, 2004.

Shipley, William C. *Tales of Sonoma County: Reflections on a Golden Age.* Charleston, S.C.: Arcadia Publishing, 2000.

Siu, Paul C. P. *The Chinese Laundryman: A Study in Isolation.* New York: New York University Press, 1987.

"Stabbing His Partner. A Chinaman Carves Up His Business Associate." *New York Times,* Aug 28, 1886, 8.

Stewart, Cal. *Uncle Josh's Punkin Centre Stories.* Chicago: Thompson and Thomas, 1905.

Storti, Craig. *Incident at Bitter Creek: The Story of the Rock Springs Chinese Massacre.* Ames, Iowa: Iowa State University Press, 1991.

Sun Grill menu. Fredericton, New Brunswik, Canada. http://eda.cs.unb.ca/ccanb/ENGLISH/Index/HISTORY/cnbhist/photos.html (accessed Jan. 12, 2007)

Sung, Betty Lee. *The Story of Chinese in America. Their Struggle for Survival, Acceptance, and Full Participation in American Life.* New York: Collier Books, 1967.

"Switches from Soap to Soup," *Pittsburgh Post-Gazette*, June 10, 1975.

Tchen, John Kuo Wei, *New York Before Chinatown. Orientalism and the Shaping of American Culture, 1776-1882.* Baltimore, Md.: Johns Hopkins University Press, 1999.

Telemaque, Eleanor Wong. *It's Crazy to Stay Chinese in Minnesota.* Nashville: Thomas Nelson, 1978.

"The Chinese in Georgia. History of the Waynesboro Trouble—A Mongolian Wins a White Wife." *New York Times*, June 11, 1883, 5.

"The Chinese Washermen. A Visit to the Laundry at Belleville, New Jersey." *New York Times*, Dec. 26, 1872, 2.

"The City of Churches." *National Laundry Journal* 59, no. 1 (1908): 25a.

"The Life of Yee Jock Leong." http://fuzzo.com/genealogy/YeeJo#E34FA (accessed June 15, 2006).

"The Passing of a Prejudice." The Laundry Manual. Chicago: *National Laundry Journal*, 1898: 14.

"The Rock Springs, Wyoming Massacre." *New York Times,* Sept. 5, 1885, 5.

"The Theory of Yee Lee." *New York Times,* May 10, 1883, 2.

"Tracking the Dragon - A guide for finding and assessing Chinese Australian heritage places," http://www.ahc.gov.au/publications/chineseheritage/trackingthedragon/background.html#e (accessed Dec. 17, 2006).

Tubin, Carole. *Working Women of Collar City: Gender, Class, and Community in Troy, New York, 1864-1886.* Urbana and Chicago: University of Illinois Press, 1978.

Tucker, George. "Norfolk's Chinese Heritage Dates Back More than a Century." *Virginian Pilot,* April 2, 1995, J3.

U. S. Census, *General Report, Occupations,* Table 6, 95-97. 1930.

U. S. Census, *Special Report, Occupational characteristics.* Table 2, 12-37. 1970.

U. S. Health Service. *Public Health Reports,* 32, no. 6 (1917), 230-231.

U. S. v. Ju Toy 198 US 253 (1905).

United States v. Wong Kim Ark 169 US 649 (1898).

Wang, Joan. "'No Tickee, No Shirtee:' Chinese Laundries in the Social Context of the Eastern United States: 1882-1943." PhD diss., Carnegie Mellon University, 1996.

Wang, Joan Siow-Huey. "Gender, Race and Civilization: The Competition between American Power Laundries and Chinese Steam Laundries, 1870s - 1920s." *American Studies International,* 40 (2002): 52-74.

Wang, Joan S. "Race, Gender, and Laundry Work: The Roles of Chinese Laundrymen and American Women in the United States, 1850-1950. *Journal of American Ethnic History,* 24, no. 1 (2004): 58-99.

"Warfare of Tongs Claims New Victim." *New York Times,* Feb. 9, 1905, 1.

"Washing Will Be Cheap. What Will Happen After the Anti-Chinese Crusade." *New York Times,* March 21, 1890, 8.

Willard, John "Chinese Baby Made Q-C History in 1926." www.qctimes.com/articles/2003/01/28/faces/export48825prt (accessed Oct. 25, 2006).

Wong, Helen Hong. "I was the only Chinese woman in town:" Reminiscences of a Gold Mountain woman. In *Chinese American Voices: From the Gold Rush to the Present.* Edited by Judy Yung, Gordon Chang and Him Mark Lai. Berkeley: University of California Press, 2006: 157-164.

Wong, Jade Snow. *Fifth Chinese Daughter.* New York: Harper, 1950.

Wong, Kevin Scott. *Americans First: Chinese Americans and the Second World War.* Cambridge: Harvard University Press, 2005.

Wong, William. *American Dream, Chinatown Branch,* (East Bay Express, July 30, 1999). Reprinted in William Wong, Yellow Journalist: Dispatches From Asian America (Philadelphia, Temple University Press, 2001), 10-24.

"Worked Too Late. Two Chinese Laundrymen Still Busy After Midnight." *Los Angeles Times,* April 7, 1896, 8.

Yang, Li. Laundry Trilogy. *China Daily News*, Sept. 3, 1940.

Yang, Philip Q. "Sojourners or Settlers: Post-1965 Chinese Immigrants." *Journal of Asian American Studies*, 2, no. 1 (1999): 61-91.

Yick Wo v. Hopkins 118 U.S. 356, 370.

Yiduo, Wen "A Laundryman's Song." Translator: Hsu Kai-yu. *Harvard Journal of Asiatic Studies* 21, (1958): 147-148.

Yollin, Patricia. "Git Jing Huey - Matriarch Who Loved Food, Family." *San Francisco Chronicle*, August 7, 2005, A-21.

Yu, Renqui. "Chop Suey: From Chinese Food to Chinese American Food." *Chinese America: History and Perspectives* (1987): 87-99.

_____ *To Save China, To Save Ourselves: The Chinese Hand Laundry Alliance of New York*. Philadelphia: Temple University Press, 1992, 28.

Yung, Judy. *Unbound Feet: A Social History of Chinese Women in San Francisco.* Berkeley: University of California Press, 1995.

Zhao, Xiaojian. *Remaking Chinese America: Immigration, Family, and Community, 1940–1965*. New Brunswick, N. J.: Rutgers University Press, 2002.

Index